Dimensions of Conscious Experience

Advances in Consciousness Research

Advances in Consciousness Research provides a forum for scholars from different scientific disciplines and fields of knowledge who study consciousness in its multifaceted aspects. Thus the Series will include (but not be limited to) the various areas of cognitive science, including cognitive psychology, linguistics, brain science and philosophy. The orientation of the Series is toward developing new interdisciplinary and integrative approaches for the investigation, description and theory of consciousness, as well as the practical consequences of this research for the individual and society.

Series A: Theory and Method. Contributions to the development of theory and method in the study of consciousness.

Volume 37

Dimensions of Conscious Experience
Edited by Paavo Pylkkänen and Tere Vadén

Dimensions of Conscious Experience

Edited by

Paavo Pylkkänen
University of Skövde

Tere Vadén
University of Tampere / University of Skövde

John Benjamins Publishing Company
Amsterdam / Philadelphia

∞™ The paper used in this publication meets the minimum requirements of American National Standard for Information Sciences – Permanence of Paper for Printed Library Materials, ANSI Z39.48-1984.

Library of Congress Cataloging-in-Publication Data

Dimensions of conscious experience / edited by Paavo Pylkkänen, Tere Vadén.
p. cm. (Advances in Consciousness Research, ISSN 1381–589X ; v. 37)
Includes bibliographical references and index.
1. Consciousness--Congresses. I. Pylkkänen, P. (Paavo) II. Vadén, Tere. III. Series.

BF311.D536 2001
153--dc21 2001043203
ISBN 90 272 5157 6 (Eur.) / 1 58811 125 3 (US) (Hb; alk. paper)

John Benjamins Publishing Co. · P.O. Box 36224 · 1020 ME Amsterdam · The Netherlands
John Benjamins North America · P.O. Box 27519 · Philadelphia PA 19118-0519 · USA

Table of contents

Experiential Dimensions

List of contributors

Susanne Ackers
Department of Humanities
University of Skövde
Skövde, Sweden

Elena Bezzubova, M. D.
Assistant Professor of Psychiatry
Russian State Medical College
Moscow, Russia

John Briggs
Dept. of English Language, Comparative Literature and Writing
Western Connecticut State University
Danbury, Connecticut, USA

Ronald L. Chrisley
School of Cognitive and Computing Sciences
University of Sussex
, U.K.

Gordon Globus, M. D.
Emeritus Professor of Psychiatry and Philosophy
University of California Irvine
Irvine, USA

B. J. Hiley
Theoretical Physics Research Unit
Birkbeck College
University of London
London, U.K.

Daniel D. Hutto
Centre for Meaning and Metaphysical Studies
University of Hertfordshire
Watford, U.K.

B. I. B. Lindahl
Department of Philosophy
Stockholm University
Stockholm, Sweden

Paavo Pylkkänen
Consciousness Studies Programme
Department of Humanities
University of Skövde
Skövde, Sweden

Antti Revonsuo
Department of Philosophy
Center for Cognitive Neuroscience
University of Turku
Turku, Finland

Maxim I. Stamenov
Institute of the Bulgarian Language
Sofia, Bulgaria

Tere Vadén
Consciousness Studies Programme
Department of Humanities
University of Skövde
Skövde, Sweden and Philosophy,
University of Tampere, Tampere, Finland

Introduction

Background

This book presents a selection of papers that were first presented in an international workshop "Varieties and Dimensions of Conscious Experience", held at the University of Skövde in October 1997. The idea of the workshop was to bring together a small number of researchers who share in common an interest in conscious experience but approach the phenomenon from different angles. The authors were then given the opportunity to develop their papers further, taking into account the discussions in the workshop and in subsequent exchanges. As a result, at least the following dimensions of conscious experience are covered in this anthology: subjectivity vs. objectivity, nonconceptuality vs conceptuality, language, evolution, neural level, microphysical level, creativity, art and dreams. The book provides a kind of "microcosm" of the developing interdisciplinary field of consciousness studies.

Description of the papers

We will here briefly summarize the contents of the papers, beginning with Ronald Chrisley's article. One of the key issues in understanding conscious experience is the turning of subjectivity of experience into something like objectivity of understanding. It has been suggested, for instance, by Thomas Nagel that this is an impossible project as the objectivity of the "view from nowhere" necessarily shuts out what we want to understand in the subjectivity of a perspectival experience. Ronald Chrisley suggests that Nagel's conclusion might be too hasty. Chrisley puts forth a different notion of objectivity, not as a view from nowhere, put as a view from anywhere. According to this notion, objectivity is not one kind of special view amongst other possible views, but rather a way of negotiating between different views, of maintaining something in focus while taking different perspectives on it. This does not amount to a new viewpoint, a view from nowhere, but rather to a skill or capacity of perspective-juggling. In Chrisley's view, objectivity is not a disembodied thing, it is something that ultimately depends on the constitution of the cognitive agent as a whole. This implies that the search for an objective understanding of conscious experience includes an inquiry into the possibilities and limitations of us as inquirers, thus giving new weight to the old philosophical maxim "know thyself".

Daniel Hutto's paper begins with the observation that a major reason why consciousness is a philosophically problematic phenomenon has to do with the difficulties of incorporating consciousness into our familiar object-based conceptual schema. As a number of recent philosophical studies have emphasized, our basic forms of conscious phenomenal experience are *nonconceptual* in their nature. Hutto suggests that we ought not treat conscious experiences as kinds of object at all. It is better to regard consciousness, not as what is experienced, but as the medium through which we experience. Before reaching and explaining this conclusion Hutto provides us with an elaborate critical review of recent philosophical literature on representational theories of consciousness, nonconceptual content and the nature of phenomenal experience.

Maxim I. Stamenov presents a case for a specific level of linguistic sentence formations that is necessary and sufficient for a mental content to become a conscious one. Cues can be taken from the fact that the semantic, syntactic and pragmatic levels of language are partly non-overlapping, thus creating a possibility to distinguish them from one another by comparing various degrees of discrepancy. Stamenov separates between three syntactic and three semantic on-line subsystems of sentence processing, and argues that for some language structure to become conscious an interface between two of them, the syntactic surface structure and the semantic localistic meaning structure, must be enacted. The argument is based on the analysis of transitive sentence formation, the unity of which according to Stamenov does not permit explanation in terms of an overarching conceptual metacategory or a syntactic structure. Thus the unity is a matter of interfacing the surface level of syntax and the semantic level of localistic meaning structure, the link being consciousness as a mechanism of dual-focus at this level. Thus, the transitive construction is seen as the "common denominator" between the content and the structure of consciousness.

Ingemar B. Lindahl approaches the problem of consciousness from an evolutionary perspective through a discussion of a solution to the problem of coadaptation and gradual evolution. He calls the solution the MBO-hypothesis after its first proponents Conwy Lloyd Morgan, James Mark Baldwin and Henry F. Osborne. According to this hypothesis, plasticity and learning may provide room for acquired characteristics, which in turn may be replaced by hereditary variation promoted by natural selection, thus creating an illusion of Lamarckian inheritance of acquired characteristics. This hypothesis is especially interesting when it comes to behavioural patterns, where the plasticity needed might be provided by mental processes or consciousness. It might be possible for animals to maintain a behavioural pattern intelligently or consciously until it is partly or totally replaced by overtly similar genetically transmitted variations, "hardwiring", so to speak. This, of course, leads us to a central question: is consciousness a causal factor in producing plasticity or behaviour or just another name for hardwired neural and material processes? Lindahl suggests that in Baldwin's theory problems occur because Baldwin tries to reconcile a dualistic view of consciousness with a materialistic analysis of causation. In contrast to this, Lindahl discusses the evolutionary ideas of William James and Karl Popper, who have argued for the survival value of consciousness, which in turn would imply some kind of causal efficacy of consciousness. This conclusion supports, according to Lindahl, an interactionist picture of the mind and the body. As for the existence of consciousness in animals, Lindahl mentions two important considerations. First, in a Darwinian view, nothing prevents us from positing a continuum of intentional mental life in the same way we posit a continuum of biological structure. Second, Lindahl claims that the problem of inferring from overt behaviour to "inner" mental life is not a methodological one since such inference from observed effects to unobserved causes is quite common in natural science. According to him, the decisive step is the choice of the topic of inquiry. Stopping inference from behaviour and biological evolution to experiental or mental notions is unfruitful, to say the least, if one is interested in the question of how consciousness has been preserved in biological evolution. That question, Lindahl points out, is a quite natural one to ask in view of the evolutionary facts and the fact that we quite obviously are conscious. His conclusion is that it seems likely that consciousness has been preserved because of its usefulness, part of which may lie in the generation of behavioural patterns that can prepare the way for natural selection of innate structure.

Antti Revonsuo draws attention to the central role that cognitive neuroscience plays in the emerging discipline of consciousness studies. For one of the most exciting aspects of consciousness studies has been to learn what cognitive neuroscience research says about such phenomena as blindsight, 40-Hz synchronous activity correlated with perception, neural correlates of binocular rivalry, and functional brain imaging of conscious states. Revonsuo points out, however, that cognitive neuroscience research is based upon implicit assumptions on what consciousness is, where it is to be found, and which methods can be used to reveal it. These assumptions need to be carefully scrutinized, and a kind of philosophy of cognitive neuroscience is called for. In his paper he first reviews some of the findings on visual awareness that have recently been made in cognitive neuroscience. He then raises the question of what exactly are the phenomena that have been measured in these studies. If we assume that consciousness is a level of organization in the brain, Revonsuo argues that it is not at all clear that we have directly measured that level in a functional neuroimage.

Basil Hiley and Paavo Pylkkänen begin by considering the general issue of naturalizing the mental. It has been traditionally problematic to find a place for mental properties in a physical universe, whether one is considering the causal powers of mental properties, their directedness (intentionality/ meaningfulness), or their conscious properties. The developments in contemporary physics require a new concept of the physical domain and consequently the mind-matter problem may be affected. Hiley and Pylkkänen focus on the so called ontological interpretation of the quantum theory (developed by Bohm and Hiley) which claims that in order to make intelligible the puzzling empirical and theoretical results of the quantum theory one has to postulate a new property of active information playing a role at the quantum level. This is a new ontological hypothesis which provides a new way of approaching the traditional philosophical problems concerning mental and physical properties. Hiley and Pylkkänen further consider the philosophical implications of some even more general proposals arising from physics, proposals, which are required, if we are to make progress in some of the unsolved problems of physics, such as quantizing gravity. Their paper involves some speculative metaphysics, but they emphasize the connection of their ideas to solid empirical results and mathematical formalism that correctly describes them.

Gordon Globus and Elena Bezzubova are encouraged by the new resources which Quantum Brain Dynamics (QBD) offers for philosophical discussion. QBD is a new approach which originates in the application of quantum field theory to brain functioning and is represented by, for example, Mari Jibu and Kunio Yasue. Globus and Bezzubova adopt a "postmodern" perspective which requires that QBD has to be approached with caution: a route between the Scylla of science-technology and the Charybdis of metaphysical consciousness has to be found. On the one hand one has to watch out for interpreting QBD in the traditional modernistic technoscientific sense. This would easily give rise to just another form of *Gestell*, the hidden control that technology has over our thinking according to Heidegger. On the other hand the modernistic notion of consciousness is prone to perpetuate the dualities between the mental and the physical along side many other metaphysical dualities. Globus and Bezzubova's postmodern QBD provides us with a poetic synthesis of quantum field theory, neuroscience, Heidegger and Derrida. We are encouraged, in understanding our brain-Existenz, to give attention to the dynamical fullness of interpenetrated possibilities whose probabilities are under nonlocal cognitive control.

In his article, John Briggs presents a sceptical if not ironical view of the hubris of reductive accounts of consciousness. Briggs separates between three types of ordering processes in consciousness, the primary order, the primordial order, and the order of what he denotes by the term "this*otherness". The primary ordering is one in terms of knowledge, of abstracting or filtering the plenitude of sensory information into abstract representations. This mapping might be either "built-in", hardwired, or "built-up", learned. According to Briggs, this is the process that Western society and materialist science is most aware of. The second type of order Briggs calls the primordial order, which is the process of un-abstracting the abstractions created in the primary process. Evidence of the primordial process can, according to Briggs, be found all over the human record, but an emphasis on the voiding and unabstracting primordial process is more familiar from Eastern schools of thought. Such unabstracting Briggs sees as a fundamental part of creative activity, in shaping new mappings and representations, but even more importantly, in reminding us of the inadequateness of all primary order conceptualizations. The third order, that in his view unites the primary and primordial orders, Briggs denotes with the neologism "this*otherness". The word is intended to point out the way in which for example certain works of art keep the "thisness" of primary order and the "otherness" of primordial order together in an unresolved whole. *This*otherness* brings about an aesthetic distance that makes it possible to experience the whole in an impersonal, non-objective and non-subjective way. Briggs sees *this*otherness* at work in true metaphors that neither lapse into ideas or abstractions nor into revolts or nullifications of abstractions. Thus *this*otherness* is the order which more than the primary order essentially characterises consciousness, and which by its very existence calls into question the validity of algorithmic accounts of the primary order as explanations of consciousness *tout court*.

In her article Susanne Ackers approaches consciousness through art. According to her, the history of art and history of technology should not be separated too strictly, as both reflect consciousness as *mediated* experience. Ackers analyses a contemporary work of art, Charlotte Davies' *Osmose* that can be described as a virtual space. The noteworthy aspect of the work is that it both aesthetically and technologically breaks the classical tradition that Panofsky described in his "Perspective as a Symbolic Form." In virtual spaces like *Osmose* perspective is perceivable not as symbolic form but as individual time of the like encountered in works of literature. Thus this kind of mediated art experience can give a glimpse of what a "materialization of consciousness" in the Jamesian sense might look like.

Tere Vadén discusses the division of conscious experience to dreaming and waking. A metaphysical unbalance in favour of waking and contra dreams can be discerned in many contemporary notions of dreaming. According to Vadén, this unbalance is structurally analogous to the bias in classical Freudian theory, where the notion of dreamwork is introduced as a way of implying waking-life purposes and goals to dreaming. Vadén analyses the philosophical motivation and production of the distinction through terms of asubjective experience, where the distinction of subject and object has been dissoluted. The dissolution leads, according to Vadén, also to a partial dissolution of the dream-waking duality; a dissolution that is well in agreement with recent studies in neuroscience.

Conceptual Foundation

A view from anywhere

Prospects for an objective understanding of consciousness

Ronald L. Chrisley
University of Sussex

One very compelling idea of objectivity is captured in the title of Thomas Nagel's book *The View from Nowhere.* According to this idea, since subjectivity is the condition of being bound to a single perspective, objectivity must be an escape from all perspectives, a detached view, a view of a centreless world (or: the centreless view of the world). A problem then presents itself: how can there be an objective understanding of subjectivity itself? In particular, how can there be an objective understanding of conscious experience? The essentially perspectival, subjective nature of experience seems to prevent its full inclusion in a truly objective, non-perspectival world view.

In what follows, I suggest how it might be possible to remove this obstacle to an objective understanding of consciousness (which is not to say that there are not other obstacles to be overcome!). I do so not by rejecting the subjectivity of experience, but by appealing to a non-standard but compelling notion of what objectivity is, a notion which has been recently and lucidly presented by Brian Cantwell Smith.

Physical vs. mental objectivity

Can there be an objective understanding of subjectivity itself? Nagel's answer is: it depends. It depends on what kind of objective understanding is in question. He distinguishes Physical Objectivity from Mental Objectivity. The former is a reductionistic enterprise which seeks to explain everything, and thus experience, in terms of objective — specifically, physical — facts. Yet this conflicts with the nature of experience, since

> every subjective phenomenon is connected with a single point of view, and it seems inevitable that an objective, physical theory will abandon that point of view. (Nagel 1980: 160).

Nagel states the conflict again when he writes:

> For if the facts of experience — facts about what it is like for the experiencing organism — are accessible from only one point of view, then it is a mystery how the true character of experiences could be revealed in the physical operation of that organism. The latter is a domain of objective facts par excellence — the kind that can be observed and understood from many points of view. (Nagel 1980: 162).

For this kind of objectivity, then, the answer to our question is "no" — a Physically Objective understanding of consciousness is impossible.

However, Mental Objectivity (or "objective phenomenology", as he calls it in his well-known paper "What is it like to be a Bat?" (Nagel 1980)) is intended to fare better. It is not a reductionistic enterprise, but it is objective nonetheless in that it is

> ... not dependent on empathy or the imagination. Though presumably it would not capture everything, its goal would be to describe, at least in part, the subjective character of experiences in a form comprehensible to beings incapable of having those experiences. (Nagel 1980: 166).
>
> The aim of such understanding, the deeper aim it shares with the reductionist views I reject, is to go beyond the distinction between appearance and reality by including the existence of appearances in an elaborated reality. Nothing will then be left outside. But this expanded reality, like physical reality, is centerless. Though the subjective features of our own minds are at the center of our world, we must try to conceive of them as just one manifestation of the mental in a world that is not given especially to the human point of view. (Nagel 1986: 18).

Nagel sees this objective phenomenology as the only way forward in an attempt to achieve an objective understanding of consciousness, but it appears to me that it falls afoul of the very arguments Nagel makes against Physical Objectivity. That is, there is a direct conflict between the essentially perspectival nature of experience and the "centerlessness" which Nagel takes to be essential to Mental Objectivity and Physical Objectivity.

Nagel admits as much in the sentence that follows the passage just quoted:

> This is, I recognize, a paradoxical enterprise, but the attempt seems to me worth making. (Nagel 1986: 18).

On its own, this might seem puzzling. But in the introduction *to The View From Nowhere*, Nagel acknowledges the existence of "the conflicts between the [objective and subjective] standpoints and the discomfort caused by obstacles to their integration" and says of them:

> Certain forms of perplexity — for example, about freedom, knowledge, and the meaning of life — seem to me to embody more insight than any of the supposed solutions to these problems. (Nagel 1986: 4).

And a few pages later:

> I shall also point out ways in which the two [objective and subjective] standpoints cannot be satisfactorily integrated, and in these cases I believe the correct course is not to assign victory to either standpoint, but to hold the opposition clearly in one's mind without suppressing either element. (Nagel 1986: 6).

But if this is all that Nagel has in mind for his objective phenomenology, one wonders in what way it is an advance on reductionist, Physical Objectivity. Indeed, doesn't the latter paint the opposition of subjective and objective, of perspectival and centreless, in starker colours of greater contrast?

I would like to defend the possibility of an objective understanding of consciousness, in all its subjective glory. The problems that Nagel encounters stem, I believe, from his "view from nowhere" conception of objectivity. I will argue that this conception of objectivity is problematic, and will therefore employ a different notion of objectivity, one which is not precluded by Nagel's arguments from applying to an account of experience, yet which nevertheless merits being called a notion of objectivity.

Objectivity as coordination

The problem with the "view from nowhere" conception of objectivity, be it Physical or Mental, is that it takes objectivity to be a particular kind of view. Once this is done, the conflict Nagel documents is unavoidable. How can one take an objective perspective, which contains no privileged points of view, on experience, without eradicating the subjectivity at its heart?

Note that even the phrase "the view from nowhere" has an air of the paradoxical; indeed, that is its attraction. All views, even the Physical, are from *somewhere.*

This raises an important constraint on any notion of objectivity relevant to the question I am considering: "Can there be an objective understanding of consciousness?" The constraint is this: we should not (perhaps cannot) require any more of an objective understanding of consciousness than we require of an objective understanding of the physical. That is, the question is really asking "Can there be an understanding of consciousness which is *as* objective as physics is about the physical world?" If, as many think likely, physics has some limitation to its objectivity, then it cannot be an argument against the objectivity of an account of consciousness that it has the same limitation. My account of consciousness as subjective as my account of physical phenomena? I should be so lucky.

So I am proposing that objectivity is not the view from nowhere. On the other hand, objectivity does involve views on the world. So perhaps objectivity is not itself a particular view, but a virtuous way of negotiating perspectival, subjective views. Brian Cantwell Smith has referred to this notion of objectivity as "a view from somewhere" or "a view from anywhere":

> …one of the most important facts about the inherently participatory picture of registration being painted here is that the form of objectivity available to it cannot be achieved by mistakenly trying more and more to completely disconnect from the world, in a vain attempt to achieve the infamous view from nowhere. On the contrary, the ability to register — *the ability to make the world present, and to be present in the world,* which is after all what this is a theory of — requires that one inhabit one's particular place in the deictic flux, and participate appropriately in the enmeshing web of practices, so as to sustain the kinds of coordination that make the world come into focus with at least a degree of stability and clarity. (Smith 1996: 305–306).

As the passage suggests, Smith is forced into this view of objectivity as perspective coordination by his constructivist, participatory metaphysics. But even if one is not forced into such a notion of objectivity by one's metaphysics, there is much to commend it, not least the fact that it can allow for an objective understanding of subjectivity.

Smith's idea is that the fundamental nature of objectivity is the creation, stabilization, and maintenance of objects in the face of the underlying non-objectual nature of reality. And such an active role in objectivity requires one to have exquisitely perspectival views on and actions in the world, and to juggle these in a way which preserves one's intentional connection with the object. Thus objectivity not only tolerates, but downright demands, subjectivity.

Smith illustrates this point with an analogy:

> Imagine an acrobat leaping and jumping about on a somewhat darkened stage, putting their body through all kinds of fantastic gyrations, and yet throughout this crazed dance keeping a flashlight pointing absolutely reliably towards some fixed point — a point about four feet off the ground, say, towards the left front center of the stage. What the acrobat would need to do, through a complex series of hand and arm motions — handing the light back and forth from hand to hand, reaching it around behind themself, and so forth as appropriate — would be to do the opposite with one part of their body (arm and hand, plus flashlight) of what the rest of their body was doing (leaping and dancing), in such a way that the two, when added up together, nullified each other, leaving the focal point of illumination unchanged. (Smith 1996:237).

At this point in the analogy, we already have enough, perhaps, to provide an alternative to the view from nowhere, and to overcome Nagel's problems with objective accounts of subjectivity, since acknowledging the perspectival stances of the acrobat is not inconsistent with also acknowledging that the acrobat is maintaining a perspective-independent link with a particular location. But Smith goes on to show how the objectivity is not just consistent with the juggling of perspectives, but requires it:

> Except of course the word "opposite" is not right. If the acrobat were to leap up four feet, it would not be necessary for them to do the exact opposite — i.e., to drop their arm down four feet, if that were even possible — in order to hold constant the full six-coordinate position and orientation of the flashlight. In fact not a single one of the flashlight's six coordinates needs to remain fixed. It is not the *flashlight* that needs to be stabilized, after all. To freeze the position of the flashlight outright might seem to be overkill, and would anyway be impossible, for example if the acrobat were to rush to the other side of the stage. Ironically, moreover, there is a sense in which keeping the light itself locked into position, as if it were epoxied to a particular point in space, would be underkill, *since there would then be no way to be sure where it was pointing.* For a fixed moving flashlight, that is, no single point along its path of illumination is uniquely singled out; all you have is a long gradually dissipating path of light. Fortunately for the acrobat … there is a better way: it is only necessary to rotate the wrist in just the appropriate manner. The normative requirement is that there be a fixed point at the "end" of (i.e., at some point along) the line along which the flashlight is pointing — a point that remains stably located in exocentric 3-space. So the dance does not

> merely compensate for the acrobats movements; as a method for stabilizing the object, it is superior. … All told, the focal point is much more stably and redundantly identifiable through the acrobat's motion than it would have been had the acrobat stayed put. (Smith 1996: 237–239).

It is the notion of maintaining an invariant in the face of changing conditions that allows us to make sense not only of what it is for a subject to think of something objectively, but also of what it is for something to be an objective particular: to be, or at the very least to be able to be, so singled out by an acrobatic dance of coordinated intentionality.

Despite its rejection of the "view from nowhere" notion of objectivity, Smith's "a view from anywhere" notion conforms with another conception of objectivity found in Nagel's writings:

> A view or form of thought is more objective than another if it relies less on the specifics of the individual's makeup and position in the world, or on the character of the particular type of creature he is. (Nagel 1986: 5).

If one reads this passage with an emphasis on the relations between individuals, then it yields the view from nowhere notion of objectivity: facts are objective facts inasmuch as they can be known by other, different individuals. However, if one reads it emphasizing intra-individual relations, Smith's notion is the result: an individual's interactions with a subject matter are objective inasmuch as they don't rely on the particular, perspectival views the individual in fact took; if the details of the interaction had been different, the individual would have compensated accordingly, employing alternative, yet just as perspectival, views of the subject matter. So the independence required is not (thank heavens) of one's own individuality as a whole, but of one's particular subjective engagement at any one time.

This conception of objectivity has its clearest application, perhaps, in the case of spatial thought.[1] One way that one might have an objective conception of a territory is through the possession of a map, and possession of the capacity to interpret and use the map. One who espouses the "view from nowhere" notion of objectivity could stop here, since presumably a map is a paradigmatic instance of such a view (with all the attendant difficulties of that view: a bird's eye view is not a view from nowhere, there is no such thing as a map from no point of view, etc.). But the conception of objectivity I am recommending has it that the objectivity of the map user lies not in the map, but in the abilities that the map affords: an ability to know the egocentric direction and distance of arbitrary landmarks in the territory given one's position and orientation on the map.

This objectivity is a view from anywhere: no matter where I move in the territory, I have the appropriate intentional relations to any other location.[2] And the important point is that I can have this ability without a map, in any conventional sense of the word, any sense in which possessing a map is more than just having the right kind of perspective-juggling capabilities. That is, objectivity consists in being able to adopt the right perspective-bound view at the right time, not in having a single, perspectiveless view — an incoherence which, fortunately, is not necessary.

A view from anywhere of experience

So much for stage-setting. It's high time to apply this notion of objectivity to consciousness. The idea is that we can have an objective understanding of consciousness through the skilled adoption of the appropriate subjective viewpoint on the experience of the person in question, just as the acrobat keeps their perspectivally-oriented torch focused on the same location. And like the case of navigating a territory, we have an objective understanding of consciousness just in case we are able to adjust our dispositions toward the experience in an appropriate way, as the context changes. But there are disanalogies as well. In both the acrobat and the navigational cases, the change that was being compensated for was that of the understander, whereas it is equally important to compensate for changes in the subject matter. Also, the changes in both illustrations were entirely spatial, whereas that is unlikely to be the flux against which objectivity arises for the case of experience — rather, we will be trying to understand the changes in the physiology, psychology, and experience of the subject, as well as ourselves.

Of course, I don't have an objective understanding of experience, so I don't know how the story will go. But the point is that Nagel has not given any a priori reasons for thinking that this kind of objective understanding of experience is impossible. Objectivity as a view from anywhere doesn't encounter the problems the view from nowhere encounters when one tries to apply it to the case of consciousness.

Recall that the defining strength of the view from nowhere is that it does not contain any privileged, subjective points of view. But this is also its limitation, since it *cannot* contain any such points of view, even if the task — understanding experience objectively — demands it. However, as we saw, Smith's notion of objectivity not only allows but exploits the perspectival in order to bring forth the objective *as* objective. At no point is the understander required to adopt anything other than a perspectival, subjective point of view. So there need be no conflict between the perspective of the understander and the perspective of who is being understood.

But there is a concomitant limitation to this form of objectivity. The whole upshot of Nagel's famous discussion of the impossibility for us to know what it's like to be a bat, was this:

> [The] ascription of experience is possible only for someone sufficiently similar to the object of ascription to be able to adopt his point of view — to understand the ascription in the first person as well as in the third, so to speak. (Nagel: 1980).

That is, to have a view from anywhere on the experience of some organism, it won't be enough to just have some perspectival view or other. One will, if Nagel is right, have to have the very same (or a very similar) perspective as the organism being understood. This is only possible if understander and understood are sufficiently similar[3]; although Nagel emphasizes the sensory system, it seems that there will have to be much else that is similar besides. And many would-be understanders, it can be assumed, will not be similar enough.

The consequence is that we must shed one of our intuitions about objectivity: an objective view of experience, while independent of any particular perspective I happen to be taking, is not independent of my capacities and constitution as a whole. Thus, there are objective views which are not available to all subjects. This is not as problematic as it may at first seem. Why should an objective understanding be available to all others? Why should we expect that what allows me to compensate for my own particularities in order to make available an objective reality should also do the same for you, given our differential situatedness and embodiment? If I am standing, facing north, tracking an airplane landing from east to west across the sky, the movements I have to make with my arm to track the plane with my index finger have little in common with the adjustments you, facing west and lying on your side, have to make in order to track the plane's descent with your finger or — even worse — your tentacle, sonar, or whatever. If objectivity is a way of factoring out the subjectivity of both oneself and one's subject matter in order to yield an objective invariant, it should not count against a conception of objectivity that it imply that not every subject can achieve this for the same subject matters. Nagel himself seems to admit as much when he says that objective facts are "the kind that can be observed and understood from many points of view..." (Nagel 1980: 162).

That's "many", not "every", and as such, it allows for an objective understanding of experiential facts, once we see that objectivity is, or can be, a view from anywhere.

Even if we grant that not everyone will be able to understand objectively a given experiential state, due to them not being sufficiently similar to the subject enjoying that state, why should we think that those who can understand that state must be unable to do so objectively? Consider the difference between two subjects: one who can be in a particular experiential state, and one who can be in that same state, but also possesses the ability to go into that state in all and only theoretically appropriate contexts for the understanding of the experience of some organism who also shares that same experiential state. Why is this difference not a difference in objectivity?

The constraint, stated earlier, on conceptions of objectivity, can be invoked here. I stipulated that a conception of objectivity should not be so stringent as to rule out physics as an objective account of the physical world, since I would be happy with any account of consciousness that is at least as objective with respect to its subject matter as physics is to its. But any opposition to an objective understanding of experience of the kind I am proposing that is based on the unavailability of such understanding to all subjects is in danger of violating the aforementioned constraint. That is, it seems to demand more of an objective account of experience than is demanded of physics. Is it really the case that our physical conception of the world can be had by *any* subject? Those of an anti-realist bent could make such a capacity a requirement for us making sense of someone as a subject, and therefore a requirement for them *being* a subject. But Nagel's strong realism prevents him from making this move; he attacks the "significant strain of idealism in contemporary philosophy according to which what there is and how things are cannot go beyond what we could in principle think about" (Nagel 1986: 9). Although this realism works against a view from nowhere account of subjectivity, because it prevents that view from dismissing as non-existent that which we cannot understand, it supports the claim that the view from anywhere understanding of experience is an objective understanding. Strong realism prevents us from moving from the impossibility (if there is such) of our conceiving of subjects who cannot access our physical understanding of the world to the actual impossibility of such. Thus, it destroys the view of objectivity as a view which is accessible by everyone. What remains is the view from anywhere conception of objectivity.

Know thyself

There is another way to defend the kind of objective understanding of consciousness that I am favouring. The foregoing attack on the objectivity of "a view from anywhere" understandings of consciousness assumed that the goal was to have an objective understanding of a particular experiential state of a particular individual. That individual's particularity, combined with the particularity of the understander, yielded the possibility of failure to have an objective understanding, since the understander may be unable to adopt the necessary subjective perspectives. Thus, there is no view on subjectivity which is available to all. But there is a sense in which "a view from anywhere" understanding of consciousness may be available to all conscious subjects. Although not every subject will be able to have an objective understanding of all instances of experience, it is plausible that all subjects are theoretically capable of having an objective understanding of at least some instances of conscious experience. At a minimum, there is no philosophical barrier, on the account I am offering, to a subject having an objective understanding of its own experiential states. The problem of consciousness is not just that we don't have an objective understanding of this or that token instance of experience, but that we don't know how we could have an objective understanding of experience at all. The person who requires an objective understanding of all particular cases of experience in order to solve the riddle of consciousness reminds me of the joke about the scientist who, upon hearing that philosophers had been struggling for millennia with the question "if a tree falls in a forest and there is no one around to hear, does it make a sound?", went away with a look of concentration and determination on her face, only to come back a few days later saying "I've solved it for elm and birch, but I'm still working on the general case." The kind of solution to the problem of consciousness we want isn't one that would still be missing if we were able to have an objective understanding of a few cases of conscious experience. Once we have one case of an objective understanding of experience, the in-principle objections, puzzles, doubts and worries vanish — all that is left is the steady acquisition of further instances of objective understanding where it can be had, and an acknowledgement of our limitations where it cannot.

Notes

1. See Cussins (1990) for a similar attempt to illustrate the differences between Nagel's and Smith's conceptions of objectivity.

2. Compare the "Pure Realigner" in Peacocke (1983).

3. Indeed, this could serve as a theoretical definition of subjectivity: an aspect A of an organism O is subjective to the extent to which an objective understanding of A requires the understander to be (physically) similar to O.

References

Cussins, A. 1990. "The Connectionist Construction of Concepts" In M. Boden (ed.), *The Philosophy of Artificial Intelligence*, Oxford: Oxford University Press: 368–440.

Cussins, A. 1992. "Content, Embodiment and Objectivity: The Theory of Cognitive Trails." *Mind*, 101: 651–688.

Evans, G. 1982. *The Varieties of Reference.* Oxford: Oxford University Press.

Nagel, T. 1980. "What Is It Like to Be a Bat?" In N. Block (ed.), *Readings in Philosophy of Psychology*, vol. 1, Cambridge: Harvard University Press.

Nagel, T. 1986. *The View from Nowhere.* Oxford: Oxford University Press.

Peacocke, C. 1983. *Sense and Content: Experience, Thought and their Relations.* Oxford: Clarendon Press.

Peacocke, C. 1989. "No Resting Place: A Critical Notice of The View from Nowhere by Thomas Nagel", *Philosophical Review*, 98: 65–82.

Smith, B.C. 1996. *On the Origin of Objects.* Cambridge: MIT Press.

Consciousness and conceptual schema

Daniel D. Hutto
University of Hertfordshire

> "In philosophy one is in constant danger of producing a myth of symbolism, or a myth of mental processes. Instead of simply saying what anyone knows and must admit."
>
> — Wittgenstein, *Zettel* § 211.

Introduction

There are two importantly different ways in which consciousness resists incorporation into our familiar object-based conceptual schema which, when analysed, help to explain why it is regarded as such a philosophically recalcitrant phenomena. One concerns the nonconceptual nature of basic forms of conscious experience. The other concerns the fact that attempts to understand the nature of such experience in an object-based schema, as is demanded by some forms of physicalism, is inappropriate. My concern in this paper is to show how certain central problems concerning our attempts to understand consciousness can be recast or dissolved if we take note of these aspects of phenomenal experience.

Before addressing these issues a few words of clarification are in order. Without refinements, talk of schema has Kantian overtones. For example, consider Tye's claim that, "Once the sensory input is brought under the appropriate schema, belief formation can take place" (Tye 1996: 66).[1] Nevertheless, it is useful to talk of "schema" specifically in order to waylay confusion with an issue, which Davidson long ago advertised about the impossibility of there being radically different conceptual schemes. Since I will be denying that our concepts of phenomenal consciousness can be incorporated into an object-based schema, it might be thought that advocating the existence of incommensurable conceptual schema ignores Davidson's important lesson concerning radically different conceptual schemes. But it does not. Davidson's point concerns the radical interpretation of an alien language of which we can make no sense. In contrast, what we have here is two different schema, both of which we can make sense of separately, but which we cannot make intelligible in terms of one another (cf. Hutto 1996: § iii).

One further caveat wants making. As should be transparent from the discussion, I am not here concerned with higher-order consciousness or self-consciousness both of which may well involve conceptualisation and an object-based schema in various ways (cf. Dretske 1995: 104–105; Cassam 1997). My concern is with the qualitative nature of the most basic form of phenomenal experience (Dretske 1995: 1; Tye 1996: xiii; Chalmers 1996: 4).

Nonconceptual content and phenomenal experience

Recently, two authors, Dretske and Tye have advanced representational theories of consciousness. They both advocate versions of what might be called the strong representationalist thesis, which proposes that, "...phenomenal conscious states are *essentially* representational states of a certain sort" (Tye 1996: 66, emphasis mine; cf. also Tye 1996: 151; Dretske 1995: 1). Interestingly, they also crucially agree in regarding the phenomenal character of the basic forms of consciousness as being nonconceptual in character (Tye 1996: 137–139; cf. also 102–104, 128; Dretske 1995: 9–12). In this section I will discuss the merits of this latter claim but suggest reasons for rejecting any *strong* version of the representational thesis before outlining a softer and more appropriate thesis in section three.

Minimally, advocates of nonconceptualism about experience believe it is possible to perceive or be consciously aware of something without being able to conceptually identify it.[2] This basic approach has an ancient and respectable pedigree. For example, it is a key feature of Aristotle's understanding of sense perception. This can be seen in his discussion of the three possible kinds of objects of perception. He writes:

> The term "object of sense" covers three kinds of objects, two kinds of which we call perceptible in themselves, while the remaining one is only incidentally perceptible. Of the first two kinds one consists of what is special to a single sense, the other to what is common to all of the senses. I call by the name of special object of this or that sense that which cannot be perceived by any other

> sense than that one and in respect of which no error is possible; in this sense colour is the special object of sight, sound of hearing, flavour of taste... Each sense has one kind of object which it discerns, and never errs in reporting that what is before it is a colour or sound (though it may error as to what it is that is coloured or where that is, or what it is that is sounding or where that is). Such objects are what we call the special objects of sense.
>
> Common sensibles are movement, rest, number, figure, magnitude; these are not special to any one sense, but are common to all....
>
> We speak of an incidental object of sense where, e.g. the white object which we see is the son of Diares; here because being the son of Diares is incidental to the white which is perceived, we speak of Diares being incidentally perceived. That is why it in no way affects the senses. (*De Anima*, Bk II, 418^a 7–23).

These distinctions can be clearly illustrated if we consider the overly familiar example of a frog that is perceiving a fly. We might say that it sees the fly by means of detecting darkly coloured-objects (colour being the special object of the sense of sight) and by means of detecting size and movement (common sensibles). But from the perceptual point of view the fact that the frog sees a fly rather than a bee-bee is merely incidental. Neither flies nor bee-bees are properly perceptible by sight — though they can be incidental objects of perception. In contrast, noticing a fly, in the sense of recognising it *as a fly*, involves a judgement and as such it requires concepts.[3] It is judgements that can be either true or false. Thus conceiving, as opposed to mere perceiving, comes into to its own when, and only when, it is possible to err with respect to truth or falsity.[4]

The idea is that, like other animals, we can be conscious of colours, pains (in certain bodily locales), sounds and the like without always being conscious of these items in an intellectual or conceptual fashion. *Prima facie*, this is evidenced by the fact that in many cases we act and respond in sophisticated ways without giving thought to our behaviour (cf. Searle 1992: 138). For example, imagine a situation in which someone throws an object at you unexpectedly and that this happens so quickly that — at the time — you are unable to give any *thought* to what the object might be. In such a case you undoubtedly see something and react regardless of your ability, or lack thereof, to put the experience into concepts. Often, even in cases where we do not have the time to *think,* we are aware of things in our environment and manage to deal with them effectively (see also Burge 1977: 349–350).

Another intuitive way to illustrate this divide would be to ask you to note the kind of things of which you are aware in your surroundings at this very moment. It would be ludicrous to think that all the while you are reading this paper that you were also paying detailed conceptual attention to these items (at least I hope not!). Nevertheless, it would be equally ludicrous to suppose that you are completely unaware of such features because of this. Consider the case of the long-haul truck driver who manages to drive successfully without giving much thought to the performance of this task (cf. Tye 1996: 115; Dretske 1995: 104–105). Although this case is frequently cited in order to highlight the distinction between mere consciousness and its higher-order, reflective forms, it also serves to remind us that a great many, perhaps the majority, of our actions are normally performed without attendant propositional thoughts. As Searle suggests, "...we need to distinguish the conscious/unconscious distinction from the center of attention/periphery distinction" (Searle 1992: 138).

The distinction between the conceptual and nonconceptual is also useful in helping us to understand certain perceptual illusions. For example, appeal to this distinction is a natural way to explain why the Müller-Lyer illusion has continued effects on those who are familiar with it.[5] It appears to be a case in which we see one thing but believe another (cf. also Crane 1992: 150–151; Tye 1996: 102). That is to say, once the illusion is explained, we know the lines are the same lengths, even so one line still looks longer. This is illustrated by a version of the illusion in Figure 1 below.

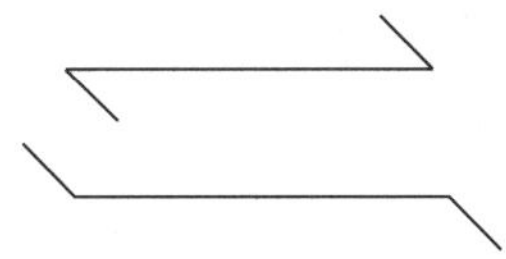

Figure 1. A version of the Müller-Lyer illusion.

The point is that a judgement with the propositional content "the lines are the same length", must be characterised in terms of concepts which we possess (or as some would say: it is composed of them). In contrast, the purely perceptual response to the illusion is distinguished by the fact that those same concepts are inappropriate in a principled description of its content.

Like the strong representationalists I claim that giving attention to the nonconceptual character of phenomenal experiences promises to unravel several old chestnuts concerning conscious experience. But I also think that Dretske and Tye are working with the wrong theories of representation. Furthermore, I claim that in its strong form the representational thesis is strictly false. It fails to provide an adequate account of phenomenal experience. Before suggesting amendments I begin with a bit of nut cracking.

Let us start with Frank Jackson's "knowledge argument" against physicalism. Jackson set up a famous thought experiment which featured Mary, a super-scientist who knows all the physical facts[6] that can be known. But she has been confined from birth in a black-and-white environment and has only had access to the outside world *via* black and white media. Given this, according to Jackson her collection of facts is incomplete (and thus so is physicalism). Specifically, Mary lacks knowledge of certain facts about colour experience. She does not know what it is like for others to experience colours[7] and this is not something that she can learn about until she, herself, has been released and has experienced them firsthand (cf. Jackson 1990; Tye 1996:172). Eschewing eliminativism and confessing that he is a *qualia freak*, Jackson concludes from the case of Mary that if he were told everything that there was to be told from a physical point of view, he would not have been told everything that there was to have been told. Thus, a complete physical and functional description of our sense organs and the kinds of worldly things that stimulate them would not include, capture or mention such mundane phenomenal experiences as of the-smell-of-a-rose (Jackson 1990:469).

Armed with the idea that rudimentary forms of experience are nonconceptual in character we are in a good position to assess the success and limits of the knowledge argument. As Churchland has recognised, the argument gains its force because it equivocates in its talk of knowledge and erroneously treats phenomenal experience as a form of propositional knowledge (cf. Churchland 1989:68). In a similar vein Nemirow's and Lewis' analysis of the knowledge argument led them to endorse what they variously call the ability equation or the ability hypothesis. In Lewis' words, "The Ability Hypothesis says that knowing what an experience is like just is the possession of....abilities to remember, imagine, and recognise. It isn't possession of any kind of information, ordinary or peculiar... It isn't knowing that. It's knowing how." (Lewis 1990:516; cf. also Nemirow 1990:493).

Both Nemirow and Lewis hoped to convince us that a phenomenal experience could be described as the gaining or having of certain abilities; the abilities to imagine, remember, recognise, and the like. Thus being capable of experiencing *red* equates to having abilities to imagine a red colour, to recognise red things, and to remember when I see red things again. I agree that we ought to concentrate on the abilities phenomenal experience imparts to a subject however, in so far as advocates of the ability hypothesis intend to equate such discriminatory abilities with phenomenal experience *per se* the approach is wanting. While the suggestion that phenomenal experience underpins such abilities is innocuous and plausible enough when advanced non-reductively, the idea that experience can be reduced to a set of abilities is a bridge too far. To be credible the ability hypothesis needs to be supplemented with an account of phenomenal experience. My suggestion is that this can be done by appeal to a nonconceptual form of experiential content. There are good independent reasons to think that the abilities of most organisms are underpinned by some form of nonconceptual content whether experiential or not (see Cussins 1990, 1992b; Chrisley 1993; Clark 1997). It is a short step from acknowledging this to seeing the appeal of the idea that some abilities may require experiential, nonconceptual content (Cussins 1992b: 655, 673, 683).[8]

If a solid link can be forged between certain abilities, basic forms of phenomenal experience and the most rudimentary kind of nonconceptual intentionality, then the limited virtues of the knowledge argument become clear. It reveals that when we talk of *knowing* what-it-is-like to experience we are gesturing at the basic phenomenal experiences that underpin certain abilities. We are not asking after a form of propositional knowledge which the physicalist could be expected to provide. If we accept this proviso it becomes safe to agree with Dretske's remark that "In order to eat, dogfish have to know about the configuration of the electric field. They do not have to *know that* it is an electric field that has this configuration" (Dretske 1995: 86, emphasis mine). This tallies with the conclusion reached by Nagel in his variant of the "what it is like" problem. In Nagel's eyes there is something-that-it-is-like for sentient beings to see colours, feel pain, or hear sounds and, further, that these *somethings*[9] or phenomenal experiences are forever beyond the reach of the objective categories employed by physicalists and functionalists.[10]

However, in drawing this conclusion on nonconceptualist grounds we must keep two issues separate. The first concerns our ability give expression and describe the character of our phenomenal experiences to each other and the second concerns our ability to understand the quality of experience of other forms of life (or kinds of minds, cf. Dennett 1997: ch. 1). For example, we might ask how is it possible that we, human beings, manage to understand the quality of each other's phenomenal experience? In our case it is our common language which enables us to finely describe and compare how things appear to us. Hence, we mark the relative differences between what-it-is-like to be hungry during a lecture, to feel a gentle rush of wind on one's face on a warm spring day, to recognise a face but be unable to place the name, to look down from a dizzying height, and so on (cf. Searle 1992: 81).

Under the sway of Cartesianism, some philosophers have denied that we are able to speak freely about the quality of phenomenal experiences. They hold that our conscious lives are logically private and hidden and argue that an understanding of another's phenomenal experiences is beyond our ability to grasp, simply because such experiences are isolated to unique points of view.[11] If this thesis were correct then we would be unable to talk sensibly to others about our phenomenal experiences since their nature would be radically inexpressible. For an example of the kind of thinking which this view promotes, consider this passage from Farrell:

> When, for example, we look at a red patch, we all just *know* what it is like to have the corresponding experience, and we all just *know* how it differs from the experience we have when looking at a green patch. *We cannot describe this difference* (Farrell: 1950: 32, emphases mine).

We must ask what can Farrell mean by such remarks? For surely, as linguistic beings, we can and do use words to describe such differences all the time. If I say "I see an olive green boat in the harbour" these words count as an adequate description of what I see but it also describes my experience, albeit not in a particularly detailed way. We might remind Farrell of his own example of seeing the colours red and green. For in making reference to these colours he seems to differentiate two distinct kinds of colour experience perfectly well. In describing *how things appear to us* we are giving descriptions of our phenomenal experiences. Farrell's confidence that we know to which type of colour experiences he is referring is grounded on the fact that he is writing for fellow human beings whose language we can interpret. The possibility of such interpretation rests on the fact that, expect in special circumstances, no question arises about whether others see things as we do. We learn our concepts of experiences against this background and with reference to items, such as colours, pains and the like, which occupy a public, or intersubjective, space. Of course, we may come to discover that another does not see things as we do, as in the case of those who are colour-blind. Yet, such cases do not provide good reason to think that experiences are essentially or initially private. Rather, they explain why we have the important practice of distinguishing first and second-order remarks about experience.[12] The point is that it does not follow that if experiences are best understood as nonconceptual that this precludes the possibility of providing adequate linguistic description of them. Nevertheless, this point must be kept separate from the claim that it is possible for us to understand the conscious life of other non-verbal animals. There the game is quite different. For it can be argued that it is impossible to understand what it is like to be a non-human creature on the grounds that such creatures, not being of our ilk, would be unable to triangulate or share experiences with us. Hence, they cannot learn our experiential concepts or descriptively index their experiences (see Hutto: forthcoming).[13]

Following in Farrell's footsteps, Nagel asks us to consider the conscious experience of a bat in his classic example.[14] He claims that in order to fully understand what it would be-like-to-be a bat we would need to do much more than simply give a description of its moth-chasing behaviour, its physio-chemical make-up, or even the inputs and outputs of the causal mechanisms that underpin its capacity for echolocation. None of these kinds of description provide any insight into the fundamentally inexpressible *way of being* in the world that the bat allegedly enjoys. As a consequence of this *Gendanken-experiment,* Nagel concludes that there are clearly facts about ourselves and our animal neighbours which are not susceptible to objective analysis — therefore functionalism (indeed any form of physicalism) is, and always will be, incomplete when it comes to understanding such aspects of phenomenal experience.

One way of reading the claim that phenomenal experience at least in its basic forms, is not conceptual in nature and for this reason alone it is beyond analysis. If we focus on the issue of expressiblity this reading of Nagel's position becomes trivially true. Thus, consider his remark that:

> Reflection on what it is like to be a bat seems to lead us, therefore, to the conclusion that there are facts that do not consist *in the truth of propositions expressible in a human language* (Nagel 1979: 171).

However, Nagel also forces us to confront the question: How can we tell if a non-human creature is conscious, or what it's conscious experiences are like, if we cannot interpret it? His analysis bids us to expect not only that creatures experience the world nonconceptually but they may be aware of or directed at *different aspects* of the world that are invisible to us. Moreover, they may experience the same things we are directed at *differently* because they do so by means of alien sensory apparatus. Again a word of caution is in order. In accepting this claim we need not endorse a purely introspectionist or solipsistic account of consciousness. Indeed it is because ascriptions of conscious life are not logically private that we, like Nagel, can be so confident that consciousness is a, "...widespread phenomena...which occurs at many levels in animal life" (Nagel 1979: 166). Our problem is not creeping scepticism about other minds, but that, "...our concepts of consciousness ...[will be]...constrained by our own form of consciousness" (McGinn 1991: 9; Dennett 1997: 4–5).[15] The fact is that what-it-is-like to be a bat is unbridgeablely different from what-it-is-like to be a human. Even if we can appreciate and understand what-it-is-like to experience nonconceptually in some general sense there are clearly limits to what we can know about which animals have experiences and what those experiences are like. Understanding the character of some other minds is barred because of the differences in our makeup. For this reason it is not a puzzle which the intellect, alone, can solve (Wittgenstein 1980b: §§ 659–663, cf. also § 644, § 558).

The right conclusion is that Nagel and Jackson are wrong, in so far as they are arguing that knowing-what-it-is-like to undergo a conscious experience imparts a special kind of phenomenal *knowledge* that could not be gained in any other way than by having the experience itself. *A fortiori* there is no such knowledge. Nonetheless, the real focus of their critique still has bite. Their thought-experiments cast serious doubt on physicalism's capacity to *give an account* of phenomenal experience. For, if we are talking about nonconceptual experiences, no account is either needed nor, indeed, possible. To chase after it is to be under the spell of *ignis fatuus* (foolish fire). While this may not establish that physicalism is flawed because it is factually incomplete, it does reveal its limits. There is no knowing-what-it-is-like in the case of those whom we cannot interpret without actually undergoing the experiences of the other. This requires transformation not knowledge, *per se.* Dennett's reply to Nagel's challenge is, particularly interesting in this light (Dennett 1991: 441–444). He claims that the, "…task [of understanding bat consciousness] would require us to subject ourselves to vast transformations…[but] we could use our research to say what these transformations would be" (Dennett 1991: 442, 444). For instance, with reference to the case of the bat, he says our biological and ecological research would help by showing, "…us a great deal of what a bat could and could not be *conscious of* under various conditions" (Dennett 1991: 444, emphasis mine).

We must tread carefully here, for it is easy to confuse what one is conscious of with the way in which one is conscious of it. This is a fatal confusion, one which the advocates of the strong representationalist thesis must of necessity fall prey to. Consider this passage from Dretske:

> …in running discrimination tests on dogfish, Mary is determining just which deformations of the electric field the dogfish is sensitive to and which it is "blind" to. Mary is thereby learning exactly what it is like (for dogfish) to sense electric fields. (Dretske 1995: 87)

That Dretske conflates the objects of experience with the experiences themselves is further illustrated when he illegitimately moves from talk of mechanisms detecting differences in speeds to talk of them *feeling* speeds in different ways, having different *quales* for them and *experiences* of them (cf. Dretske 1995: 75).[16] Consider his example of the parasite:

> Since in the case of our parasite, the property the object (the host) has when the perception is veridical is the property of being 18°C, that has to be the quale of the parasite's experience of the host whether or not the parasite is perceiving the host veridically. So anyone who knows what 18°C is, knows what this property is, knows what quale the parasite's experience has. (Dretske 1995: 84, cf. also 83).

What is lost in Dretske's description is an account of how things appear *to the tick*. Here is a quotation, from Clark, concerning a tick's *Umwelt* which also highlights the means by which the animals respond to their environment.

> Butyric acid, when detected, induces the tick to loose its hold on a branch and to fall on the animal. Tactile contact extinguishes the olfactory response and initiates a procedure of running about until heat is detected. Detection of heat initiates boring and burrowing. (Clark 1997: 24)

Clark employs the euphemism of "niche-dependent sensing" and reminds us that this notion originates with Von Uexkull's account in terms of imagining an invisible world. Yet, it is not for nothing that Von Uexkull's work is entitled *A Stroll through the Worlds of Animals and Men: A Picture Book of Invisible Worlds* (cf. Clark 1997: 24). The worlds are invisible precisely because neither Dretske's nor Clark's descriptions give us any insight into how things look or feel to the parasite in question. Dretske doesn't see this problem because, as a strong representationalist, he focuses solely on what the experience is meant to represent as opposed to how it represents. Thus he tells us "What makes…an experience — the experience it is what it is an experience of" (Dretske 1995: 36). This apparently runs contrary to the idea that physicalism is limited in its capacity to tell us about phenomenal experience. However, at one stage he writes:

> There is one thing dogfish *can do* that Mary cannot do…Suppose a fish experience[d] an electric field pattern P. If these fish could think, this fish could think that *this* (referring to the experienced electric field) has pattern P. Mary cannot. *Not being aware of* any electric field, Mary knows nothing that can be expressed in quite this form. (Dretske 1995: 87, first and third emphases mine, cf. also Tye 1996: 142)

While I agree fully with the tenor of this second remark, this approach will only work if one is willing to say more about the phenomenal character of nonconceptual content which acts as a *basis* or *ground* for such indexical and perceptual judgements (cf. also Tye 1996: 137–138; Hutto 1995: 473–475). As suggested above, if we see our abilities as grounded in our capacity for nonconceptual experience, then this can act as a basis for conceptual judgement. But it need not. There can be unexpressed, and in the case of non-verbals, inexpressible phenomenal experiences.

In this light Nagel and Jackson are right to think there will be an inexplicable residue (even though wrong to characterise it as a special kind of knowledge) after the process of seeing is fully characterised, functionally and neurologically speaking. This residue is the qualitative character of phenomenal experience. But the reason why a neurologist cannot give an account of it is not, to borrow Dretske's terminology, because it is "a representational fact" which concerns representational content as opposed to the vehicle of that content, which is located in the brain (cf. Dretske 1995: 3). Although it is true that representational contents are invisible to those concerned only with inputs and outputs and neurology, this is not the reason, as we have seen above, why phenomenal experience eludes detection from the physicalist's point of view.[17]

The best of intentionality

Thankfully, it is not necessary to accept the strong representationalist thesis in order to reap the benefits of a nonconceptualist understanding of phenomenal experience. Even if we acknowledge, as I think we ought, that there is an nonconceptual, intentional (or representational) *aspect* to experience, this should not be confused with its phenomenal character. To make this, and some related points clearer, it will prove useful to say something more about current theories of intentional content. Both Dretske's and Tye's representational accounts suffer, in different ways, from inadequacies inherent in their theories of representation. Tye endorses a causal-computational account of representation (cf. Tye 1996: 100–101). Whereas Dretske advances his own, much more developed and elaborate account of teleofunctional semantics which rests on a information-theoretic account of content (Dretske 1995: 4–7; 1981, 1988). Both of these theories of representation are riddled with internal difficulties, as revealed by the suite of problems about misrepresentation, disjunction and transitivity which I will not dally to discuss here (cf. Hutto 1999). In so far as

Dretske addresses the issue of normativity by appealing to the biological function that indicators serve in order to unpack the notion of representations, his account is to be preferred. Nonetheless, the central and common problem from which these accounts mutually suffer is that, at base, they hope to clarify the notion of representation wholly in terms of indicative relations of different sorts without giving any serious care and attention to what consumes the representations. This is a problem in representational theory in general but it has very serious consequences in the context of understanding phenomenal experience.

The problem is best exposed if we consider a superior theory of intentional content which hails from the biosemantist camp (Millikan 1984, 1993; Neander 1991, 1995; Godfrey-Smith, 1989, 1992, 1993, 1994a, 1994b). Like Dretske, such theorists claim that if we appeal to a principled notion of biological function it is possible to explicate the nature of intentionality. But, crucially, they do not rest their theories on a pre-given, information-theoretic notion of indication. Millikan's work avoids the problems of both information-theoretic and causal theories of content by distinguishing proper functions from mechano-functions and by advancing a selectionist account of the former. For our purposes, the primary thing to note is that the very idea of a proper function is essentially normative. As she never tires of observing, abnormality and dysfunction only make sense against a background understanding of proper functioning. Furthermore, the norms introduced by a selectionist account must not be confused with statistical norms (Millikan 1993: 165). Thus, on her account, a completely malformed device, provided it is a member of a reproductively established family, can have a proper function even if it rarely, or never succeeds, in performing it. One of her favourite ways to illustrate this is by appeal to the case of sperm and the ovum (cf. Millikan 1984: 4, 29, 34). She writes, "It is the biological purpose of the sperm to swim until it reaches an ovum. That is what its tail is for. But very few sperm actually achieve this biological end because ova are in such short supply." (Millikan 1993: 223).

For Millikan, the source of the normativity of proper functions stems from natural selection and is decidedly etiological, or historically-based. To understand proper functions requires reference to a device's normal conditions, or ideal conditions, of operation. She fleshes out her theory by appeal to the interlinked notions of *normal explanations* and *normal conditions*. The former, "...explains the performance of a particular function, telling how it was (typically) historically performed on those (perhaps rare) occasions when it was properly performed" (Millikan 1993: 86). With respect to "normal conditions" her position is that they must, "...be mentioned when giving a full normal explanation for the performance of that function" (Millikan 1993:86). Thus, she maintains that normal conditions could also be described as historically optimal conditions (Millikan 1993:87, cf. also 28).[18]

Bearing these points in mind, Millikan rightly insists that the first place it is appropriate to speak of "content" is with respect to biological devices that she calls "intentional icons" (cf. Millikan 1984: ch. 6; 1993: ch. 5).[19] Such icons are intentional (not intensional) in Brentano's sense in that they can be *directed at* features, objects or states of affairs which may or may not exist (cf. Millikan 1993:109; 1989:96). There are several features that all intentional icons share. These are that: (a) they are relationally adapted to some feature of the world (which she dubs an *adaptor*) by means of a mapping rule (mathematical conceived); (b) they have the adapted derived proper function to produce an appropriate response in the consumer *via* such a mapping; and (c) they have the direct proper function to guide a co-operating device in the performance of its direct proper function(s) (adapted from Millikan 1993:106–107).[20]

Millikan's own paradigm example of a simple intentional icon is the bee dance. Such dances are meant to generate an appropriate response in a co-operating consumer mechanism(s); the watching bee or bees. In this case, the response is a patterned flight response ought to take the bee(s) to the location of nectar.[21] A bee dance, like other intentional icons, has both indicative and imperative aspects. If the relational conditions for this characteristic type of dance are normal then it will successfully map the location of nectar *via* some mathematically describable projection rule. This is the icon's indicative aspect. If all is well on this score, then the consumer mechanism(s) ought to produce the appropriate, adapted response of taking the bee(s) to the nectar. This is the icon's imperative aspect (cf. Millikan 1984:99). The point is that to rightly understand the referential features of intentional icons it is necessary that we focus on their direct proper functions. This in turn requires us to focus on the end for which they are consumed.

Although in the case of the bee dance there are two organisms, the account works just as easily with distinct mechanisms within a single organism. Millikan is explicit about this intended use. She writes:

> Put (an analogue of) the bee dance inside the body so that it mediates between two parts of the same organism and you have…an inner representation (Millikan 1993:164).

The strong contrast between the biosemantic theory of content and causal/informational theories is transparent if we bear in mind that the functions of intentional icons are determined by considering the proper functions of production and consumption devices with reference to their normal, historical, conditions for operation. Thus, Millikan stresses that:

> [I]ntentional icons do not, as such or in general, carry "natural information". Nor do they "covary" with or "track" what they icon. Their definition makes no reference to how likely or unlikely they are actually to correspond to their designated environmental features, nor how likely these features are to get mapped by them (Millikan 1993: 107).

The point is that we cannot understand the direct proper function of intentional icons by sole reference to what they regularly map, statistically understood. Neither can we understand the direct proper function of sperm or livers by sole reference to their mechanical dispositions. Rather the direct proper functions of icons need to be explicated with reference to what effect they produce on or for their consumer devices given the normal, or ideal, conditions for the operation (cf. Jacob 1997: 110). With this in hand, we are now in a position to see how all this relates to representational theories of experience. Consider Tye's remark:

> Experiences nonconceptually represent that there is *a* surface or *an* internal region having so-and-so features at such-and-such locations, and thereby they acquire their phenomenal character (Tye 1996: 139).

If we adopt the biosemantic theory a better formulation would be as follows:

> Experiences nonconceptually direct an organism O towards a surface or an internal region because doing so produces an effect that, in the past, has helped the ancestors of organism O with this response to proliferate.

There are several reasons to prefer the second formulation over the first. One immediate advantage is that it gives us a foothold in understanding the origins and nature of the so-called secondary qualities, such as colour experiences. For example, because Tye relies on a causal theory with a notion of tracking at its heart he is forced to face up to the difficult problem of making sense of colour objectivism (see Tye 1996: 144–150). Noting the absence of any external features of the world that can be neatly identified with the various colours, we might take seriously Dennett's proposal. He suggests that, "Some things in nature 'needed to be seen' and others needed to see them, so a system evolved that tended to minimize the task for the latter by highlighting the salience of the former. Consider the insects. Their color vision co-evolved with the colors of the plants they pollinated, a good trick of design that benefited both." (Dennett

1991: 377, cf. also 378, 381). If we regard colour experiences as primary examples of creature-relative responses then their metameric nature need not trouble us (Dretske 1995: 89).

Another major advantage is that the biosemantic is that it does not mislead one into supposing that surfaces or regions are represented *as* having features. Any theory concerned to emphasise the nonconceptual character of experiences needs to exercise caution on this front. Moreover, biosemantic theory is helpful in clarifying the nature of nonconceptual content in a yet more positive way. A major stumbling block for advocates of nonconceptual content is that if one wishes to speak about representational content at all it is generally supposed that one must also speak of correctness conditions of some kind. However, the very idea of correctness conditions conjures up the image of conceptual, intensional content that relates to objects or features of the environments in ways that involve truth and reference. But taking this line threatens to rule out the attractive possibility of appealing to nonconceptual content as a means of understanding how the subjective/objective contrast develops. Recognising this, Cussins has advanced a formulation of nonconceptual content, discussed earlier, in terms of the "realm of embodiment" (which he equates with experience). He explicitly contrasts this with accounts of content that appeal to the "realm of reference". Thus he denounces accounts which, "...suppose that representation in embodied practice is to be explained in terms of the prior, and therefore *given*, notions of truth and the realm of reference" (Cussins 1992b: - 652, emphasis mine). His is an attempt to prioritise our capacity for experiential response over our capacity to refer when theorising about our most basic cognitive performances (cf. Cussins 1992b: 653). His notion of nonconceptual content is meant to provide, "...a genuine notion of significant representation" which does not require taking "truth" or "reference" as basic notions. However, talk of embodied experience alone is not sufficient to underpin or explain the directedness of intentionality because it leaves us without a principled account of the norms that govern nonconceptual responses in relation to worldly things and features.

It is precisely here that a suitably modest account of biosemantics supplies the requisite *kind* of normativity for nonconceptual content without relying on notions of truth or reference as given. There is nothing wrong in thinking that the most basic nonconceptual contents have "correctness conditions" provided we are careful in understanding their source and nature. According to a modest biosemantic theory of content although intentional icons are normatively directed at features of the world their "correctness conditions" are not best understood as "truth conditions".[22] For example, biosemantists need not, and should not, hold that content of the frog's intentional icon is anything like the conceptual content of the English sentence "There is an edible bug". Millikan notes:

> bee dances, though (as I will argue) these are intentional items, do not contain denotative elements, because interpreter bees (presumably) do not identify the referents of these devices but merely react to them appropriately (Millikan 1984:71).

We identify the object that the bee is directed at *as* nectar using our own conceptual schema, but the bees do not. For this reason when we attempt to characterise the content of such icons, in a principled manner, it is inappropriate to deploy our standard scheme of reference. The consequence of taking this view is that:

> One can, therefore, speak of the mechanism detecting flies, or enabling the frog to detect flies, but this is only in a secondary and derivative sense... (Rowlands 1997:295).

Finally, and connectedly, by focusing on the issue of the icon consumer, we must confront the spectre of *the way in which* the organism responds to or uses the representation. For although the consumption of an icon will have, at some point, benefited the ancestor organisms, it would be wrong to think that in doing so the organism, itself, need have any awareness of it. Looking at things in this light uncovers a vitally important question that tends to get obscured in these discussions. What is "consuming" or "interpreting" the icon? In cases involving nonconceptual intentionality, following Millikan's model, we must not assume that even the whole organism is involved, for it may merely a subpersonal mechanism. In either case we are not dealing with a "subject" which is capable of "identifying" the icons as anything at all. This affords Millikan a neat reply to the problem that Dennett once labelled *Hume's problem* (Dennett 1985:122).[23] According to Dennett, Hume's worry was that the only sensible use of the term representation was to describe a representation to or for *something*. Problems start if that *something*, "...takes the form of a little man in the machine, a homunculus, a demon or a goblin..." (Dennett 1985:57). For if such an internal viewer (or interpreter) is needed in order to make sense of the original representation then we will need another internal viewer in its head in order to explain how it views, and so on *ad infinitum*.

Returning to case of the bees once more, it is clear that there can be intentionality without the existence of any internal interpreters. Yet although this is good news for our understanding of intentionality, it highlights a crucial reason why phenomenal experience must be treated differently. For when it comes to understanding experiences we must rightly wonder: *who* or *what* is having them? Unless we wrongly and illicitly paper over this difficulty by equating "the internal operations of the system" with the "subject of experience" we will have no answer to this question. Strong representationalists have no answer to the questions "Who consumes the experience?" and "In what way it does so?". This is the Achilles' heel of their approaches (cf. Chalmers 1996:-296–297). Crucially, this is why experience cannot be understood solely in terms of intentionality and the two, while intertwined, should not be conflated.

Functionality, conceptual schema and the hard problem

In defending the claim that experience cannot be equated with mere capacities or intentional responses, it would appear that I am endorsing something akin to Chalmer's distinction between phenomenal and functional awareness (cf. Chalmers 1996:29). That being so it may appear as if I must face up to his hard problem of consciousness, as exemplified by his question: "Why should there be conscious experience at all?" (Chalmers 1996:4).

Yet, this explanatory version of the "hard problem" is not really so very hard. It loses its teeth in light of the mere observation that conscious experience makes a difference to the performance of many general tasks (Dretske 1995:-116–122). We know that in the execution of our daily routines responses to the environment which are mediated by experience generally convey real advantages over those that do not. For example, consider the case of blindsight. It is amazing that the afflicted subjects can perform better than chance when describing aspects of their environment, despite their reported lack of experience. Of course, to do this they need to employ the roundabout means of being prompted by experimenters in order to access such information (cf. van Gulick 1989:220). Yet, as Dretske notes, although this is remarkable the fact is blindsighted subjects, "...cannot avoid bumping into lampposts, even if they can guess their presence or absence in a forced-choice situation" (Dretske 1995:121; cf. van Gulick 1989:218–220; Marcel 1988). The point is that although blindsight is remarkable, subjects who have the full complement of experiences navigate the world much better.

All of this fits well with the supposition that the capacity for experience confers advantages. These observations are enough to put to rest worries raised by the question: Why is there consciousness? Even so, if this reply is on the right track it only further highlights a more genuinely hard question: How is phenomenal consciousness possible?[24] I have elsewhere labelled this second problem the metaphysical problem (Hutto 1998d).[25] At its heart is the difficulty we have in providing an intelligible account of the relation between consciousness and the physical. Indeed, it is a problem best understood against the backdrop of the metaphysics of physicalism.

Physicalism holds our ultimate ontology is physical, even though it isn't entirely clear how to define the scope of "the physical" (cf. Tye 1996: 38- 39).[26] Reductive physicalists, as the name suggests, hope to show how all higher-order phenomena reduce without residue into lower-order phenomena. Non-reductive physicalists tend to appeal to softer notions of supervenient composition and realisation when attempting to understand the relation between consciousness and its physical base (cf. Tye 1996: 40–42; Charles 1992). However, I claim that the reason consciousness resists incorporation into a physicalist framework, of either sort, is because it cannot be understood in terms of an object-based schema.

What does it mean to say that consciousness does not fall within an object-based schema? The point is that in its humble beginnings, classical physics was essentially concerned with explaining the behaviour of familiar, macro-physical objects. Hookway, in an attempt to provide a broad definition of the physical, proposes, "...a property is physical if it has a fundamental role in the explanatory practice which grows out of our initial concern to master the behaviour of spatio-temporal physical things. This leaves it open what the physical world is actually like, while keeping that world anchored through those *spatially extended objects* which were our first paradigms of the physical" (Hookway 1988: 74, emphasis mine). What is right about Hookway's suggestion is that even though physical science has undergone considerable theoretical transformations, it remains a vital hallmark of classical physics that its entities can be spatio-temporally located (cf. Einstein and Infeld 1961: ch. 1; Hodgson 1991:-208–209, 259). To approach the study of consciousness from such a starting point or in a parallel fashion generates confusion. It promotes a misleadingly picture of consciousness based on the model of an inner world populated with objects which can be viewed by introspection. Here lies not only monsters, but nonsense (cf. Hutto 1995: 465–467).

This is why physicalism looks most plausible if we consider the interrelations between domains such as chemistry and physics where it is possible to see, in a fully transparent fashion, how all the elements link together (cf. P.S.

Churchland 1986: 279). That is to say, it is possible to understand how chemical molecules decompose into their atomic basis, be they compounds or elements. All that is needed is a specification of the kinds of bonds that would have to exist between the atoms in order to form the molecule. Thus, there is nothing puzzling about the idea that a chemical molecule is composed of certain types of atoms, in the right mix, bonded together in the right kind of way. There is also no intractable problem in giving an intelligible account of the mechanisms that forge such links, such as sharing or trading electrons. The reason such relations can be made transparent is that although atoms, electrons, elements, compounds and molecules are all different they all partake of a common conceptual schema. Specifically, be they on a micro or macro scale, such things can be understood according to an object-based schema in that, at the very least, all such items occupy three-dimensional properties and spatio-temporal locations and have identifiable properties that can be quantified. This is not the case with consciousness, and it is the source of difficulty in making it intelligible within any physicalist framework (cf. Tye 1996: 64–65).[27]

Although many denounce this picture they are inclined to take seriously problems that simply do not make sense without in some way presupposing it. For example, some philosophers have been tempted to ask: Where is my experience of pain located? They take the sense of this question to be akin to the query: Where is my pen located? But trying to establish the location of experiences leads directly to the problem of phenomenal space. It is the problem of finding a place for the world of experience within the world of physical space (McGinn 1995: 149–153; Rundle 1997: 26–27, 40–41). Yet, if we decline to locate objects of experience in the physical world we might be inclined to locate them in some world of secondary qualities — a world with spatial boundaries that are phenomenal as opposed to physical. But this invites the legitimate question: "What is phenomenal space? Is it physical space inside the brain? Is it the on-stage space in the theater of consciousness located in the brain?" (Dennett 1991: 130). In the very question one can hear the echoes of the long-standing debate over the issue of objects of perception between the representational sense-data theorists and their naive realists opponents. Are the objects of perception in the mind, in virtue of which we see the world or are they items in the world which we see directly? Neither answer is satisfactory as we shall see.

If we take seriously the idea that there is an intentional, or directed aspect to most experience, as discussed in section three, we can throw some light on this issue. The thought is that our most basic conscious responses, and those of non-linguistic creatures, are nonconceptual responses directed at aspects of an environment — be that environment internal, like a damaged lining in the stomach or external, like a thrown object.[28] In this I agree with Tye when he claims that the objects of experience are not located in the mind or head (Tye 1996: 135–136). He reminds us that:

> When you turn your gaze inward and try to focus your attention on intrinsic features of these experiences, why do you always seem to end up attending to what the experiences are *of*? Suppose you have a visual experience of a shiny, blood-soaked dagger. Whether, like Macbeth, you are hallucinating or whether you are seeing a real dagger you experience redness and shininess as outside you, as covering the surface of the dagger…In turning one's mind inward to attend to the experience, one seems to end up scrutinising external features or properties. (Tye 1996: 135–136).[29]

This compares well with Wittgenstein's remark on this topic when he writes:

> What actually is the "world" of consciousness? There I'd like to say: "What goes on in my mind, what's going on in it now, what I see, hear…Couldn't we simplify that and say "What I am now seeing"? (Wittgenstein 1992: 74e).

When we are not regarding the world through the eyes of physicists, it makes perfect sense to say that colours are out there, not in here. Nevertheless, while I think we can make sense of the idea that the *objects* of consciousness are features of the world I would not wish to claim, as Dretske does, that experiential content *per se* can be identified with the properties of things which our experiences are meant to represent (cf. Dretske 1995: 36). Although this would solve the location problem by placing the contents of consciousness in the world, it wrongly conflates the object or focus of consciousness with its experiential content. For example, it is always possible to distinguish the object's properties from the way they appear to *certain kinds* of creature, or to a *particular* creature of a certain kind, or to a particular creature of a certain kind in conditions x and y, and so on. If we wish to talk of consciousness as "a mode of presentation" we must distinguish between the properties *of the thing* itself (the object) and *the way* they are presented (the content).[30]

McGinn is right to note that when confronted with the problem of finding a home for experiences in the world there is a pervasive tendency, amongst philosophers, to try to locate the experiences in the brain of the subject on the basis of causal considerations (McGinn, 1995: 151). Thus, despite adopting the strong representationalist line we find Tye suggesting a cerebral location for experience. He writes, "…if I have a pain in my leg, intuitively, I am aware of something in my leg (and not in my head, *which is where the experience itself is*) as painful" (Tye 1996: 116, emphasis mine; cf. also Tye 1996: 91). Presumably, as with Dretske's account, the idea is that the brain state which is identified with the experience is simply a vehicle of content and hence can be located in the brain.[31] Yet, it is not plausible to simply regard experiences as mere neural vehicles of representational content. We cannot identify them with brain states in this casual manner. Unless the intelligibility of some form of reductive identity theory is illicitly presupposed, we come face to face with the full complement of unanswered questions all over again.

My suggestion is that we ought not treat conscious experiences as kinds of object at all. Hence we must surrender the attempt to locate them in this way. Putting aside our other differences, Dennett is right in thinking that we must altogether rid ourselves of the misleading picture of consciousness as the "cinema show of the senses" with an internal viewer. This applies just as much to the issue of the location of conscious experiences as to the question of the location of the subject of consciousness (cf. Chalmers 1996: 297).[32] It is simply the wrong model for understanding consciousness. As Aristotle noted long ago, when we see something we do not "see" our seeing it. There is no sensory means of sensing conscious experience. It is not seen, it is the *medium* through which we see. Long before Hume gave expression to his problem, Aristotle wrote, "...if the sense concerned with sight is indeed different from sight, either there will be an infinite regress or there will be some sense which is concerned with itself; so that we had best admit this of the first in the series" (*De Anima*, 425^b 15–18). The point is that if we wish to avoid intractable difficulties it is better to regard consciousness, not as what is experienced, but as the *medium* through which we experience.[33] This is not to bury or avoid the problems associated with our attempts to understand subjective experience. It is simply to reiterate that things in the ordinary spatio-temporal world are the *targets* of perception, but this world is not co-extensive with the world of consciousness itself (cf. Searle 1992: 131). In taking this line we can agree that the representationalists get the story generally right about the distal locations — internal or external — of the *objects* at which conscious experience is directed. We can also agree with them about the bodily or neural locale of the *means*, or mechanisms, by which experience is made possible. But experience itself cannot be identified with either of these. The consequence of this view that it is not possible to give something like our *experience* of the colour red a location in the way we can locate our car keys or a pencil on our desks (cf. McGinn 1995: 150). To borrow McGinn's summary, "In advance of theoretical reconstruction consciousness is not spatially well-behaved" (McGinn 1995: 153).

Conclusion

In light of the fact that consciousness cannot be understood in an object-based schema my claim is that the metaphysical problem is not a problem to be solved — but one to be avoided or unravelled. By its very formulation it is linked to a materialist or physicalist metaphysics. It arises in different ways for those who favour reductive and non-reductive versions of the doctrine. I have elsewhere proposed that the way around this problem is first to accept that consciousness cannot be understood in an object-based schema and then, on this basis to rethink our current metaphysics and adopt a more tolerant naturalism as provided by a version of absolute idealism (Hutto 1998d, 1999, 2000).

Notes

1. Or as he puts it elsewhere, "Seeing-as demands bringing the sensory input under the appropriate schema" (Tye 1996: 104).

2. This understanding fits with Jackson's criticisms of Berkeley on the objects of sense perception (cf. Jackson 1977: 7–8).

3. Aristotle supposedly believed that we have a "…sense faculty [which] we share with animals and [an] intellectual apprehension [which] we share with God or gods" (Kahn 1979: 30). This contrasts with the Cartesian doctrine according to which human minds are uniquely identified by their thinking essences. Thus, the ability to think, as exemplified by the reasoning required to conceptually recognise that we exist, is the essential distinguishing feature of mentality. Hence, "…the term 'thought' served as the most general expression for the common property of all mental acts" (Kahn 1979: 23). Thus by its all-pervasive intellectualist bias Cartesianism constrains our understanding of phenomenology in unacceptable ways. The result is that, "…[i]f every human sensation includes thought, and if thought is propositional content together with propositional attitude, then at the very centre of every sensation of ours there is a proposition" (Malcolm 1977: 45; Kenny, 1973). This is a major source of inspiration for the overly intellectual account of phenomenal awareness.

4. This is why Aristotle writes, "…thinking is also distinct from perceiving — I mean that we find rightness and wrongness — rightness in understanding, knowledge, true opinion, wrongness in their opposites; for perception of the special objects of sense is always free from error, and is found in all animals, while it is possible to think falsely as well as truly, and thought is found only where there is discourse of reason" (*De Anima*, Bk III, 427^{b} 7–14).

5. Tye believes that this gives us reason to regard vision as modular, or cognitively impenetrable. It suggests that the, "…perceptual processes that operate on the retinal input in a largely fixed, autonomous manner" (Tye 1996: 102).

6. The physical is broadly construed to include the behavioural, neurological, functional and so on.

7. He writes, "…after Mary sees here first ripe tomato, she will realize how impoverished her conception of the mental life of others has been all along." (Jackson 1997: 568).

8. Cussins writes, "Evans saw that contents can be canonically specified by the theorist's referring to abilities of the organism, where the abilities are not (or need not be) part of the realm of reference….These abilities are not available to the subject as the content's referent, but they are available to the subject as the subject's experience-based knowledge of how to act on the object, and respond to it." (Cussins 1992b: 655). He has spoken of a contrast between the world presented as truth-maker as opposed to it being presented as the realm of activity ("Nonconceptual Content Conference", University of Hertfordshire, 1st November, 1997).

9. According to Nagel, "…fundamentally an organism has conscious mental states if there is something that it is like to *be* that organism — something it is like *for* the organism" (Nagel 1979: 166). To highlight this Dretske notes the distinction between creature consciousness of the kind of which Nagel speaks and state consciousness, where "conscious" is an accolade we apply to certain mental states as opposed to others (Dretske 1995: 98).

10. Functionalism and physicalism generally come together if the former insists that "mental" items must be *identifiable* in terms of their objectively specifiable causal roles. As Hornsby says, "Such a theory contains terms of two sorts, which David Lewis has called the T-terms and the O-terms. The T-terms are, intuitively, mental terms to be thought of as receiving implicit definition; in a functional theory, their denotations are accorded functional roles that are specified using only the non-mental O-terms…physical states [which] occupy the functional roles of mental states" (Hornsby 1986: 99). Or as Shoemaker says: "Functionalism, as a general theory of mind, should be understood as the thesis that all mental states are functionally definable in the strong sense [i.e. …that no mental terminology occurs in the *definiens*]" (Shoemaker 1984: 311).

11. As Nagel sees any given experience is relative to *a single point of view* and it is impossible to objectively describe these individual *points of view* (Nagel 1979: 167). Adoption of this view is usually bound up with acceptance, tacit or explicit, of some form of Cartesianism or aspect thereof. As Kenny notes, "The introduction of *Cogito* as the defining characteristic of the mind is tantamount to the substitution of privacy for rationality as the mark of the mental" (Kenny 1973: 119). Or again in the same paper, "Descartes' innovation was to identify the mental with the private" (Kenny 1973: 120).

12. An example of a first-order remark about my experience would be one, "…concerning not the experience itself but the object of experience" (cf. Chalmers 1996: 175). Chalmers contrasts these with second-order judgements that directly focus on conscious experiences themselves. Thus, he says, "When I have a red sensation, I sometimes notice that I am having a red sensation" (Chalmers 1996: 176). Like Johnston, I claim that such second order *talk* about is derivative and is based on our first learning to speak about things around us (cf. Johnston 1993: 55–57).

13. Dennett remarks, "If the bat could talk, for instance, it would generate a text from which we could generate a heterophenomenological world, and that would give us exactly the same grounds for granting it consciousness that serve for any person. But, as we have just noted, bats can't talk" (Dennett 1991: 445–446).

14. Farrell anticipated Nagel's argument by some years, even by coining the phrase "what-it-is-like-to-be-a-bat". His statement about experience is remarkably similar to Nagel's (cf. Farrell 1950: 35). Nagel acknowledged this debt (see Nagel 1986: 15).

15. In the case of animals and other pre-verbals, as Dennett says, "we start naturally, from our own experience and most of what then springs to mind must be adjusted (mainly downward)" (Dennett 1991: 447).

16. It is of interest, in this context, that the biologist is concerned with the lowest level of a mechanism's proper functions because it is at such a level that the explanation of a device's capacities can be "discharged" in non-teleological terms. It is the hand over point for a different kind of (mechano) functional analysis (cf. Godfrey-Smith 1993). By focusing on the things that mechanisms (devices, responses, etc.) are in fact capable of doing, we are able to understand how such capacities can be broken down into purely physio-chemical (mere causal processes). Rosenberg supplies some detailed examples of the way this kind of homuncular discharge of function takes place, "at the border of molecular biology and organic chemistry" (Rosenberg 1985: 59).

17. For Nagel, the fact that we are conscious aware is the source of the *real* mind/body problem (cf. Nagel 1979, 1986). In this light the fact that proponents of the strong representationalist thesis attempt to subsume consciousness under the notion of representation is ironic. Consider McGinn remark that "Books and articles appear apace offering to tell us exactly what mental aboutness consists in, while heads continue to be shaken over the nature of consciousness" (McGinn 1991: 24). Or consider Dennett's remark that: "[c]onsciousness is regularly regarded, especially by people outside the field of philosophy, as the outstanding (and utterly baffling) challenge to materialist theories of mind. And yet, curiously enough, most of the major participants in the debates *about mental content*...have been conspicuously silent on the topic of consciousness. No theory, or even theory-sketch, of consciousness is to be found in the writings of Fodor, Putnam, Davidson, Stich, Harman, Dretske, or Burge, for instance" (Dennett 1987: x). Searle also comments that "one of the most amazing things about the past half century or so in analytic philosophy of mind is the scarcity of serious work on the nature of consciousness" (Searle 1989: 193).

18. However, it is also vital to note, as Millikan does, that "The notions of "function" and "design" should not be read...as referring only to origin. Natural selection does not slack after the emergence of a structure but actually preserves it by acting against the emergence of less fit structures" (Millikan 1993: 86).

19. She quite rightly borrows the term "icon" from Peirce because it does not carry with it a legacy of confusion and disagreement.

20. Millikan was initially wont to speak of "producer and interpreter devices" in *Language, Thought and Other Biological Categories*, but given that she explicitly did not require that the interpreter, "understand *what* the sign signs" the term "consumer" is less misleading (Millikan 1984: 96).

21. She writes, "The production and 'consumption' of the icon may be accomplished by any mechanisms designed, biologically or in some other way, to co-operate in the iconing project. For example, the dances that honey bees execute to guide fellow workers to nectar are paradigm cases of intentional icons" (Millikan 1993: 107).

22. This sits well with the idea that, "natural selection does not care about truth; it cares about reproductive success" (Stich 1990: 62).

23. Millikan explained how her account of intentionality solves this problem in her talk "Intentionality: A Naturalist Approach", presented to the Philosophy Society of the University of Hertfordshire, 5th March, 1998.

24. This is Chalmers' later way of formulating the problem: "The hardest part of the mind-body problem is the question: how could a physical system give rise to conscious experience" (Chalmers 1996: 25).

25. Tye effectively divides the metaphysical problem into the problems of mechanism and mental causation (cf. Tye 1996: 15–19).

26. As Dennett reminds us, "The prevailing wisdom, variously expressed and argued for, is *materialism*: there is only one kind of stuff, namely *matter* — the physical stuff of physics, chemistry, and physiology — and the mind is somehow nothing but a physical phenomenon. In short, the mind is the brain." (Dennett 1991: 33).

27. In his article "Why is Consciousness Puzzling?" Peter Bieri identifies the source of the trouble in a similar fashion. In discussing the relation of wholes to parts, he makes the following important remark: "...whereas all other laws to which we get accustomed relate perfectly *objective* phenomena, we are here talking about the case where something *subjective* emerges from purely objective factors... there is an essential point we are not willing to give away: sensing or experiencing is something different and new relative to all other systematic properties" (Bieri 1995: 52). Bieri's point is that there is a problem about intelligibility in the case of consciousness.

28. Given the account of intentionality I wish to sponsor, it is important to note that when it comes to understanding proper functions the internal/external dichotomy is largely artificial. The only important difference is that often internal, bodily conditions are homeostatically regulated and hence, more under the organism's control than those of an external environment (Millikan 1993: 161).

29. As Searle notes, "...the vocabulary I use to describe the table — "There's a lamp on the right and a vase on the left and a small statue in the middle" — is precisely that which I use to describe my conscious visual experiences" (Searle 1992: 131). He also gives excellent reasons for thinking the entire introspectionist understanding of consciousness is ill-motivated and based on a naive metaphor (cf. Searle 1992: 97).

30. Dretske takes this path when he suggests that, "...qualia are supposed to be the way things seem or appear in the sense modality in question" (Dretske 1995: 83).

31. Dretske regards brains states as the mere vehicles of experiential content which ought not to be confused with the experiential content itself (cf. Dretske 1995: 35, cf. also 3).

32. A cruder means of locating conscious experience as taking place wherever the person or organism that is having the experience is, of course, not ruled out by this suggestion. I owe this observation to my friend and colleague Dr. Paul Coates.

33. For a fuller discussion of this see (Hutto 1998b).

References

Aristotle. 1984. *The Complete Works of Aristotle: The Revised Oxford Translation.* Vol I & II, J. Barnes (ed.), New Jersey: Princeton University Press.

Bermudéz, J. 1994. "Peacocke's Argument Against the Autonomy of Nonconceptual Representational Content." *Mind and Language* 9(4): 402–418.

Bermudéz, J. 1995. "Nonconceptual Content: From Perceptual Experience to Subpersonal Computational States." *Mind and Language* 10(4): 333–369.

Bieri, P. 1995. "Why is Consciousness Puzzling?" in Metzinger, T. (ed.) *Conscious Experience.* Schöningh: Imprint Academic: 45–60.

Burge, Tyler. 1977. "Belief *De Re.*" *The Journal of Philosophy.* LXXIV: 338–362.

Cassam, Q. 1997. *Self and World.* Oxford: Clarendon Press.

Chalmers, C. 1995. "Facing up to the Problem of Consciousness" *Journal of Consciousness Studies,* 2, no. 3: 200–219.

Chalmers, C. 1996. *The Conscious Mind: In Search of a Fundamental Theory.* Oxford: Oxford University Press.

Charles, D. 1992. "Supervenience, Composition and Physicalism" in Charles, D. and Lennon, K (eds.). *Reduction, Explanation and Realism.* Oxford: Clarendon Press: 265–296.

Chrisley, R. 1993. "Connectionism, Cognitive Maps and the Development of Objectivity". *Artificial Intelligence Review* 7: 329–354.

Churchland, P.M. 1989. *A Neurocomputational Perspective.* Cambridge, M.A. MIT Press.

Churchland, P.S. 1986. *Neurophilosophy.* Cambridge, M.A: MIT Press.

Clark, A. 1989. *Microcognition: Philosophy, Cognitive Science, and Parallel Distributing Processing.* Cambridge, MA. MIT Press.

Clark, A. 1997. *Being There: Putting Brain, Body and World Together Again.* Cambridge, MA. MIT Press.

Coates, P. and Hutto, D. (eds) 1996. *Current Issues in Idealism.* Bristol: Thoemmes Press.

Crane, T. 1992. "The Nonconceptual Content of Experience" in Crane, T. (ed.) *The Contents of Experience.* Cambridge: Cambridge University Press: 136–157

Cussins, A. 1990. "The Connectionist Construction of Concepts" in Boden, M. (ed.) *The Philosophy of Artificial Intelligence.* Oxford: Oxford University Press: 368–440.

Cussins, A. 1992a: "The Limits of Pluralism" in Charles, D. and Lennon, K (eds.). *Reduction, Explanation and Realism.* Oxford: Oxford University Press: 179–223.

Cussins, A. 1992b. "Content, Embodiment and Objectivity: The Theory of Cognitive Trails" *Mind,* 101: 651–688.

Davidson, D. 1980. *Essays on Actions and Events.* Oxford: Clarendon Press.

Davidson, D. 1987. "Problems in the Explanation of Action" in Pettit, P., Sylvan, R. & Norman, J. (eds.). *Metaphysics and Morality.* Oxford: Blackwell: 35–49.

Davidson, Donald. 1991. "Three Varieties of Knowledge" in *A.J. Ayer: Memorial Essays.* Cambridge: Cambridge University Press.

Dennett, D.C. 1985. *Brainstorms.* Cambridge, M.A: MIT Press.

Dennett, D.C. 1987. *The Intentional Stance.* Cambridge, M.A: MIT Press.

Dennett, D.C. 1991. *Consciousness Explained.* New York: Penguin.

Dennett, D.C. 1997. *Kinds of Minds: Towards an Understanding of Consciousness.* London: Phoenix.
Dretske, F. 1981. *Knowledge and the Flow of Information.* Cambridge, Mass. MIT Press.
Dretske, F. 1986. "Misrepresentation" in Bodgan, R. (ed.) *Belief.* Oxford: Oxford University Press: 17–36. Reprinted in Lycan, W. (ed.) 1990. *Mind and Cognition.* Oxford: Blackwell: 129–143.
Dretske, F. 1988. *Explaining Behaviour: Reasons in a World of Causes.* Cambridge, MA. MIT Press.
Dretske, F. 1995. *Naturalizing the Mind.* Cambridge, MA: MIT Press.
Einstein, A and Infeld, L. 1961. *The Evolution of Physics.* Cambridge: Cambridge University Press.
Farrell, B.A. 1950. "Experience." Mind. Reprinted in Chappell (ed.) 1962. *The Philosophy of Mind.* New Jersey: Prentice Hall: 23–48.
Flanagan, O. 1993. *Consciousness Reconsidered.* Cambridge, MA: MIT Press.
Fodor, J.A. 1992. "The Big Idea." *The Times Literary Supplement* July 3.
Godfrey-Smith, P. 1989. "Misinformation." *Canadian Journal of Philosophy* 19(4): 533–550.
Godfrey-Smith, P. 1992. "Indication and Adaptation." *Synthese* 92: 283–312.
Godfrey-Smith, P. 1993. "Functions: Consensus Without Unity." *Pacific Philosophical Quarterly,* 74: 196–208.
Godfrey-Smith, P. 1994a. "A Modern History Theory of Functions." *Nous* 28(3): 344–362.
Godfrey-Smith, P. 1994b. "A Continuum of Semantic Optimism" in Stich, S. and Warfield, T. (eds.) *Mental Representation: A Reader.* Oxford: Blackwells: 259–277.
Hodgson, D. 1991. *The Mind Matters: Consciousness and Choice in a Quantum World.* Oxford: Oxford University Press.
Hookway, C. 1988. *Quine: Language, Experience and Reality.* Oxford: Polity Press.
Hornsby, J. 1986. "Physicalist Thinking and Conceptions of Behaviour" in Pettit C. and McDowell (eds.), *Subject, Thought and Context.* Oxford: Oxford University Press: 95–115.
Hutto, D. 1995. "Consciousness Demystified: A Wittgensteinian Critique of Dennett's Project." *The Monist* 78: 464–478.
Hutto, D. 1996 "Was the Later Wittgenstein a Transcendental Idealist?" in Coates, P. and Hutto, D. (eds.) *Current Issues in Idealism.* Bristol: Thoemmes Press: 121–153.
Hutto, D. 1998a. "Bradleyian Metaphysics: An Healthy Scepticism." *Bradley Studies* 4: 82–96
Hutto, D. 1998b. "Nonconceptual Content and Objectivity." *Eletronic Journal of Analytic Philosophy: Special Issue on Gareth Evans.* http://www.phil.indiana. edu/ejap/ejap.html
Hutto, D. 1998c. "Davidson's Identity Crisis." *Dialectica* 52: 43–61.
Hutto, D. 1998d. "An Ideal Solution to the Problems of Consciousness." *Journal of Consciousness Studies* 5.
Hutto, D. 1999. *The Presence of Mind.* Amsterdam, Philadelphia: John Benjamins.
Hutto, D. 2000. *Beyond Physicalism.* Amsterdam, Philadelphia: John Benjamins.
Hutto, D. Forthcoming. "The World is not Enough: Shared Experiences and Other Minds." in Goldie, P. (ed.) *Understanding Emotions.* Hampshire: Ashgate.
Jackson, Frank. 1977. *Perception: A Representational Theory.* Cambridge: Cambridge University Press.
Jackson, F. 1990. "Epipehomenal Qualia" in Lycan, W. (ed.) *Mind and Cognition.* Oxford: Blackwell: 469–477. Reprinted from *Philosophical Quarterly* 32: 127–136.

Jackson, F. 1997. In Block, N, Flanagan, O and Güzeldere, G. (eds.) *The Nature of Consciousness: Philosophical Debates.* Cambridge, MA: MIT Press: 567–570. Reprinted from 1986. "What Mary Didn't Know." *Journal of Philosophy* 83: 291–295.

Jacob, P. 1997. *What Minds Can Do.* Cambridge: Cambridge University Press.

Johnston, P. 1993. *Wittgenstein: Rethinking the Inner.* London: Routledge.

Kahn, C. 1979. "Sensation and Consciousness in Aristotle's Psychology" in Barnes, Schofield & Sorabji (eds.) *Articles on Aristotle. Vol. 4: Psychology and Aesthetics.* London: Duckworth: 1–31.

Kenny, A.J. 1973. "Cartesian Privacy" in *The Anatomy of the Soul: Historical Essays in The Philosophy of Mind.* Oxford: Blackwell: 113–128.

Kuhn, T. 1970. *The Structure of Scientific Revolutions.* Chicago: University of Chicago Press.

Kirk, R. 1995. "How is Consciousness Possible?" in Metzinger, T. (ed.) *Conscious Experience.* Schöningh: Imprint Academic: 391–407.

Lewis, D. 1990. "What Experience Teaches" in Lycan, W. (ed.) *Mind and Cognition.* Oxford: Blackwell: 499–519.

Malcolm, N. 1963. *Knowledge and Certainty: Essays and Lectures.* New York: Cornell University Press.

Malcolm, N. 1977. "Thoughtless Brutes" in *Thought and Knowledge.* New York: Cornell University Press: 40–57.

Malpas, J.E. 1992. *Donald Davidson and the Mirror of Meaning.* Cambridge: Cambridge University Press.

Marcel, A. 1988. "Phenomenal Experience and Functionalism" in Marcel and Bisiach (eds.) *Consciousness and Contemporary Science.* Oxford: Oxford University Press: 121–158.

McGinn, C. 1991. *The Problem of Consciousness.* Oxford: Blackwell.

McGinn, C. 1995. "Consciousness and Space" in Metzinger, T. (ed.) *Conscious Experience.* Schöningh: Imprint Academic: 149–163.

Millikan, R. 1984. *Language, Thought and Other Biological Categories.* Cambridge, MA. MIT Press.

Millikan, R. 1993. *White Queen Psychology and Other Essays for Alice.* Cambridge, MA: MIT Press.

Nagel, T. 1979. "What It Is Like to Be a Bat" in *Mortal Questions.* New York: Cambridge University Press: 165–180.

Nagel, T. 1986. *The View from Nowhere.* Oxford: Oxford University Press.

Nagel, T. 1994. "Consciousness and Objective Reality" in Warner, R. & Szubka, T. (eds.) *The Mind-Body Problem.* Oxford: Blackwell: 63–68.

Neander, K. 1991. "The Teleological Notion of Function." *Australasian Journal of Philosophy* 69: 454–468.

Neander, K. 1995. "Misrepresenting and Malfunctioning." *Philosophical Studies* 79: 109–141.

Nemirow, L. 1990. "Physicalism and the Cognitive Role of Acquaintance" in Lycan W. (ed.) *Mind and Cognition.* Oxford: Blackwell: 490–499.

Price, H.H. 1967. "Some Considerations about Belief" in Griffiths (ed.) *Knowledge and Belief.* Oxford: Oxford University Press: 41–59.

Rosenberg, A. 1985. *The Structure of Biological Science.* Cambridge: Cambridge University Press.

Rowlands, M. 1997. "Teleological Semantics". *Mind* 106: 279–303.

Rundle, B. 1997. *Mind in Action.* Oxford: Clarendon Press.

Searle, J. 1984. *Minds, Brains and Science.* Cambridge, M.A: Harvard.

Searle, J. 1992. *The Rediscovery of the Mind.* Cambridge, M.A: MIT Press.

Shoemaker, S. 1984. *Identity, Cause and Mind.* Cambridge: Cambridge University Press.

Stich, S. 1990. *The Fragmentation of Reason: Preface to a Pragmatic Theory of Cognitive Evaluation.* Cambridge, Mass.: MIT Press.

Tye, M. 1996. *Ten Problems of Consciousness: A Representational Theory of the Phenomenal Mind.* Cambridge, MA: MIT Press.

van Gulick, R. 1989. "What Difference Does Consciousness Make?" *Philosophical Topics* 17: 211–230.

Wittgenstein, L. 1953. *Philosophical Investigations.* Oxford: Basil Blackwell.

Wittgenstein, L. 1967. *Zettel.* Oxford: Basil Blackwell.

Wittgenstein, L. 1969. *On Certainty.* New York: Harper Torchbooks.

Wittgenstein, L. 1980a. *Remarks on the Philosophy of Psychology Vol. I.* Oxford: Basil Blackwell.

Wittgenstein, L. 1980b. *Remarks on the Philosophy of Psychology Vol. II.* Oxford: Basil Blackwell.

Wittgenstein, L. 1982. *Last Writings on the Philosophy of Psychology: Preliminary Studies for Part II of the Philosophical Investigations Vol I.* Oxford: Blackwell.

Wittgenstein, L. 1992. *Last Writings on the Philosophy of Psychology. Volume II.* Oxford: Blackwell.

Language structure and the structure of consciousness

Can one find a "common denominator" between them?

Maxim I. Stamenov
Institute of the Bulgarian Language, Sofia

Introduction

In contemporary cognitive psychology there are two approaches to consciousness which seem especially pertinent from a linguistic point of view:

a. The first approach deals with the problem how a content of consciousness becomes constructed out of its components each of which is incapable of becoming conscious by itself. This is one of the main concerns of the *constructive approach* to consciousness (cf. Mandler 1985, 1989);

b. The second approach deals with the structure of consciousness and the prerequisites and consequences for some mental content (from some mental module) of gaining access to consciousness. This is an approach advocated by, e.g., Baars (1988) in his Global Workspace theory of consciousness. This theory places an emphasis on the consequences for some mental content gaining access to consciousness. We may call it an *integrative approach* to consciousness although here what we have in mind is not integration of the parts of the future explicit mental content of some state of consciousness, but rather integration as an outcome of the work of some set of mental structures capable of unifying and widely (re)distributing some aspects of the mental information currently processed in the brain.

In this article, I will discuss some aspects of both constructive and integrative approaches to consciousness. I will address, more specifically, the following two aspects of the problem:

i. What are the "components" of language structure, if any, whose binding, linking or union can or must necessarily lead to an act of becoming conscious of all of them as parts of some unified conscious mental content? and
ii. What are the "components" (modules, subsystems) of mental structure which can and/or must causally support the formation of a conscious language-specific mental state with qualitative mental content?

Language structure is implemented in the mind as a highly stratified hierarchy of patterns activated in a parallel distributed way from long-term memory (LTM) stores and constructed from on-line structures in the working memory (WM). We can conjecture, in the first approximation, that there must be some level(s) of integration of sentence and/or discourse structure and meaning which critically enable (parts of) them to become accessible to consciousness. Components of structure at these levels may turn out to be identical to some "standard" concepts in making sense of sentence/discourse pattern formation, such as

a. predicativity (the capacity to integrate on-line two or more mental contents which by themselves cannot function as an implementation of consciousness);
b. some other specific features of sentence structure like grammatical relations and/or syntactic transformations (analogical transforms) operating on grammatical relations; or
c. referentiality (the requirement imposed on sentence structure obligatorily to undergo truth-conditional and/or possible worlds semantic interpretation). This requirement, if reformulated, would be reduced to the claim that there is no possibility in the mind for the syntactic processor to function in an encapsulated way for its own sake, i.e., without necessarily triggering an attempt of semantic interpretation. This is a strong claim because, in this way, we posit a link of necessity in the relation from syntax to semantics (but not in the direction from semantics to syntax); and/or
d. a (sub)set of semantic roles (e.g., the explication of trajector/ landmark; cf. Langacker 1997) and their schemata-motivated (quasi-)localistic mental spaces may require as part of their realization becoming conscious of mental content.
e. conscious cognitive states are implemented not just by one but by the interfacing of two or three subsystems of cognitive processing, e.g., of syntax/semantics, semantics/pragmatics or syntax/semantics/pragmatics. In the case patterns from each of them are mapped (or blended; cf. Fauconnier 1997), we will experience a conscious mental state. Formulated in a different

> way, we can expect that whenever some formal pattern of language structure is identified with some *pattern of* meaning, the interface of form and meaning would be what we experience as a conscious mental state having an appropriate qualitative content "what it is like" to be in a situation like that. For example, when I utter *This tomato is red,* I experience a conscious mental state to the degree I manage to unify the syntactic structure of the sentence, its meaning (conceptual structure) and an indexical external (represented in my perceptual mental state) or an internal (imagined) situation of looking at and seeing a red tomato.

In this article I will try to explore the possibility of identifying some level of sentence and/or utterance formation as the one where consciousness must necessarily emerge due to the accrual of some set of necessary and sufficient conditions (statable in terms of structure, function and/or specificity of qualitative mental content). It should be clear from the beginning that conditions (a)–(d) would be conscious-state-internal conditions for the formation of a state of consciousness, while (e) posits a difference between the structure of consciousness (as interface between different components of the system supporting consciousness) and its mental content which can be generated in one or two of them but is by no means identical to the structure of consciousness itself. In other words, in the case of (e) there is always a difference between the implicit (supporting) structure of consciousness and the conscious language-specific content one experiences at any moment of time.

The problem of "correspondence" and "dissociability" at the interface between syntax, semantics and pragmatics of natural language

One of the widely shared (implicitly or explicitly) beliefs in linguistics is that the minimal unit of language structure which is compatible with the structure of both thought and reality is that of the sentence. It is standardly claimed that a sentence expresses (implements) a well-defined thought. The thought itself is prototypically a representation of some discrete event in the external world. In this way, we have a mapping between the structure of language, cognitive structure and structure of the world.

If every sentential syntactic pattern had a unique matching type of semantic pattern (in the mentalese of thought) and referred to a well-defined type of event in reality, we should have had serious trouble in differentiating between these types of structure. There is, however, no one-to-one mapping between these three types of structure. In other words, the other side of compatibility is the capacity to dissociate language structure, cognitive structure and the structure of reality from each other. This dissociability can be illustrated by the already famous passive transformation, where one and the same situation in the world and its conceptualization in the form of semantic roles is expressed by means of two different clausal syntactic constructions:

(1) a. *John kissed Mary.*
    b. *Mary* was *kissed by John.*

In (1a–b) we have one and the same meaning exemplified by the identity of John as Agent (A) and of Mary as Patient (P). While (la) is an active transitive construction with a subject and a direct object, (lb) is a passive construction with a subject and an indirect object. (la) and (lb) implement an identical semantic pattern, while differing in syntactic terms. What distinguishes (la) from (lb) is the difference in structure (subject + direct object vs. subject + indirect object) as well as the asymmetry in the relationship between the two constructions on syntactic grounds — the active construction is "basic" (i.e., somehow closer to meaning from the point of view of the directness of mapping or linking), while the passive one is "derived", a result of a syntactic "transformation" (Chomsky 1965: 130–131), perhaps the most basic transformation or movement in syntax. To the extent that we reveal differences and asymmetries at the interface between syntax and semantics we prove the tenet of the autonomy of syntax. The higher the asymmetry at the syntax/semantics interface, the higher the margin of uncertainty in the possibilities of mapping between them; the higher will also be the unpredictability and "creativity" of linking them on-line. These features (indeterminism, variability, on-line decision, creativity) are among the ones frequently cited when we speak about consciousness.

The hypothesis that the syntax/semantics interface may be, indeed, the interface between conscious and unconscious language-specific mental processing has been with us for a long time (cf. de Beaugrande 1997). Representatives of different grammatical traditions have expressed similar opinions on this subject. Chomsky's (1990) views about the "deeply unconscious" nature of the syntactic rules are well-known. The doyen of dependency grammar, Lucienne Tesniere, also expressed quite a compatible (from a certain point of view) opinion (cf. Tesniere 1966: 20.13) that the processing of syntactic structure is "subjective" and unconscious. It is a deep, elementary phenomenon which is obligatory in its realization. It is impossible to control willfully the formation of this level of mental structure. This structure becomes possible to analyze only retrospectively with the help of "intuitive introspection".

On the other hand, Tesniere claims that cognitive activity as it reveals itself on the level of semantic structure, is "objective" and accessible to consciousness. It is a surface and a "purely accidental phenomenon". The speaker, at this level, feels free to choose which thoughts to express and in what way. It is at this level that we can and do monitor and control what we say (cf. Tesniere 1966: 20.15).

If syntax and semantics are defined by Tesniere (1966) as nonoverlapping aspects of the structure of language, it is quite logical to assume further that the ways of determination of the syntactic and semantic structure in the sentence must *complement* each other. This idea has never been, to my knowledge, consistently followed in terms of its possible implications. The point of Tesniere (1966: 21.5–6) was that syntactic relations are directed from the head to its complement, i.e., from the top to the bottom of the stemma according to the stemmatic way of representation developed by him. The semantic relations, on the other hand, point from the complement to the head in the corresponding relation, i.e., are bottom-up oriented in the stemmatic representation of the structure of the sentence. In this way, one and the same stemmatic structure represents both syntactic and semantic relations. Depending on the specificity of the analysis one can make explicit the semantic or the syntactic aspect of it using one and the same (from a structural point of view) stemma. The point is that even in the case where we have "identical" components of structure from a semantic and syntactic point of view, the relationships between them differ in some way.

It is also interesting to note that the "bias" of Tesniere (1966: 21.14) was on the semantic side, because he emphatically pointed out that there are no syntactic relations without the semantic ones while the opposite is not true. This "bias" seems to be opposite in orientation to Chomsky's view about the "radical autonomy" (encapsulation) of syntax.

The possibility to dissociate meaning from the situation in the world that it represents is frequently illustrated by examples (cf. Talmy 1994 for discussion) providing alternative construals (via "fictive motion") of one and the same objective situation in the world:

(2) a. *This mountain range extends from Orinoko to Machu Pikchu.*
b. *This mountain range extends from Machu Pikchu to Orinoko.*

The possibility to dissociate syntactic and semantic structure from pragmatic structure is most evident when we change the word order or accentual and intonational contour of the constituents of the sentence depending on the theme-rheme (topic-comment) configuration imposition:

(3) a. *John came to the window* (Who came to the window?)
b. *John came to the window* (Where did John come?)
c. ?*To the window John came* (Where did John come?)

Here the pragmatic imposition of the context on the way of interpretation of the sentence in (3) is dependent on the question to which it can be taken as an answer.

It is appropriate to point out that (in a broader perspective) pragmatic mappings (interfaces) are supposed to deal with the following relationships:

i. the way the argument structure of the current sentence is related to the arguments of the previous sentences in the context of text and/or discourse processing, e.g., via anaphora, topic-comment (old-new information; cf. Gergely 1997) distribution, presuppositions, entailments, conventional implicatures;

ii. the way the structure of the sentence is related to (mapped onto) some situation in the world, e.g., by the use of deixis and the adjuncts "projecting" it onto the non-linguistic situation during some time moment in which it is uttered and to which it fits; and

iii. the way the current sentence is interpreted as a speech act of some type by the speaker and the other interlocutors (cf. Searle 1969) involved in a conversation and the conversational implicatures (cf. Grice 1975) required for its proper understanding as an expression of intention by the speaker. In everyday conversation, the hearer aims at becoming conscious of the true (real) intention of the speaker in talking to him/her. This is the default teleology of communication.

In my exposition below I will not deal with the wider set of problems related to the pragmatics of language understanding in the context of discourse interpretation, as sketched above (for further information cf. Levinson 1995; van Dijk 1997). I will take into "pragmatic" account only the necessity to bind the language-specific syntactic/semantic structure to some kind of languagenon-specific mental representation, the latter being a representation of reality in a medium not necessarily completely isomorphic (according to its structural specification) to the medium of language-specific conceptualization. This means that I will concentrate on the nature of the obligatory (and minimal) clause-specific argument structure and its relation to the structure of reality (as represented in the non-language specific conceptualizations). In the very first approximation, we can identify semantic and pragmatic interpretation with each other as prerequisite to representing the meaning in a medium comparable to, yet different from, syntactic structure proper. Still, it is quite appropriate not to lose sight completely of the wider pragmatic context of language processing in order not to arrive at a rather reductionist interpretation of what happens in the "ordinary mind" when we consciously process language.

If the syntactic, semantic and pragmatic structure of the sentence can diverge, it is only reasonable to try to trace the "origin" of their mappability and dissociability. The hypothesis to be explored here can be summarized in the following way: If semantic and syntactic structures can deviate from each other, it is reasonable to expect that this can occur to a different degree and we can find structures where they come closest to identity. It is at this level that we will try to locate the primary reasons to dissociate syntax from semantics.

The clause and its components

In linguistics the analysis of the possibility to relate to each other different words in order to form sentences and texts came down to the necessity to posit as fundamental and impossible to derive from others the relationship between the subject and the predicate of the sentence. The subject must be prototypically a noun phrase (NP) capable of referential or contextual interpretation, while the predicate is a verb phrase (VP) which "predicates" (attributes something) to the subject. It is worth noticing that this way of splitting of the content of the sentence looks quite "pragmatically" oriented, because it is comparable to the dichotomy in the topic-comment distinction. This is the case because, psychologically speaking, the split in question is some kind of an operation which first analyzes (separates two parts of) some entity in order afterwards to unify it again in the act of forming the content of the sentence. This is most evidently the case with the so called "analytic propositions" (cf. Lyons 1977: 147 for discussion):

(4) *Every sun is a star.*

Here a characteristic inalienably belonging to an object (as a concept in the LTM) is singled out (dissociated from its unity) and afterwards re-united with it in the process of ascertainment.

The action of predication is, in other words, ideally an action which unifies two mental contents which were previously dissociated or originated in different quarters of the mind. A fuller explication of the content of (4) would reveal that it means *Every star is a star.* This is, strictly speaking, a tautological assertion (i.e., nothing "new" is ascertained) unless we assume that its function is just to bring to consciousness a mental object from a certain perspective. Ontologically, any member of the class of suns does not need to be perspectivized. It is identical to all its characteristics all the time. Instead, the act of becoming conscious of a sun requires perspectivization. With this double action of first analyzing (or dissociating, or activating from different quarters) and then unifying two mental contents we achieve the possibility to become aware of some "object" of consciousness under some "aspectual shape" (cf. Searle 1992), i.e., ascertain the status of the sun under the rubric of its belonging to the conceptual class of stars.

The act of "unification" depends on different conditions. The analytic propositions represent an ideal situation from the point of view of the possibility to practically eliminate the pragmatic component in the interpretation of the corresponding assertion. This is the case because in analytic propositions nothing "new" is claimed, i.e., they serve to combine and re-combine (re-call) some knowledge which is already available in the semantic LTM. In other words, the act of interpretation, in this case, requires only the activation of the lexical meanings of words plus the syntactic subcategorization frame of the verb to *be* (which has practically no representational content of its own).

If we, however, claim that the filling of the argument positions (minimally that of the subject) of an activated verb (the core of the predicative VP) by appropriate NPs is enough for becoming aware of the meaning of the corresponding sentence, it is possible immediately to point out counterexamples with verbs which take no arguments whatsoever, e.g.:

(5) *Vali* "It rains"

To rain, both in Bulgarian and in English, does not take any arguments. In English it takes the dummy subject *it*, while in Bulgarian there is no subject explicated. The syntactic conditions for the realization of the subject position may diverge from the semantic conditions of filling this same position, i.e., in some cases the syntactic subject remains without semantic interpretation. And this is the case on a very basic level.

If the requirement for filling the argument positions of the verb is a necessary but not a sufficient condition for forming a well-defined sentence, we may try to add further requirements for the fulfilment of predication as a binding relation capable of implementing the consciousness cathexis. This is, in principle, possible because the account of integration developed thus far tries to identify the components, but not the manner of unification to be performed.

The possibility to develop a model according to which consciousness is generated "from within" is highest if we maintain that the activation of some finite verb (as the minimal predicate form) is identical to the "action" of unifying some mental contents into a single conscious mental representation. This looks most plausibly to be the case simultaneously on syntactic, semantic and pragmatic grounds with the so called performative speech acts (cf. Searle 1969). Imagine that I have undergone religious conversion and a priest now is performing a religious ritual on me. At this particular moment he utters:

(6) *I hereby christen you with the name of John-Paul.*

I am now supposed to become a different man. With the performance of the utterance (6) the priest changes my own self-identity (= self-consciousness) and the way I am seen by him and all interested others (i.e., the social reality in which I am embedded). The meaning of the verb *to christen*, the mental action of generating the sentence in filling its argument and adjunct positions, the behavioral action of uttering it, and the action of changing the world with it seem to come to coincidence in this case as close as possible. A speech act changes the way we are aware of us and the world.

Even in this case, however, it is quite apparent that the mental action, the behavioral action (uttering the sentence) and the consequences from it (the change in the social world) do not coincide completely. Actually, they follow from each other. The problem about the interface between language and consciousness is much more complicated and troublesome (cf. Stamenov 1997a for discussion). Thus it becomes apparent that there is a set of events (constructive actions) and associations (mappings, blendings) responsible for the construction of potentially conscious sentence-specific meaning which we must analyze in more detail.

The verb as a "mirror" of clause structure

It is quite apparent from the beginning that mental events (actions) are discrete and sometimes the outcome of their performance becomes part of the conscious mental representation. It is also close to intuitive appeal that they can have sentence-like structure. The gestalts of sentence-specific mental actions are coded by the verbs according to their lexicalization patterns (i.e., the way the action in question is represented in the meaning of the verb), syntactic subcategorization frames and semantic selectional restrictions. Whenever some verb's argument positions become filled, we can become aware of the meaning of some sentence-like structure. In this section I will analyze the "minimal" argument structures, as they are determined by the verb-specific lexical representation, expecting that in this case it would be most straightforward to identify the basic reasons for mapping and mutual deviation of the structures of language, explicit cognition, and reality.

Patterns of action in the verb's meaning — the interface between lexicalization patterns and the subcategorization frame

In traditional grammar the problem of the patterns of action denoted by different verb classes has been considered under the rubric of the basic grammatical category of "voice". The standard practice has been to discern active and passive voice, as well as reflexive and reciprocal one:

i. active voice: A → B; *John kissed Mary;*
ii. passive voice B ← A; *Mary was kissed by John;*
iii. reflexive voice: A=B: *Anton se mie* "Anton washes himself"; cf. *Anton se bie* "Anton beats (somebody)"; *Anton i Petar se miyat* "Anton and Petar wash themselves";
iv. reciprocal voice: A →← B: *Anton I Petar se biyat* "Anton and Petar beat each other".

Please notice that while the differentiation between active and passive voice is implemented by the regular means of grammar in great many languages of the world, the difference and juxtaposition between reflexive and reciprocal voice is much more idiosyncratic and dependent on the specificity of the individual lexical meanings of the verbs. In the Bulgarian examples given above, the reflexive particle *se is* used not only for reflexivization, but also to express reciprocity and intransitivization. The ascription of reflexive or reciprocal voice in the examples above depends on the lexical meaning of the verbs *biya vs. miya.* The *se* particle in *Anton se bie* is used for the sake of turning the transitive verb *biya* into an intransitive one but not for the sake of marking a reflexive voice as in *Anton se mie.*

In other words, the relation between lexical meaning of the verb and the syntactic structure it may enter can vary. Sometimes what can be ascribed to the verb as a subcategorization frame "belonging" to it (e.g., with reciprocal or reflexive voice), can be considered also to be an aspect of sentence-level, e.g., not part of verb-specific, language processing. This is appropriate to acknowledge in looking for the boundaries and interfaces between lexical meaning and syntactic structure. In other words, it seems impossible to differentiate in principle where lexicalization patterns end and where syntactically-specific sentence-level processing starts. This interface depends on a set of conditions starting with those that are highly generalizable over many verbs in the case of active-passive transformation and finishing with idiosyncratic (lexically specific) reflexive and reciprocal ones. One and the same grammatical category (voice) turns out to be implementable by different mechanisms in language processing — either in lexis or in syntax.

Looking for the minimal sentence structure at the interface between selectional restrictions and the subcategorization frame of the verb

If we consider explicit (or overt) syntactic (predicative) structure, we can distinguish at least three different types of basic-looking formal patterns:

a. with a transitive verb, e.g., *John hits Fred;*
b. with an intransitive verb, e.g., *The lake froze;*
c. other cases like *to be, to have,* etc., expressing the static-looking relationships of identity, possession, equation, ascription, etc.

It seems as if identification of the minimal well-formed structure would be most straightforward when applied to overt syntactic structure as determined by the verb's valency. According to this approach, the intransitive verbs have, evidently, less structure than the transitive ones. Still, there are controversial examples of the following type. Since the 1980s, syntactically distinguishable subclasses of intransitive verbs have been identified — unaccusatives and unergatives. The former, which include *arrive, descend,* etc., have surface subjects which are hypothesized to be the result of movement from object position in deep structure (D-structure). The surface subjects of unergatives (which include, e.g., *bark, bloom, jump, walk)* have not undergone any such movement (cf. Burzio 1986):

(7) a. Unaccusative verb — [vP V NP]: *The bottle broke.*
b. Unergative verb: NP [vP V]: *Peter thinks.*

The unaccusative hypothesis is based, as a matter of fact, on the idea that the subject of an unaccusative verb is a derived subject, being a direct object at some underlying level of syntactic representation (= D-structure), while the subject of an unergative verb is a subject at all levels of syntactic representation.

The point of the present analysis is that unaccusative intransitive verbs are not processed and interpreted in the way unergative verbs are. This is the case because they require a movement of the object to the subject position. The movement presupposes the availability of two argument positions for a supposedly intransitive verb (cf. 7a). The very possibility of juxtaposition of unaccusative and unergative verbs, in other words, is based on the presupposition that the matrix model is that of two-argument structure and that the representation of the subcategorization frames of the verbs may have empty slots to be filled at some level of syntactic parsing different from that of S-structure of the sentence and the subcategorization frame of the verb "belonging" to the corresponding lexical entry.

What is the minimum syntactic and semantic structure of a clause capable of being implemented in a verb?

Tenny (1994: 137–138) posited as minimal (from a semantic point of view) the unaccusative event structure of change-of-state which has only an internal argument (object of the action), as in *The lake froze.* It should be clear that this minimal event structure is impossible to implement at the level of surface structure in English. It is a hypothetical construct which can surface only after an operation of Move-α of the object (O) of the verb to the subject (S) position. From this point of view, we can claim that the requirement for an overt subject in English serves as quite an appropriate syntactic balance to the asymmetric minimal semantic event structure. If the minimum of surface syntactic structure amounts to S-V, the minimum of semantic structure amounts to V-O (in syntactic terms). If this is the case, we must posit that the primary structure which can support the possibility for a mutual asymmetric deviation of syntactic and semantic structure must be the transitive construction:

(8)	S ————————		V	[syntactically motivated minimality of structure]
	V ————————		O	[semantically motivated minimality of structure]
	S	V	O	[the "common denominator" between them]

The point for this dissociation in the possibilities to minimize overt and deep syntactic and semantic structure seems to be as follows: Something must be done on-line in the mind in order to balance the asymmetry. Syntactic and semantic structure turn out to be complementary, according to this account, too (cf. also the opinion of Tesniere 1966 cited above).

The structure of the transitive construction

The standard formulation of the nature of the transitive clause is that this is a clause which contains an object. The activity or action denoted by the finite verb is "transitive" in the sense that it "goes across" from the subject to the object. The object is "affected" by the activity in question and in the great majority of cases transitive clauses can undergo a passive transformation. Please notice that both suggestions about the "going across" and the "affectedness" of the object directly suggest the visibility and visualizability of the action/activity denoted by the transitive clause as a whole.

Another aspect of the specificity of the transitive construction was pointed out by Tsunoda (1985). The terminology of distinguishing transitive vs. intransitive clauses contains the implicit suggestion that they are opposites in a single dimension. The intransitive clauses are supposed to lack a direct object and no activity is transferred. The problem is, however, that the intransitives do not seem to form a well-defined set according to its syntactic specificity. If this is the case, the "unity" of the transitive construction must be defined by criteria shared by the members of the set in question.

Attempts to define transitivity through analysis of the argument structure of the verb

In the analysis of transitivity we must initially return once again to the level of the lexically specific verb representation. The traditional statement on the nature of transitive verbs is that of verbs having minimally two arguments — one external and one internal. The latter is defined either syntactically as "direct object" or semantically as "patient"; the former is defined as "subject" or "agent" (or "actor"). A verb is called "transitive" only if it takes a subject and an object which are both noun phrases. This is the case according to the syntactic treatment of the notion of transitivity. It is appropriate to point out, however, that all the verbs which have two valencies (take two arguments), as. e.g., *The bottle floated into the* cave, may be considered as semantically transitive. Furthermore, there are many verbs with a valency of three arguments which are transitive, i.e., denote a transitive relationship between the first and the second argument. In other words, the relationship between the syntactic and semantic aspects of transitivity may impose partially syncretic and partially different conditions for the fulfilment of the relationship in question.

The syncretic aspect of the determination of the transitive relation can be illustrated by the definition of Pinker (1995) that the entity specified as "affected" by the transitive action denoted by the verb ends up as the object, while the entity specified as "affecting" ends up in the position of the subject. The differentiation of this two-argument relationship from other possible two argument ones is due to the nature of the relationship of "the object being directly affected by the action denoted by the verb" (Pinker 1995: 170). "Direct affectedness" looks suspiciously localistically semantic in its specification: In the sentences *John kicked Peter* and *John criticized Peter* we treat *Peter* as "directly affected" by the action referred to by the corresponding verbs. In this way, we equate the manner of physical action with that of (physically invisible and indirect) interpersonal mental actions. Pinker's definition is localistic, i.e., semantic, while he uses syntactic concepts like subject and object for the "components" of the transitive construction.

The position of the internal argument (object) and some complications in defining it uniquely from a syntactic point of view

The position of the direct object (as sketched above) looks relatively well defined until we consider some complications related to the possibilities to treat the intransitive, ditransitive, and three-argument constructions. Verbs with three arguments belong, predominantly, to two *Aktionsarten* — of giving and speaking. There are borderline cases where we can speak not about a verb with three different arguments (subject, direct object and indirect object) but about the so called ditransitive constructions where we have a subject and two direct objects:

(9) a. *Doceo pueros*-ACC.
"I teach boys"
b. *Doceo grammaticam*-ACC.
"I teach grammar"
c. *Doceo pueros*-ACC *grammaticam*-ACC.
"I teach grammar to boys"
d. *Doceo grammaticam*-ACC *pueros*-ACC.
*"I teach to boys grammar"

The accusative case in Latin is considered as a marker of the direct object. It treats *pueros* and *grammaticam* in the same way and gives the possibility of their alternation in (9c) and (9d) — a symmetric figure-ground reversal between them which is prohibited in English. In the latter language the asymmetry between the first (direct) and the second (indirect) object is epitomized in the dative shift construction:

(10) a. *John gave Mary a book.*
b. *John gave a book to Mary.*

The alternation in (9c-9d) in Latin is even more exemplary having in mind that Latin is a pro-drop language, i.e., a language in which it is not necessary always to explicate the syntactic subject, as is the case in English.

The problem in tracing the boundaries between transitive, ditransitive and three-argument constructions can also be illustrated in considering the possibilities for passivization (one of the tests for proving that some construction involves a transitive verb) in the case of verbs with three valencies. The latter verbs can form the passive voice in two distinct ways (cf. Tesniere 1966: 106.11):

(11) a. *Alfred donne le livre* a *Charle.*
"Alfred gives the book to Charles"
b. *Le livre est donne par Alfred* a *Charles.*
"The book is given by Alfred to Charles"
c. *Charles is given the book by Alfred.*
d. *The police refused a licence to the motorist.*
e. *The motorist was refused a licence (by the police).*

The alternative (11c) is available in English but not in French or Bulgarian. The possibility to use the passive construction in English in foregrounding not the second but the third argument (the indirect object) is specific to English (cf. 11d vs. 11e) only and may be quite confusing for learners of English with native languages which prohibit this type of passivization.

We can conclude that there are cases where the difference between direct object and indirect object becomes blurred and some languages tend to treat them as closer to or more distant from each other in syntactic terms. If this is the case, it would be quite difficult to give a vigorous definition of the direct object in syntactic terms alone which would be of universal validity.

The position of the subject (external argument)

Valency grammarians like Tesniere (1966) and Allerton (1982) consider the subject to be an elaborator of the verb like the direct and indirect object. Still it is recognized that the subject has some specific characteristics which accord it a special status from a syntactic point of view. It appears as an NP in first position by default, i.e., before all other arguments of the verb, in the SVO, SOV, and in VSO languages, e.g., in more than 90% of the languages of the world. From the point of view of the syntactic conditions for occurrence, the subject has a higher priority than the object in the sense that the subject's explication in many languages is a sine qua non (except in pro-drop languages like Latin and Bulgarian), while the object's explication is required only by some set of verbs (e.g., the transitive ones). As regards inflectional morphology, in languages that have grammatical cases there is a case like the nominative (or absolutive in the so called ergative languages; cf. Dixon 1994, Palmer 1994) that is selected for the subject in the formation of the transitive (active) construction regardless of the lexical verb used, whereas verbs may govern objects in at least two different cases (as Accusative and Genitive in Russian or Polish).

These grammatical aspects of the subject's uniqueness are supplemented by some features of phonetico-phonological realization, as the subject is often marked through a separate intonation unit. Finally the subject (but not the object) has a special status from the point of view of the pragmatics of text and discourse formation in being the typical sentential theme (topic) — the one often carrying forward some information from previous sentences.

In sum according to valency grammarians, the subject stands apart from all other verb arguments due to its specificity, but it is still under the dominion of the verb. This is the case because it is impossible to tear apart and define on independent grounds the autonomy and dissociability of the subject from the other arguments of the verb. This means that we cannot make a straightforward case that the integration of the external argument with the frame of the verb (and its internal arguments) is the default integration during which some mental content (= the meaning of the sentence in question) must become conscious.

There are problems, however, with the unambiguous identification of the subject, too. For example, there are verbs, termed sometimes "ergatives", which have both transitive and intransitive forms. Their peculiarity lies in the fact that the object of the transitive form of the verb becomes the subject of the intransitive form of this same verb:

(12) a. *The burglar burnt the house* [Transitive, Causative]
b. *The house burnt* [Intransitive, Anticausative]

Here we have a lexically specified transformation (intransitivization) for the promotion of the direct object of the transitive form of the verb into the position of the subject, while the previous subject-agent of the transitive form is demoted and must remain implicit. For this reason the intransitive form was named "anticausative".

There is a closely related alternation between forms of verbs with three vs. two valencies:

(13) a. *Napoleon marched 100, 000 soldiers up the hills near Leipzig.*
b. *100, 000 soldiers marched up the hills near Leipzig.*

Here the direct object of the transitive form of the verb has a semantic specificity of being an animate, agent-like entity, unlike the direct object of (12a) above.

The causatives of *march, walk, gallop,* etc., in English are often called "double agentives". The first and second agent become the subject and the direct object, respectively. In the case the first agent (instigator of the action) remains implicit, the second one takes its place, i.e., moves to the subject position. The point is that the decision which agent is available for allocation to the appropriate position is an on-line decision. In other words, this cannot be done via automatic mapping of the semantic structure of the verb-specific meaning to its own subcategorization frame or a larger clause-specific syntactic construction. It is enacted by some other module of language processing.

The examples above display the point that the uniqueness of the position of the subject as an inalienable part of the explicable structure of the sentence is also questionable. It turns out, upon scrutiny, that both the position of the subject and object do not form well-defined classes with a fixed set of criteria for membership. They form classes with relatively well-defined "centers" and a fuzzy "periphery". The point in discussing double subjects and double objects here is that they display the impossibility to provide with syntactic or semantic means the conditions necessary and sufficient to define them in a way that makes them categorically different from each other and from indirect objects.

The place of the features of Tense and Agreement

The syntactic, semantic and pragmatic constraints on the realization of the category of predication do not coincide as a rule. If there is integration in processing the information leading to the formation of a sentence meaning gestalt, it is achieved in many discrete steps in different compartments of the mind. This becomes also evident when we consider that during any act of predication the verb must also acquire the features of Agreement (Agr) with the subject of the sentence (in the languages where the verb agrees with the subject; there is a controversy in this respect in considering the features of accusative vs. ergative languages; cf. Dixon 1994; Palmer 1994) and of Tense (Tns). The feature of Agr, in some way, underscores the special status of the subject of the sentence, while Tns is supposed, basically, to bind the sentence to the present (or some other) moment of time as a true or false representation of some situation in the world. While Agr is a sentence-internal requirement for well-formedness, Tns is a requirement to interpret the sentence by language-structure-non-specific cognitive means.

Tense and Agreement are grammatical categories marking the finite verb and licensing it, in this way, as the matrix of the clause. It is interesting to note, how different they are in the requirements they impose on the conditions of well-formedness of the sentence. These requirements are requirements for the establishment of appropriate interfaces with different subsystems of language processing.

The case for implicit conditions of well-formedness of sentence structure

The very idea about the necessity to posit transformations in the generation of the surface syntactic structure of the sentence was based on the intuition of Harris (1952) and Chomsky (1957, 1965) that some aspects of sentence structure must be generated (=constructed, integrated) on-line, but are not something activated ready-made from the LTM. The explicit motivation for this claim was put in terms of the "economy" of syntactic derivation of a potentially open set of sentences from a finite set or rules for their construction. The other aspect — that they are constructed on-line, i.e., with a different mental mechanism compared to the one responsible for the activation of the mental structure from LTM — remained for a time in the background. Later on this "syntactic mechanism" started to acquire features like innateness, universality, etc. It also tended to multiply itself from one implicit module of D-structure to two modules — D-structure and Logical Form (LF) — each of them being a kind of an interface with other modules of the mind. What makes this approach especially challenging in our context, is that Chomsky (1990: 600–601) maintains that those aspects of language structure formation are "deeply" or potentially "in principle" inaccessible to consciousness.

In the latest Minimalist Program of the generative grammar tradition (cf. Chomsky 1995), there are two versions of the structure of the syntactic module of the language capacity. According to the first version, the derivations from D-structure to Phonetic Form (PF) and LF are postulated to have a common part: D-structure is mapped to S-structure by some operation (Affect α), and the derivation then branches off into two independent paths — PF and LF (Chomsky 1995: 64). The S-structure is "the sole point of interaction among the three fundamental levels" (Chomsky 1995: 132) of D-structure, LF and PF, no matter from which of them we initiate the derivation. In the second and "most recent" version there are three components altogether — PF, LF and the "computational system" (the latter includes the previous S- and D-structure) (cf. Chomsky 1995: 378; Marantz 1995: 357).

The point in developing different versions of the structure of the syntactic processor is in distributing the "responsibilities" between different modules of the language capacity in generating and processing in an optimal way the syntactic representations in different languages. For example, there is an overt wh-movement in English while there is no such movement in a language like Chinese. Huang (1995: 149) made the point, on the basis of some facts relating to scope and extraction, that despite this difference in the S-structure, Chinese resembles English in that at the LF level wh-phrases move to the initial position of the clause. The difference between English and Chinese reduces to the fact that in the former wh-movement applies in the surface syntax and LF, while in the latter it applies only to LF. The wh-movement remains "invisible", i.e., inaccessible to consciousness, and the syntactic S-structure is not available for introspection not in the "shallow" way, but in some "deeper" way. In other words, the further away we deviate from the transitive construction, the more significance and volume is acquired by this "deeper" or "in principle inaccessible" component of syntactic and semantic processing of language structure.

Multiple semantic tiers in interpreting the transitive construction?

Jackendoff (1990: 126) points out that conceptual representations can be organized into independent tiers, not unlike the way phonological information is analyzed and represented in contemporary phonological theory. He identifies two tiers of conceptual roles — the thematic tier, dealing with motion and location, and the action tier, dealing with agent-patient relationships. Possible ways of correlating them are illustrated by Jackendoff (1987: 395) as follows:

(14)	a.	*Sue*	*hit Fred.*	
		Theme	Goal	(thematic tier)
		Actor	Patient	(action tier)
	b.	*Pete*	*threw the ball.*	
		Source	Theme	(thematic tier)
		Actor	Patient	(action tier)
	c.	*Bill*	*entered the room.*	
		Theme	Goal	(thematic tier)
		Actor	-	(action tier)
	d.	*The car hit the tree.*		
		Theme	Goal	(thematic tier)
		-	Patient	(action tier)
	e.	*Bill*	*received the letter.*	
		Goal	Theme	(thematic tier)
		-	-	(action tier)

The interesting point to notice is that the "mapping" is sometimes of the schema-to-schema type, while in other cases some member(s) of one schema map(s) onto (blends with) member(s) of another as part to whole (in a metonymic way). The blend becomes imaginable even if some of its constitutive parts are not available for visualization (or possible to represent in a visible format). It is appropriate also to note that while the action tier is possible to represent by means of the thematic tier, the opposite is not true. This asymmetry is apparently used as (implicit) motivation for developing localistic theories for the interface between syntax and semantics. The dynamics sketched above of partial "visibility" and accessibility as a qualitative content of consciousness is quite controversial and requires further specification.

Looking for the "common conceptual format": The transitive construction and its semantic content

Comparing the requirements for formation of the overt semantic and syntactic structure, as well as for the implicit syntactic derivation, we were looking for the common denominator between them. This common denominator (= matrix construction) seemed to approximate the features of the transitive syntactic construction.

What is called a "transitive relation" in syntax is a "common denominator", however, of at least three different prototypical schemata of meaning (cf. Stamenov 1997a: 321–324 for a more extended discussion):

a. The localistic *schema of motion* where *figure*$_1$ and *figure*$_2$ *(trajector* and *landmark;* or *theme* and *source/goal)* determine a relationship of movement, location and change of location of primarily physical entities, as in "The ball hits the rock";
b. The *schema of self-initiated action,* e.g., "Fred hits John (the ball)", where the *agent* and *patient* form a transitive relationship due to a pattern of action which is initiated by the agent and affecting the patient (animate or inanimate). The patient may undergo some changes due to the realization (complete or incomplete) of the action;
c. The schema of *dialogical communicative interaction* with *speaker* and *hearer* or *agent* and *counter-agent* (cf. Fillmore 1971), or *agonist* and *antagonist* (cf. Talmy 1988) as basic roles, e.g., "Fred criticizes John".

The problem of looking for the interface between semantic and syntactic structure seems to boil down to the possibility to identify the transitive construction as the one where the semantic and syntactic structure come closest to each other. It turns out, however, that it is quite difficult to give a definition of this construction exclusively in syntactic or semantic terms (cf. the discussion above). The reason why the transitive construction still tends to be defined in syntactic but not in semantic terms is due to the problem of the higher level of ambiguity of the semantic description. As was shown, the meaning of this construction can be reduced to three prototypes which seem mutually incommensurable. It is due to the semantic incommensurability between them that the bond between syntax and semantics becomes loosened and the possibilities for reanalysis of the transitive constructions and its derivatives and blendings become open for the learner and user of language.

How many systems of syntactic vs. semantic processing should we posit in order to justify the possibility of both conscious and unconscious sentence processing?

If I am right in the argument I have developed thus far, we should posit the following set of subsystems responsible for sentence processing on-line in the mind (according to the possibility for representing in them the transitive construction and its transformational derivatives at the levels of their syntax and semantics):

Syntax:	*Semantics:*
1. S-structure;	1. *Localistic* meaning structure;
2. D-structure;	2. Agent-Patient *Causative* structure;
3. LF;	3. Agent-Counteragent *Interactional* structure.

We may hypothesize that the relations between the subsystems of the syntactic and semantic processing can be realized in multiple ways, e.g., from D-structure to Causative and from LF to Interactional subsystems and *vice versa*. The point, however, is that for some language structure to become conscious there must be actualized, however fleetingly, an interface between S-structure and the Localistic meaning structure. This was intuited in the context of cognitive grammar and was put forward as its adage "grammar as image" (cf. Langacker 1986: 13). The interfaces between all other subsystems of syntactic and semantic origin are enacted unconsciously and support cognitive structures which is impossible directly to actualize as qualitative contents of consciousness. They still resemble or map onto each other due to the primacy of the bond between localistic semantics and the surface syntactic structure. This view is epitomized in generative grammar in the claim that the sole point of interaction and interface between LF and D-structure is S-structure (within the syntactic system of the verbal mind). The same, generally speaking, view is epitomized in cognitive linguistics in accepting the primacy of localistic meaning (image schemata, mental spaces, etc.).

It remains presently unclear how LF and D-structure, on the one hand, and the causative and interactional semantic modules, on the other, can interact. Chomsky (1995) seems to be inclined to relate the syntactic system to the nonlanguage specific cognitive (conceptual-intentional) computation only through the LF-interface. This would be the "deeply unconscious" way of their interaction, while the one which can implement consciousness is the interface between S-structure and the localistic qualitative meaning. We may conjecture that the only direct route for eliciting consciousness (as an on-line phenomenon associated with the mind's performance) is due to the binding of PF, S-structure and the localistic semantic module. This is the unique route along which some conscious language-specific content can become conscious. On the other hand, it is possible for the other modules of language processing to interface each other in different ways without their interaction being acknowledgeable as qualitative conscious representation.

The accessibility of the transitive construction and the ideomotor theory of consciousness, or why we need localistic meaning

Leading psychologists like William James and Sigmund Freud maintained the tenet about the "perceptual connection" of consciousness, i.e., that consciousness is affiliated primarily, if not exclusively (if we speak about its possible contents), to the perceptual end of the continuum between perceptual and cognitive processes. The idea of William James (1890) about the role of conscious mental images in volition and control of mental and motor performance was used by Baars (1988:261) for proposing the concept of the "ideomotor control of conceptual thought". In his Global Workspace theory, the "conscious goal-image" is a global consistent representation that provides information and coordinates the action of numerous specialized processors. The goal-image can trigger both the specialized subordinate modules for the realization of a motor response, as well as activate and/or modify the intentional goal context that constrains planning and execution of behavior without itself becoming conscious.

The main point of the ideomotor control of thought and behavior is that the images can "impulsively" (cf. James 1890) evoke and recruit conceptual processes that are more abstract and impossible to access by themselves as qualitative contents. By means of the perceptual image one gets, instead, access to abstract conceptual representations and means for manipulating them (cf. Baars 1988: 285). Furthermore, the qualitative images may start to represent these abstract conceptual structures becoming their conventionalized signs in visual or aural form. The whole edifice of language is grounded on the possibility to have the aural images of sounds and their concatenations, as well as of visual images of letters and their concatenations.

According to this orientation, language-specific consciousness consists of a vertical two-layered interface between cognition and action. The first "layer" is formed by the interface between categorical perception and willfully controlled articulatory action (the so-called "articulatory loop"; cf. Baddeley 1986). The second "layer" is constituted by the interface between the structures of syntax and localistic imagery (semantics). In order to become conscious, we must have some qualitative content at some level of mental processing. At the "high" level of cognitive language-specific processing this is realized in the imperative to map onto each other the surface structure of the sentence with its schematic localistic conceptual counterpart (as discussed above regarding the way the transitive contraction can become mapped into different cognitive schemata which are more or less capable of visualization).

Conclusion

The transitive construction seems to mirror (in its fundamentality) primarily not some basic (or root) mental or behavioral action (as conjectured in developmental psycholinguistics) or its language-specific formal correlate. If the problem was simply that of cognitive structure, there are other species, e.g., monkeys and dolphins, who are perfectly capable of performing the behavioral and cognitive correlates of the transitive construction, i.e., to do some things with some objects, e.g., to manipulate them intentionally. The basicness of the transitive construction seems to point out to a deeper and more sophisticated relationship between different faculties of the human mind.

The main point of this article could be formulated as follows:

a. What makes mutually commensurable the Localistic, Causative and Interactional transitive semantic schemas for humans is not an overarching conceptual metacategory definable according to its structure or function;
b. The unity of the transitive construction seems not to be supported in a well-circumscribed way from "below", i.e., from the syntactic system, either.

The unity in question, if possible to maintain at all, is a problem of the *interface* between syntax and semantics, i.e., of an interface between two different routes (foci) of processing and representing cognitive structures in a mutually compatible format. If this is the case, we must further assume that the specificity of the interface in question is not simply that between two different subsystems of cognitive processing (as there are more of them both in the syntactic and semantic system of the mind according to the models discussed above). I see no way to face this situation unless we assume that it is consciousness which is implemented as a mechanism of dual-focus exactly at this level (cf. Stamenov 1997a for discussion), i.e., at the interface between S-structure and Localistic meaning. The unity and dissociability of the transitive relationship seems to mirror the interface (the mappability in principle) of the minimal content and minimal structure of consciousness. In other words, the transitive construction is the "common denominator" not simply of some basic mental *content* from the point of view of cognitive processing, language structure and consciousness access. It is the common denominator, furthermore, of the content of consciousness and its structure. It is due to this final aspect of interfacing that the transitive construction acquires its very special status — its empowerment to represent a cognitive content with an active agent and a passive patient and to be orchestrated by an implicit subject (in the great majority of cases) and explicit object. The "common denominator" between language and consciousness, in the final resort, reflects the mappability and dissociability of the components of some root schema of conscious mental content vs. the components of the minimal structure of consciousness.

To summarize, syntax is necessary for the implementation of the obligatory "subject" (as an implicit cognitive structure component) of consciousness, while semantics — for the implementation of the obligatory "object" (mental content) of consciousness. The relationships between the "subject" and "object" of consciousness are those of reversible association, mappability and blending (cf. Stamenov 1997a: 336–338 for discussion) while the relationships between the grammatical subject and object are those of predication.

References

Allerton, D. J. 1982. *Valency and the English Verb.* London: Academic Press.
Baars, Bernard. 1988. *A Cognitive Theory of Consciousness.* Cambridge: Cambridge University Press.
Baddeley, Alan. 1986. *Working Memory.* Oxford: Oxford University Press.
Baddeley, Alan. 1989. "The Uses of Working Memory". In Solomon et al. 1989: 107–123.
Beaugrande, Robert de. 1997. "The 'Conscious and Unconscious Mind' in the Theoretical Discourse of Modern Linguistics". In Stamenov 1997b: 9–47.
Burzio, Luigi. 1986. *Italian Syntax.* Dordrecht: Reidel.
Chomsky, Noam. 1957. *Syntactic Structures.* The Hague: Mouton.
Chomsky, Noam. 1965. *Aspects of the Theory of Syntax.* Cambridge, Mass.: MIT Press.
Chomsky, Noam. 1990. "Accessibility 'in Principle"'. *Behavioral and Brain Sciences* 13: 600–601.
Chomsky, Noam. 1995. *The Minimalist Program.* Cambridge, Mass.: MIT Press.
Dijk, Teun A. van. 1997. "Cognitive Context Models and Discourse". In Stamenov 1997b: 1 89–226.
Dixon, Robert M. W. 1994. *Ergativity.* Cambridge: Cambridge University Press.
Fauconnier, Jilles. 1997. *Mappings in Thought and Language.* Cambridge: Cambridge University Press.
Fillmore, Charles J. 1971. "Types of Lexical Information". In Danny D. Steinberg & Leon A. Jakobovits (eds), *Semantics.* Cambridge: Cambridge University Press: 370–392.
Gergely, György. 1997. "The Role of Focus-Based Inferences in Antecedent Matching: Topic Foregrounding at the Clause Boundary". *Acta Linguistica Hungarica* 44: 111–150.
Grice, H. Paul. 1975. "Logic and Conversation". In Peter Cole & Jerry Morgan (eds), *Syntax and Semantics. Vol. 3: Speech Acts.* New York: Academic Press: 41–58.
Harris, Zellig. 1952. "Discourse Analysis". *Language* 28: 18–23.
Huang, C.-T. James. 1995. "Logical Form". In Webelhuth 1995: 127–175.
Jackendoff, Ray. 1987. "The Status of Thematic Relations in Linguistic Theory". *Linguistic Inquiry* 18: 369–411.
Jackendoff, Ray. 1990. *Semantic Structures.* Cambridge, Mass.: MIT Press.
James, William. 1890. *Principles of Psychology.* Vols. 1–2. New York: Henry Holt.
Langacker, Ronald. 1986. "An Introduction to Cognitive Grammar". *Cognitive Science* 10: 1–40.
Langacker, Ronald. 1997. "Consciousness, Construal, and Subjectivity". In Stamenov 1997b: 49–76.
Levinson, Stephen. 1995. "Three Levels of Meaning". In Frank R. Palmer (ed.), *Grammar and Meaning. Essays in honour of Sir John Lyons.* Cambridge: Cambridge University Press: 90–115.
Lyons, John. 1977. *Semantics. Vols.* 1–2. Cambridge: Cambridge University Press.
Mandler, George. 1985. *Cognitive Psychology: An essay in cognitive science.* Hillsdale, NJ: Lawrence Erlbaiun.
Mandler, George. 1989. "Memory: Conscious and Unconscious". In Solomon et al. 1989: - 84–106.

Marantz, Alec. 1995. "The Minimalist Program". In Webelhuth 1995: 351–439.
Palmer, Frank R. 1994. *Grammatical Roles and Relations.* Cambridge: Cambridge University Press.
Pinker, Steven. 1995. "Language Acquisition". In Lila Gleitman & Mark Liberman (eds), *An Invitation to Cognitive Science. Vol. 1: Language.* 2nd ed. Cambridge, Mass.: MIT Press: 135–182.
Searle, John. 1969. *Speech Acts.* Cambridge: Cambridge University Press.
Searle. John. 1992. *The Rediscovery of the Mind.* Cambridge, Mass.: MIT Press.
Solomon, Paul R. *et al.* (Eds), 1989. *Memory. Interdisciplinary approaches.* New York: Springer-Verlag.
Stamenov, Maxim. 1997a. "Grammar, Meaning and Consciousness: What Sentence Structure Can Tell Us about the Structure of Consciousness". In Stamenov 1997b:-277–342.
Stamenov, Maxim. (ed.). 1997b. *Language Structure, Discourse and the Access to Consciousness* (Advances in Consciousness Research, 12). Amsterdam & Philadelphia: John Benjamins.
Talmy, Leonard. 1988. "Force Dynamics in Language and Cognition". *Cognitive Science* 12: 49–100.
Talmy, Leonard. 1994. "The Windowing of Attention in Language". In M. Shibatani & S. Thompson (eds.), *Essays in Semantics.* Oxford: Oxford University Press: 235–289.
Tenny, Carol L. 1994. *Aspectual Roles and the Syntax-Semantics Interface* (Studies in Linguistics and Philosophy, 52). Dordrecht: Kluwer.
Tesniere, Lucien. 1966. *Elements de syntaxe structurale.* 2-nd ed. Paris: Klincksieck.
Tsunoda, Tasaku. 1985. "Remarks on Transitivity". *Journal of Linguistics* 21: 3853–96.
Webelhuth, Gert (ed.). 1995. *Government and Binding Theory and the Minimalist Program.* Oxford: Blackwell.

Biological Perspectives

Consciousness, behavioural patterns and the direction of biological evolution

Implications for the mind–brain problem*

B. I. B. Lindahl
Stockholm University

Introduction

The decline of the Lamarckian theory of inheritance of acquired characteristics — which may be said to have seriously started in the 1880s with August Weismann's development of the theory that in the early ontogenesis of individual organisms the germ cells are separated from the body cells and that changes in the body cells cannot influence the germ cells and therefore cannot be naturally transmitted to the next generation (Mayr 1982) — was accompanied by an intensive discussion of the possibilities of explaining merely by Darwin's theory of natural selection the evolution of animal structures and behavioural patterns. Two problems were at focus: (1) How is it possible for characteristics to evolve *gradually* by natural selection? (2) How is a *coadaptation* of characteristics possible by natural selection? Gradual evolution by natural selection was a problem, some critics argued, because characteristics have to reach a certain level of development before they can make a difference in the struggle for existence and reproduction, and in order to reach this level of development, some other factor would have to ensure the preservation of the incipient characteristics in each generation. For example, to make it possible for a new innate behavioural pattern, say a certain feeding habit, to gradually emerge in the phylogenetic development of a species, various new elements of innate muscular movements, which are not in themselves, not even in combination, sufficient for performing an adaptive feeding behaviour, would have to be preserved in previous generations. Coadaptation of characteristics by natural selection was a problem, some argued, because the characteristics would have to evolve in synchrony with each other, and in order to maintain this balance, some additional adjusting factor would be needed. For example, to make it possible for an existing structure, say the antlers of a species, to increase in size in the phylogenetic lineage, the variation in size of the antlers would have to coincide harmoniously with appropriate variations in all parts of the body that support and move this structure.

In 1896 a solution to these problems was suggested by three men, to all appearances independently of each other, first by Conwy Lloyd Morgan in a paper read to the New York Academy of Sciences on January 31st (Morgan 1896), then by James Mark Baldwin (1896a) in the discussion following Morgan's paper, and later also by Henry F. Osborn at another meeting of the Academy, March 9th, the same year (Bristol 1896; Dyar 1896). The factor, or rather set of factors, they proposed to have played a crucial role in the gradual evolution and coadaptation of characteristics has become known as "Organic Selection," a name suggested by Baldwin, and also as "The Baldwin Effect." The basic idea of the hypothesis may be summed up in five points:

i. Organisms are born not only with congenitally definite dispositions, but also with a certain amount of plasticity which enables the individuals to make modifications of their structures and behavioural patterns that are not hereditary as such, but which may be repeated by future generations through learning.
ii. Those modifications that promote the survival and reproduction of the individuals acquiring them are repeated generation after generation, while the disadvantageous modifications are eliminated by natural selection.
iii. As the organisms produce their modifications each generation is also subject to variations of germinal origin.
iv. Those germinally generated variations that are in the same direction as the advantageous acquired modifications are preserved, while those that are in the direction of the disadvantageous acquired modifications are eliminated by natural selection.
v. Through (i–iv) acquired modifications may gradually be replaced by innate variations, without the acquired modifications as such being inherited.

The most elaborate formulation of the hypothesis appears in Morgan's paper. Baldwin's contribution lies primarily in that he applies the hypothesis to the explanation of the phylogenetic development of innate behavioural patterns — and this involves, as we shall see, considerable interpretation problems. Osborn's contribution seems to have been very limited. Judging from the account of the March 9th meeting (Bristol 1896; Dyar 1896), he did not seem to have come up with anything beyond what Morgan had already formulated. I will call our attempt at summation (i–v) "the Morgan-Baldwin-Osborn hypothesis" — "the MBO-hypothesis" for short. To call this "organic selection" or "the Baldwin effect" would be less satisfactory. As Simpson (1953) points out, there is nothing particularly organic about organic selection/the Baldwin effect, nor is this process really directly or solely a form of selection, in addition to natural selection.[1] And to call (i–v) "the Baldwin effect" would not give due credit to Morgan and Osborn.[2]

The MBO-hypothesis explains why acquired characteristics may seem to be inherited, when they are in fact (according to the hypothesis) *replaced* by germinally generated variations (i. e. variations caused by mutations and recombinations of genes), promoted by natural selection while the individual organisms keep repeating the acquired characteristics generation after generation through learning. As we have noted, the hypothesis is supposed to explain the evolution of both animal structures and behavioural patterns. There is, however, a fundamental difference between explaining the evolution of structures and explaining the evolution of behavioural patterns. An explanation of the evolution of animal structures may be comparatively straightforward. For example, according to the MBO-hypothesis, the coadaptation of a phylogenetic increase in size of antlers and of the parts of the body supporting and moving this structure could simply be explained by a plasticity of the supporting muscles, ligaments and bones, making it possible for each generation to adapt to the variations in size of the antlers and preserve any innate variation in the supporting and steering parts working in an advantageous direction. (The development of an existing structure and the gradual emergence of a new structure, say wings from fore limbs, with a new function, flying, may be explained even without the MBO-hypothesis. It could be explained by a plasticity in the use and strength of certain muscles making it possible for each generation to make an adaptive use of the various structures preceding the fully developed wings. This idea of a change in function was developed already by Anton Dohrn (1875) and could partly be traced back to Darwin (1859:-450–456).) However, to explain the evolution of behavioural patterns is quite a different matter. This involves special interpretation problems.

To begin with, how should the distinction made in point (i) of the MBO-hypothesis, between "congenitally definite dispositions" and the "plasticity which enables the individuals to make modifications," be understood in this connection? As long as we are discussing the evolution of structures we may think of this distinction as a division between a given genotype and a more or less plastic bodily phenotype. But what does this distinction stand for in the case of behavioural patterns? For instance, if we try to explain the evolution of innate behavioural patterns by the MBO-hypothesis, and we assume that "congenitally definite dispositions" refers to some innate and rigid neural predisposition to react in a certain way to a certain stimulus (e.g. by producing muscular movements that are not in themselves sufficiently adaptive), what is it in the organism that has the flexibility that enables the individual to adjust its behaviour and make it adaptive? Is it just another neural process? Or is it something "mental," perhaps even something conscious? And how are these processes — the rigid and the flexible — related to each other?

Our problem of understanding the distinction made in point (i) of the MBO-hypothesis brings us over to the main questions of the present paper: Could an application of the MBO-hypothesis to the problem of explaining the evolution of innate behavioural patterns shed some light on the question of the place of consciousness in the biological evolution? For example: Could it suggest an answer to the question why conscious mental processes have been preserved and developed by natural selection in the biological evolution? And could it suggest an answer to the specific question of how conscious mental processes may be understood to be related to neural processes (the mind-brain problem)?[3] Baldwin's analysis is of particular interest for a discussion of these questions.

The relevance of Baldwin's analysis to these problems has not attracted much attention in the philosophy-of-mind literature. Among the rare exceptions are Popper (Popper and Eccles 1977), Dennett (1991; 1995) and Watkins (1999). Karl Popper's analysis is rather brief, but makes clear that Baldwin's analysis (Popper mentions also Morgan, but not Osborn) may elucidate how "subjective aims and purposes" can have an evolutionary significance (Popper and Eccles 1977: Chapter P1, Section 6). Popper does not, however, go into discussing in greater detail how Baldwin's analysis of the evolution of innate behavioural patterns may be understood. Daniel Dennett tries to avoid dealing with any possible conscious mental factors in Baldwin's analysis, and attempts to reformulate the "Baldwin Effect"-hypothesis in purely behaviouristic terms (1991: Chapter 7, Section 3; 1995: Chapter 3, Section 4). It is doubtful, however, whether he fully succeeds — he still employs mentalistic terms like "recognize" and "learn" — and he turns the "Baldwin Effect"-hypothesis, about an active and partly creative role of behavioural changes in evolution, into a hypothesis about a reactive and mechanical behavioural function. Dennett's behaviouristic approach makes his discussion of the "Baldwin Effect" less relevant to our analysis.

In contrast to Dennett, and in agreement with Popper, John Watkins, takes Baldwin's emphasis on the role of mental factors seriously. However, Watkins focuses on other aspects of Baldwin's analysis than we will do. Watkins's main concern is with the question whether the "Baldwin Effect" does in fact occur and whether it would be desirable within human societies.

In his contribution to the New York Academy of Sciences meeting (Baldwin 1896a), Baldwin raises the question whether consciousness may be a causal factor in the evolution of innate behavioural patterns. In a later paper (Baldwin 1896b) he follows up this issue by a more detailed analysis of how the relation between consciousness and activities of the brain may be understood. He emphasises that "no adequate theory of the development of organic nature can be formulated without taking conscious states into account," but at the same time he rejects the idea that "consciousness is a *causa vera* whose modes of action do not have physiological parallel processes in the brain and nerves" (Baldwin 1896b: 300–301). In the present paper this position will be critically examined and compared with ideas put forward by William James (1879; 1890) and Karl Popper (1977, 1978; Popper and Eccles 1977).

To what extent characteristics actually evolve in the way Morgan, Baldwin and Osborn suggest (summed up in the MBO-hypothesis) has not been much discussed in the modern literature. Basically, this seems to be due to uncertainties as to how the hypothesis should be understood to be related to "neo-Darwinism" and "neo-Lamarckism" — the two most influential theories of evolution at the time of Weismann's development of his theory of inheritance. Neo-Darwinism was a development of Darwin's theory of evolution, amounting to a rejection of Darwin's theory of pangenesis and of any other idea of a direct inheritance of acquired characteristics. Neo-Lamarckism was an attempt to defend the Lamarckian theory of inheritance in opposition to the emerging neo-Darwinism.

Some of the early critics understood Morgan's, Baldwin's and Osborn's hypothesis as an attempt to reconcile neo-Darwinism with neo-Lamarckism, and took no further interest in the hypothesis after the Lamarckian theory of inheritance had been refuted by Mendelism and later genetic theory (Simpson 1953). Others have understood the hypothesis to suggest an alternative to the theory of natural selection, and have rejected the hypothesis on this ground (Mayr 1963). Both interpretations overstate the ambitions of Morgan's, Baldwin's and Osborn's hypothesis. Although Morgan (1896) does talk of a "reconciliation" of selectionist and transmissionist views, he makes fully clear that the hypothesis he suggests (summed up in the MBO-hypothesis, i–v) rules out the Lamarckian theory of inheritance of acquired characteristics. What the "reconciliation" amounted to was merely that "[acquired] modifications afford the conditions under which [germinally generated] variations of like nature are afforded an opportunity of occurring and of making themselves felt in race-progress" (Morgan 1896: 737). Also Baldwin (1896a) clearly concludes at several places of his analysis that he finds no need to assume "the Lamarckian factor" and the "the inheritance of acquired characters." Osborn similarly questions the relevance of the Lamarckian theory of inheritance (Bristol 1896; Dyar 1896). Nor did Morgan, Baldwin or Osborn try to develop an alternative to the theory of natural selection. On the contrary, the hypothesis they suggest explicitly presupposes natural selection.

This paper will not discuss to what extent, in what species, etc., animal characteristics may be understood to evolve in the way the MBO-hypothesis suggests and the empirical problems involved in determining this. I will confine myself to merely commenting on a few possible examples discussed in the literature. The analysis will focus on examining the distinction made in point (i) of the MBO-hypothesis between causal factors that are "congenitally definite" and causal factors that have "a certain amount of plasticity." I will discuss this distinction by first commenting on an example of gradual evolution of co-adapted characteristics, in which the characteristics are muscular movements — namely the coordinated muscular movements found in instincts; an example brought up by Baldwin (1896a). I will argue that in this context the congenitally definite factors may be understood as genetically programmed neural processes, that may generate a specific pattern of behaviour upon a certain stimulus, whereas the plastic factors may be understood as conscious mental processes, that may generate a variety of behavioural patterns upon a certain stimulus. I will discuss how processes of the first kind may be understood to be related to processes of the second kind. I will critically examine a double-aspect solution suggested by Baldwin (1896b) and compare this with an interactionistic mind-brain theory which I will argue is plausible and fruitful from an evolutionary biology point of view. I will then go over to comment briefly on an example of the gradual evolution of coadapted characteristics, in which one of the characteristics is a behavioural pattern and the other a bodily structure — the correlated changes of feeding habits and beak structures in birds, discussed by Alister Hardy (1965). I will argue that although this example does not necessarily illustrate the MBO-hypothesis, it is nevertheless relevant to a discussion of the hypothesis, because Hardy's analysis suggests a similar way in which conscious mental events may be involved in biological evolution.

Changes in behavioural patterns

There is an interesting paradox in the fact that the survival of every animal species depends both on its ability to maintain and to change its behavioural patterns. As long as the environment remains practically unchanged, an animal may benefit from behavioural patterns developed by earlier generations, but as soon as the practical circumstances change a continued adherence to these patterns may instead lead to the extinction of the species. In other words, a species may become extinct as a result of the individuals' inability to adjust their behaviour to the new circumstances. A clear example is the selection of nesting site in different species of bird. Some species of bird prove to be quite flexible in this respect. Others are more rigid. The blackbird is an example of the first category; the white-backed woodpecker of the latter. Although the blackbird prefers nesting in bushes, it may nest in trees and even adapt to nesting on projections of walls. The white-backed woodpecker, on the other hand, is highly dependent upon old deciduous trees for its survival. An efficient weeding out of these trees would most likely lead to extinction of this species. There are also situations where the preservation of a species depends on a strict conformity of behavioural patterns. An example is mating. As Niko Tinbergen points out: "In many species, copulation is even based on a series of social releasers [such as shape, colour, movements, sounds, scents, etc.], which together render inter-breeding highly improbable and, as a rule, even entirely impossible" (Tinbergen 1951: 172). A deviation in behaviour may fail to release the required reaction of the mate and cause a break in the chain of stimuli and responses normally leading to copulation.

This conflict between rigidity and flexibility is reflected in the phylogenetic development of innate behavioural patterns. The development may go in both directions, towards increased rigidity as well as towards increased flexibility. It all depends on what best promotes the survival of the species. To use our example, evolution has produced both the flexibility of the blackbird and the rigidity of the white-backed woodpecker. We might say that as a result of evolution the blackbird is born with a richer behavioural repertoire than the white-backed woodpecker regarding the selection of nesting site. But what does this imply? Does it imply that both species are born with a certain amount of dispositions to *automatically* respond to certain stimuli by producing certain patterns of muscular movements, but that the blackbird is born with a greater amount of such dispositions than the white-backed woodpecker regarding the selection of nesting site? (This would mean that individuals of both species "select" nesting site only in a figurative sense — there is no form of deliberation involved, influencing the behaviour.) Or does it imply that both species are born with a certain amount of dispositions to respond to certain stimuli by producing certain patterns of muscular movements, but that the production of these responses also depends on certain *cognitive processes*, and that the blackbird is born not only with a greater amount of dispositions but also with a greater cognitive capacity than the white-backed woodpecker regarding the selection of nesting site? (The cognitive processing would mean that the animal is at least able to associate — perhaps even *consciously* compare — incoming impulses with stored information and to attain results that may influence the animal's behaviour. It should be noted that, in the case of innate behavioural patterns, also the stored information is understood to be innate.) In other words: If we assume that a behavioural pattern is innate, does it imply that we understand the behaviour to be just a more or less complicated series of reflexes, or would it allow us to assume that the behaviour is at least partly influenced by some form of conscious mental processing? And if one species exhibits a greater innate behaviour repertoire than another, does it allow us to infer a difference not only in their neural systems but also in some innate mental capacity?

These questions have direct bearings on our problem of understanding what the plasticity, suggested in point (i) of the MBO-hypothesis, may amount to. If innate behavioural patterns are completely automatic — like the "behaviour" of a slot-machine, determined by what buttons are pressed — there could be no room for a plasticity that would enable the individual to modify its innate behaviour. But if innate behavioural patterns may be influenced by some form of conscious mental processing, this could be understood to provide the individual with the required plasticity.[4]

As we shall see, Baldwin (1896a) argues that animals may influence their behaviour by, what he calls, "intelligence," and that a species in that way may maintain a behavioural pattern generation after generation until it has been completely replaced by an innate behavioural pattern. Although he understands intelligence to be a *conscious* process (Baldwin 1896a: 561), he does not, as we noted earlier, view consciousness as something that itself causes the behaviour.

This ambivalence, to not want to deny that animals, at least not birds and mammals, are conscious, but at the same time not want to concede that this capacity may play causal role, has continued to characterise the general view of animal behaviour far onto the twentieth century. Even if no one has really intended to go as far as viewing animals as pure machines — not even Descartes

(Gaukroger 1995), although he has often been ascribed this view — many modern scientists and philosophers have tried to disregard the problem whether animals are conscious and whether subjective experiences influence their behaviour, with reference to the principle of parsimony — "Ockham's razor." To take into account subjective experiences was not considered necessary for explaining animal behaviour. Ethologists have referred to "Morgan's principle": "In no case may we interpret an action as the outcome of the exercise of a higher psychical faculty, if it can be interpreted as the outcome of the exercise of one which stands lower in the psychological scale" (Morgan 1894: 53). For a long time researchers of animal behaviour also shared the overly high ambitions of early twentieth century physicists to achieve a completely "objective" science, renouncing all interest in "unobservable" entities. To include cognitions or subjective experiences, such as feelings, in the explanation of behaviour was considered unscientific. Even such a prominent and pioneering ethologist as Tinbergen advocated these ideals. As he puts it: "Although, as we said before, the ethologist does not want to deny the possible existence of subjective phenomena in animals, he claims that it is futile to present them as causes, since they cannot be observed by scientific methods" (Tinbergen 1951: 5).

During the last thirty years, however, this trend has changed. The explanatory value of cognitive theories has gained increased acceptance in the study of animal behaviour (Burghardt 1985; Rizstau 1991). Ethologists allow themselves to explain animal behaviour in partly psychological terms. There is still, however, a resistance against dealing with questions of animal consciousness. A progressive ethologist in this area is Donald Griffin, who comparatively early emphasised the plausibility, from an evolutionary point of view, of a "physiological continuity between men and animals in brain function, and [...] a comparable continuity in mental experiences" (Griffin 1976: 52; cf. pp. 74, 104). Griffin suggests that it may in fact be more parsimonious to assume that animals are conscious, and that this capacity confers an adaptive advantage, than to adopt a behaviouristic approach: "It may be helpful, and even parsimonious, to assume some limited degree of conscious awareness in animals, rather than postulating cumbersome chains of interacting reflexes and internal states of motivation" (Griffin 1976: 85). Griffin calls attention to the degree of versatility of the behaviour as a criterion for determining whether an animal acts consciously. In *Animal Minds* (1992) he further substantiates these points by numerous examples of communicative behaviour and versatile adaptability of behaviour in various species. And he makes clear that we cannot rule out the possibility that even genetically programmed behaviour may be guided by conscious thinking (Griffin 1992: Chapter 12; See also Griffin 2001: Chapter 14).

How, then, more exactly, could conscious processes be understood to be related to genetically programmed behaviour? This is the problem Baldwin is dealing with in his attempt to explain the evolution of innate behavioural patterns. Let us examine his analysis more closely.

The evolution of innate behavioural patterns

In order to fully grasp Baldwin's criticism of the Lamarckian explanation of the evolution of innate behavioural patterns, it is necessary to first get an idea of his distinction between "intelligent actions" and "reflexes." According to Baldwin (1896a), "intelligence" is the conscious process by which an individual animal (in accordance with the MBO-hypothesis) may modify its behaviour and by that supplement and pave the way for the phylogenetic development of innate behavioural patterns — what Baldwin calls "instincts." And a basic idea in Baldwin's criticism of the Lamarckian theory is that it overrates the ability of "intelligence" to produce new habits; that the theory fails to recognise the dependence of intelligent actions on neural predispositions, some of which are innate and some acquired. Baldwin may be said to deny the existence of purely "intelligent" actions. The main difference between "intelligent actions" and "reflexes" is, in Baldwin's view, that in the former the effect of external stimuli on the bodily movements is mediated by cognitive processes, "memories," or feelings, "pleasures and pains," whereas in the latter the effect is more direct. He characterises the difference like this:

> Intelligent actions are centrally stimulated. This means that brain processes release the energy which goes out in movement, and that something earlier must stimulate the brain processes. This something is association in some shape between present stimulating agencies in the environment and memories, or pleasures and pains. In other words, certain central processes intervene between the outside stimulus and the release of the energies of movement. In reflexes, however, no such central influence intervenes. The stimulus in the environment passes directly — is reflected — into the motor apparatus. (Baldwin 1896a: 560)

Instincts Baldwin seems to view as something very close to reflexes. In fact, it is not clear to what extent he really distinguishes between instincts and reflexes. At one point he even refers to certain behaviour as "instinctive reflexes" (Baldwin 1896a: 559). As in his comparison of reflexes with intelligent actions, he emphasises that the difference between instincts and intelligent actions lies in "the connection in the brain" whereby "in instinct the muscular coördination is brought into play *directly* by a sense stimulation; while in intelligence it is brought into play *indirectly*, i. e., through association of brain processes, but by the same sense stimulation or a similar one" (Baldwin 1896a: 439). There is also an uncertainty in Baldwin's discussion as to whether or not he understands instincts to be in any degree conscious behaviour. Physiologically he characterises instinct as a tendency "embodied in the white matter and the lower brain centers" and intelligence as a tendency "embodied in the cortex of the hemispheres" (Baldwin 1896a: 441). It is not decisive for our discussion, however, whether or not Baldwin views instincts to be in any degree conscious behaviour. It is sufficient that we note that he views *intelligent* actions to be influenced by conscious processes, such as pleasures and pains, and that he views intelligence itself to be something conscious. This is sufficient because, if intelligence is something conscious, its active role in the phylogenetic development of innate behavioural patterns (assumed by Baldwin, in what appears to be an application of the principles summed up in the MBO-hypothesis) would itself highlight the question of the place of consciousness in the biological evolution. — Does Baldwin's explanation of the phylogenetic development of innate behavioural patterns not imply that conscious experiences are in some way efficacious in the biological evolution? What does he mean by consciousness not being a *causa vera* whose modes of action do not have physiological parallel processes in the brain and nerves? Let us take a closer look at his criticism of the Lamarckian theory.

According to the Lamarckian theory, Baldwin contends, the coordination of the muscular movements found in instincts could not be the result of gradual variation, because they are so coadapted and merely partially adaptive movements would not have been useful; the innate behavioural patterns must therefore have been originally produced by intelligence and developed into habits by repetition in the individual, and these habits were then transmitted to the next generation by "natural" (i. e. genetic) inheritance. Baldwin rejects this Lamarckian explanation, not only for its theory of inheritance, but also for its understanding of the function of intelligence in the ontogenesis of individual organisms.

Baldwin argues that intelligence cannot bring about coordinated muscular movements unless they are already, to some extent, in the organism's repertoire: "The intelligence can never, by any possibility, create a new movement, or effect a new combination of movements, if the apparatus of brain, nerve and muscle has not been made ready for the combination which is effected [...] So we may say that intelligent adaptation does not create coördinations; it only makes functional use of coördinations which were alternatively present already in the creature's equipment" (Baldwin 1896a: 438–439). And, Baldwin reasons, an organism may be physiologically prepared to perform certain combinations of muscular movements either from birth or as a result of acquired habits. (Even in the latter case, however, when the physiological preparation is a result of learning, Baldwin seems to assume that the ability to perform some of the most basic movements is still innate.) He illustrates this with a child's efforts to learn how to write:

> Every child has to learn how to write. If he depended upon chance movements of his hands he would never learn how to write. But on the other hand, he can not write simply by willing to do so; he might will forever without effecting a "special creation" of muscular movement. What he actually does is to *use his hand in a great many possible ways as near as he can to the way required;* and from these excessively produced movements, and after excessively varied and numerous trials, he gradually selects and fixes the slight successes made in the direction of correct writing. (Baldwin, 1896c: 548–549; emphasis in the original)

In animals, Baldwin contends, the production of excess movements and the gradual selection of movements are largely governed by sensory experiences of pleasure and pain: "Actions which secure pleasurable conditions to the organism are determined by the pleasure to be repeated, and so to secure the continuance of the pleasurable conditions; and actions which get the organism into pain are by the very fact of pain suppressed" (Baldwin 1896b: 303). Baldwin calls this feedback process "Circular Reaction."

In the phylogenetic development of innate behavioural patterns, Baldwin (1896a) argues, intelligence can only have a supportive function; the intelligence may supplement innate but yet only partially developed behavioural patterns, making them adaptive — in accordance with the MBO-hypothesis. In some cases, Baldwin contends, *imitation* may have the same supportive function. To illustrate this, he mentions what seemed to be a not fully developed instinct to drink in young chicks. Chicks have a characteristic way of drinking by throwing their heads up in the air. This behavioural pattern, Baldwin maintains, comes into action only after the chick has had the *taste* of water, either by accident or by imitation. The mere *sight* of water will not make them drink, he argues. The imitation — the tasting of the water — may then supplement the not yet fully developed instinct to drink. In this way, Baldwin reasons, the species may be preserved and have a chance of completing the development of the instinct, by becoming subject to germinal variations that establish a connection also between the sight centre and the existing behavioural predispositions, so that future chicks may start to drink at the mere sight of water. (Of course, provided that this interpretation is correct, that the tasting is really a matter of imitation and not an instinct, to complete the instinct to drink, also this part, the tasting, would have to be replaced by an innate variation. The complete instinct of drinking would then consist of three elements: the immediate effect of the visual sensation, releasing the movements of tasting, which in turn releases the movements of swallowing.) Although modern ethologists would perhaps not agree with Baldwin's interpretation — but instead view also the tasting as an instinct, activated by the behaviour of the other individuals[5] — it is easy to see how he imagined the phylogenetic development of instincts to take place. Besides, even if the whole sequence of drinking as it appears in chicks today ought to be viewed as a chain of instinctive events, Baldwin could always argue that the chain once originated through the assistance of imitation.

There are several uncertainties in Baldwin's analysis. For instance, it is not clear how generally applicable his explanation of the phylogenetic development of instincts should be understood to be. Is it supposed to explain the evolution of all types of instincts? And how far "down" in the animal kingdom is it supposed to apply? Nor is it clear if his explanation always implies that the assistant factor is conscious. Baldwin's notion of imitation is ambiguous in this respect. At one point of his analysis, he seems to view imitation as a form of instinct — he talks about an "instinct to imitate;" at another point, he calls imitation the most prominent example of "simpler states of consciousness" (Baldwin 1896a: 440, 561). Perhaps imitation should be understood as an intermediate form, that may sometimes be conscious and sometimes non-conscious. Most central to our analysis, however, is Baldwin's puzzling view on the relation between consciousness and activities of the brain in the generation of overt behaviour.

Baldwin (1896b: 307) contends that voluntary movements cannot be adequately explained neither in purely psychological terms, nor in merely the terms of physics or the natural sciences in a broader sense, including "the chemistry and physiology of the brain." He emphasises that voluntary movements are always the result of both conscious and nervous processes. He contrasts this view with an interactionistic theory that asserts that conscious mental processes, such as the experiences of pleasure and pain, may by themselves causally influence neural processes, and also with an epiphenomenalistic theory that denies any such influence. Baldwin seems to defend a double-aspect theory, according to which both conscious mental processes and neural processes are necessary and neither alone sufficient for causing voluntary movements. It is not clear, however, in what way the conscious mental processes are understood to be necessary in causing the bodily movements. On one hand, Baldwin rejects the idea of "an actual efficiency of some kind in consciousness itself for producing physical effects," that (he assumes) would violate the principle of conservation of energy (Baldwin 1896b: 307). On the other, he argues that in the production of voluntary movement consciousness is to the brain what the electric current is to an electro-magnet in the attraction of iron filings (Baldwin 1896b: 306). Perhaps Baldwin in rejecting the idea of consciousness as a "*causa vera*" should be understood to distinguish between *cause* and *condition*; and that he employs a narrow notion of cause, according to which something is a cause of something else only if the former is itself sufficient for the occurrence of the latter. An antecedent that merely *contributes* to the effect in question, as a necessary but not in itself sufficient condition for the occurrence of the effect, would then not count as a *cause* of this effect. But even this would still appear hard to reconcile with his idea that an "efficiency" in consciousness would violate the principle of conservation of energy, because even a mere contributory influence could be understood to have some degree of efficiency.

Baldwin seems to have got stuck on the classical problem of trying to reconcile an ontologically dualistic mind-body distinction (amounting to mind being something immaterial and body something material) with a materialistic notion of causality. By assuming that reference always has to be made to some state of consciousness in explaining voluntary movements and, at the same time, that a causal influence of conscious mental processes on neural processes would violate (what is generally understood to be) a universal principle, the principle of conservation of energy, Baldwin entangles himself in contradictions. This is totally uncalled for, since his problem — to explain the phylogenetic development of innate behavioural patterns — requires, not a physical, but a biological perspective. Baldwin need not adopt a material-immaterial distinction or try to analyse the existence of consciousness in the terms of physics or discuss whether or not subjective experiences, such as pleasures and pains, conform to the principle of conservation of energy. What his evolutionary problem requires, however, is that he determines the plausibility and fruitfulness of the alternative mind-body theories in relation to Darwin's theory of evolution.

William James (1879) seems to have been the first to realise the significance of an evolutionary approach to the mind-body problem. James (1879, 1890), and later also Popper (1977, 1978; Popper and Eccles 1977), argue that if the preservation and development of consciousness in the biological evolution is a result of natural selection, it is plausible (Popper appears to say even necessary) that consciousness has not only been influenced by neural processes, but has had a survival value itself; and that this in turn would entail that consciousness must have been causally efficacious. Both James and Popper conclude that Darwin's theory of natural selection tells against theories that deny that conscious mental events, such as pleasure and pain, may bring about and influence neural events. (For a discussion of James's and Popper's respective versions of this evolutionary argument, see Lindahl 1997.)

Although it may be to go too far, to argue, as Popper seems to do, that Darwin's theory of natural selection is incompatible with the theory that consciousness is merely a causally inert effect of neural processes (Lindahl 1997), it does not seem possible to explain the existence of various forms of consciousness in different species (from mere degrees of awareness in "lower" species to self-consciousness in man) as being a result of evolution by natural selection unless we assume that this capacity (consciousness) is *either* an epiphenomenon of neural processes *or* something that at least partly influences the overt behaviour. (As an epiphenomenon, consciousness could have been preserved and have developed as a consequence of the development of the nervous system and, if causally efficacious, consciousness could have been preserved and have developed as a consequence of its usefulness in the struggle for existence and reproduction. A third alternative would be to view conscious mental events and processes as ontologically identical with certain neural events and processes. But this does not seem to be a tenable position. See e.g. Popper and Eccles 1977; Smythies 1994; Svensson 1994; Lindahl 1997.) Since Baldwin rejects the epiphenomenalistic alternative, he seems from an evolutionary perspective bound to allow for, in his mind-body theory, some degree of influence of consciousness on the overt behaviour — even if this influence would be only as a contributory condition. He seems to have to embrace some form of interactionistic theory.

Despite the uncertainties we have noted about Baldwin's analysis, it seems justified to conclude that his explanation of the phylogenetic development of innate behavioural patterns, when combined with an evolutionary approach to the mind-body problem, implies that consciousness plays an active role in the biological evolution. Consciousness may be understood to influence both the ontogenetic and phylogenetic development of the neural basis of overt behaviour — the ontogenetic, through what Baldwin calls "Circular Reaction," and the phylogenetic, through the process suggested by the MBO-hypothesis (i–v). In this way, consciousness would have a survival value. Subjective experiences of sensations and emotions, as well as the conscious processes Baldwin (1896a, 1896b) calls "intelligence" and "volition," would promote the survival and reproduction of organisms having this capacity (consciousness).

Hardy (1965), in his discussion of the problem of explaining the coadaptation of behaviour and structures — for instance, the coadaptation of feeding habits and beak structures in birds — goes a step further than Baldwin and *explicitly* suggests that mental phenomena, such as the "exploratory curiosity" of animals, may causally influence the direction of the phylogenetic development of species. (Interestingly, Popper developes a similar hypothesis in his Herbert Spencer Lecture, 1961.[6]) Hardy explicitly defends a 'psycho-physical" interactionistic theory. Let us briefly examine his analysis.

The coadaptation of behaviour and structure

Hardy's problem is not primarily the two questions we have seen Morgan, Baldwin and Osborn focus on, how a gradual evolution and a coadaptation of characteristics is at all possible by natural selection. Hardy is not mainly concerned with explaining how acquired characteristics may seem to be inherited; how a basically Darwinian process of evolution by natural selection may appear to be Lamarckian. Hardy concentrates more directly on discussing how changes of habit — and ultimately the animals' "power of choice" — may affect the course of evolution.

Hardy agrees with Morgan, Baldwin and Osborn, that animal structures and innate behavioural patterns may evolve by socially inherited habits (i.e. acquired behavioural patterns that are transmitted from one generation to another by learning) making the preservation and accumulation of innate variations possible. However, Hardy does not restrict this explanation, like the MBO-hypothesis, only to cases where an acquired modification of a characteristic of a certain kind is being replaced by an innate variation of a characteristic of overtly the same kind; for example, where a certain acquired feeding habit is replaced by an overtly identical innate feeding habit.[7] Hardy does also include cases where an acquired modification of a characteristic of a certain kind enables the species to evolve an innate variation of a characteristic of an entirely *different* kind; for example, where an acquired change of a certain feeding habit enables the species to evolve a new innate bodily structure (e.g. a new shape of beak or a different length of legs). (Hardy does not seem to have noticed that this amounts to an expansion of the original hypothesis.[8])

As an illustration Hardy discusses the correlation between beak differences and differences in feeding methods found in the finches on the Galapagos Islands (analysed in Lack 1947: Chapter VI). He relates these correlations to the diversity of beaks among birds in general, and concludes: "Can it really be maintained that it is *more likely* that random mutations forced these different groups of birds to their different modes of life, rather than that they developed different habits and that such differences in feeding led gradually to beaks better and better adapted to their ways of life? Surely it must be admitted that it is change of habit which is the dominating factor influencing such selection." (Hardy 1965: 177)

The idea that changes of habit may pave the way for an evolution of bodily structures by natural selection is in itself hardly controversial. Already Darwin (1859) discusses this as a possible mechanism. He speculates:

> In North America the black bear was seen by Hearne swimming for hours with widely open mouth, thus catching, like a whale, insects in the water. Even in so extreme a case as this, if the supply of insects were constant, and if better adapted competitors did not already exist in the country, I can see no difficulty in a race of bears being rendered, by natural selection, more and more aquatic in their structure and habits, with larger and larger mouths, till a creature was produced as monstrous as a whale. (Darwin 1859: 184)

Mayr (1982: 612) goes as far as concluding that "Many if not most acquisitions of new structures in the course of evolution can be ascribed to selection forces exerted by newly acquired behaviors" (see also Mayr 1960). Ewer (1960) discusses a plausible example, the evolution of teeth and skulls of certain African Suidae, in which changes of the teeth, due to changes of feeding habit, seem to have preceded changes of the skull architecture.

What is controversial, however, in Hardy's analysis, is his emphasis on the "psychic life" of animals as a causal factor in the biological evolution. Hardy calls attention to the difference between, what he calls, "external" and "internal" selective agencies/forces. The external is the influence other organisms and the inanimate environment have on the evolution of a species, whereas the internal is an influence a species has on its own evolution through its own behaviour (Hardy 1965: 171–172). It is in the working of these mechanisms, Hardy points out, that one of the main differences between the plant and animal kingdoms lies. He explains:

> The greater part of the plant's structure is mainly, although perhaps not entirely, the result of the external selective forces, for example, those of the physical environment, of competition with neighbours, and of the browsing of herbivorous animals. Now animals are subject to as many such external forces of selection as are plants [...] but in addition, they have this "internal" behavioural selection — the effects of habits developed by active, exploring, inquisitive, initiating creatures; this makes the vital difference. (Hardy 1965: 206)

Hardy's point seems to be that, unlike plants, animals are not always victims of the environment or merely reacting to stimuli from the environment, but often appear to act on their own initiative, in a way that seem to require *mental* activity. He contends that "the internal, behavioural selection, due to the "psychic life" of the animal [...] is now seen to be a most powerful creative element in evolution" (Hardy 1965: 208). Hardy calls his view of the psychic life of animals a form of vitalism:

> ... I am not a vitalist in the old-fashioned sense of believing that there is some vital force or entelechy interfering directly with the physico-chemical reactions of the body in development. I am sure that the laws of physics and chemistry are never broken; yet [...] I am sure we have no right to assume that physics and chemistry as we at present understand them can explain the whole of life — particularly the body-mind relationship. I am not committed as to whether the universe is a dualistic one or not, but I think it more likely that it is. Space and time form a dualism in a sense — perhaps only a dualism of our perception; the physical and psychical may well have a similar relationship. My "vitalism" is a belief that there is a psychic side of the animal which, apart from inherited instinctive behaviour, may be independent of the DNA code that governs the form of the physical frame, but that it may interact with the physical system in the evolutionary process through organic selection. (Hardy 1965: 254)

It is not fully clear how Hardy defines the "psychic life" of animals. Unfortunately, the last two chapters of his work, where he deals in more detail with mental issues, is obscured by parapsychological and religious associations. But he seems to suggest that at least mammals, and perhaps also birds, may possess *conscious minds* (Hardy 1965: 257, 278).

Ethologists with a strict behaviouristic bent may argue that Hardy goes too far in his explanation of how changes of habit may affect the course of evolution. They may argue that his reference to the psychic life of animals as an underlying cause is superfluous or downright wrong. They may argue that his distinction between "external" and "internal" selective agencies/forces has an explanatory value only to the extent it amounts to a distinction between, on the one hand, the environmental influences and, on the other, the influences of the overt behaviour of the animal itself. And this is all his distinction may appear to amount to, as he first formulates it, as a division between "*external* selective agencies, meaning those acting from outside the organisms concerned, i.e. the selective forces acting from both the animate and inanimate environments; and [...] an *internal* selective force due to the behaviour and habits of the animal itself" (Hardy 1965: 171–172). The trouble begins, some behaviourists may argue, when it turns out that Hardy seems to put more into his notion of internal selective force than the influence of the overt behaviour; that he seems to mean by "internal selective force" the influence *mental* events and processes have *through* the animal's overt behaviour.

From a behaviourist point of view there is no need to invoke mental events and processes to explain the evolution of animal structures and innate behavioural patterns, even when changes of habit are understood to play a role. There is no need to go beyond the overt behaviour, some behaviourists would argue, or at least not to take into account other influences on the behaviour than external stimuli. Tinbergen is an interesting exception in this respect. He admits internal factors such as hormones acting upon the central nervous system, sensory stimuli, like "hunger" (understood as a physiological condition), and "intrinsic or automatic nervous impulses generated by the central nervous system itself" (Tinbergen 1951: 66, 67, 74, 101). He calls these internal factors "motivational factors," because, he argues, they are usually not in themselves sufficient for generating the overt behaviour, but merely determine the threshold of the response to sensory stimuli (Tinbergen 1951: 122). His use of the term "motivation" does not seem to imply anything more, however, than a mere physiological excitation.

Is there anything to this criticism of Hardy's analysis? It all depends, of course, on how broad Hardy's evolutionary problem should be understood to be. Of course, the significance of changes of habit for the evolution of animal structures and innate behavioural patterns could be accounted for merely in terms of overt behaviour and environmental influences. But, one may object, this would be to miss Hardy's point about the difference between animals and plants. Such an explanation would miss the point that animals, unlike plants, seem to be able to act on their own initiative. There would be no decisive difference between the acts of animals and the reactions of plants (their tropic and nastic movements). However, also this point could be considered without reference to mental phenomena. All we need to add, a critic might argue, is Tinbergen's idea of internal factors. An animal might be said to act on its own initiative when the behaviour is initiated by such internal factors. Perhaps some of these factors would be too simple to satisfy Hardy's distinction between animals and plants, but the *neural* factors would no doubt be sufficient, the critic might add. All the behaviour Hardy understands characterise "active, exploring, inquisitive, initiating creatures" could, according to this view, just as well be performed without a "psychic life." To see this, the critic might continue, we need only imagine an advanced robot, the overt movements of which is initiated by a genuinely random mechanism, working independently of any external factors. The random mechanism could be understood to generate impulses to a complex computer network (analogous to a nervous system), processing previously stored information and determining the content and running of certain motor programmes for the overt movements. (In order for the robot to "survive," these internally initiated movements would then, of course, very soon have to be supplemented by impulses from various sensors and feedback systems. It is hard to see how the robot would manage to continue relying merely on internally initiated movements.) But perhaps this is to make too light of Hardy's distinction between animals and plants. Perhaps Hardy means to say that the difference lies in that animals, unlike plants, act *intentionally* (one might even say that this is what is meant by an animal "acting"). Animals would then differ from plants in that animals are able to behave with anticipation and planning, based on beliefs, desires and, at least among certain "higher" species, reasoning and creative thinking. There is no compelling reason for assuming that humans are the only species that can act intentionally, in some sense. Nothing prevents us from assuming that there are similarities between humans and other species in this respect. Darwin's idea of evolution as a gradual process ought to apply to this particular trait, the mental, to the same extent as it applies to other phenotypical structures and functions. (It should be noted that even if we assume that conscious mental processes are *emergent* phenomena, we may understand the mental to evolve gradually, by a gradual evolution of the nervous system giving rise to different degrees and forms of conscious minds. And the occurrence of emergent phenomena within a population is fully compatible with the idea of a gradual evolution of the population as a whole (Mayr 1997). Rogers (1997: 187), without discussing the problem of emergent phenomena, comments on the difference between degrees and forms of consciousness and she boldly suggests that "rather than being a matter of more versus less it may be one of different kinds of consciousness in different animals.")

Hardy's evolutionary problem cannot be caught in strict behaviouristic or even Tinbergenian terms. Hardy's problem resembles more the problem that James and Popper discuss — to explain the place of consciousness in the biological evolution. And Hardy's explanation is, as we have noted, that the psychic life of animals (e.g. their "active, exploring, inquisitive, initiating" capacities) causally interacts with physical processes, such as the phylogenetic development of bodily structures, and thereby affects the course of evolution. To try to analyse Hardy's problem in strict behaviouristic or Tinbergenian terms would be to miss not only his distinction between animals and plants, but the very fundamental idea of his analysis — that conscious mental events and processes might make a difference in the biological evolution.

Although Hardy discusses his evolutionary problem much in terms of how changes of various forms of "behaviour" and "habits" may alter the course of evolution, and devotes comparatively little of his analysis to clarifying his idea of the nature and role of the underlying "psychic life," it is clear that his main point is that modern evolutionary theory has not paid enough attention to the problem that animals may be *conscious* active agents. And this is the decisive difference between biologists of the strict behaviouristic and Tinbergenian tradition and biologists of the kind Hardy represents. Whereas biologists of the former kind make every effort to avoid the problem of explaining the place of consciousness in the biological evolution, and why conscious mental processes have been preserved and developed in nature, this is exactly the questions biologists of the latter kind try to answer.

Concluding remarks

Whether animals really are conscious and whether their subjective experiences then influence their behaviour or only are epiphenomena of some neural activity, are questions we can only speculate about, by studying their overt behaviour, neuroanatomy and neurophysiology. There will always be objections, even against the most well-founded and cautious conclusions. But this is the case in all scientific contexts. The inferences made from overt behavioural patterns to assumptions about conscious mental activities are not fundamentally different from the inferences made from observed effects to their unobservable and alleged causes that we accept as evidence in other sciences, like chemistry and physics. The crucial question is not really methodological, although that is what is most often discussed, but has to do with the choice of *problem*.

For those who want to find an answer to the question why the remarkable capacity we call "consciousness" — and which we know at least ourselves to possess — has been preserved in the biological evolution, it does not carry the matter forward to apply an approach that avoids every assumption about subjective experiences and their possible survival value. If we can only accept a strict behaviouristic or Tinbergenian methodology, we are forced to waive investigating one of the most challenging problems in evolutionary biology. If we instead choose to tackle the problem, a fundamental question will be the one we have seen James (1879, 1890) bring up, and which has later been discussed by especially C.D. Broad (1925) and Popper (1977, 1978; Popper and Eccles 1977), namely whether consciousness should be understood to have been preserved because of its survival value (which, as we noted earlier, seems to imply an interactionistic mind-brain theory) or only as a causally inert side-effect of some neural activity (which implies an epiphenomenalistic theory). Broad (1925) contends, in contrast to Popper, that both alternatives are compatible with the idea that consciousness has been preserved as a result of natural selection.

If Broad is correct, which to me seems quite obvious (Lindahl 1997), the epiphenomenalistic theory cannot be ruled out on logical grounds, as being incompatible with Darwin's theory of evolution by natural selection. The question is then which of the two mind-brain theories seems most plausible in the light of Darwin's theory. And this may be analysed in several ways, each putting the question in a more concrete form. For example, we may do it from an "economic" perspective: Is it not more plausible that subjective experiences, such as pleasure and pain, influenced the individuals' chance of surviving and producing offspring, than that nature would have wasted energy on preserving the capacity of having such experiences without avail? Or we may do it from a perspective of explaining the evolution of certain structures or functions in animals. For instance, as we have seen Hardy reason regarding the evolution of beak structures: Is it not more plausible that changes of feeding habits, due to the psychic life of the animal, contributed to paving the way for a natural selection of certain beak structures, than that changes in beak structures led to a natural selection of certain feeding habits? And, as we have seen Baldwin reason regarding the evolution of instincts: Is it not more plausible, at least in "higher" animals, that learned modifications of behavioural patterns, due to conscious processes such as "intelligence" and "volition," paved the way for a natural selection of innate muscular-movement predispositions, gradually replacing the learned behavioural patterns, than that the innate predispositions were naturally selected to gradually form complete and advantageous behavioural patterns, without any assistance of conscious processes?

Of course, it is quite possible that nature preserves an energy-wasting function. And it is also quite possible that changes in bodily structures precede changes in habits, and that innate muscular-movement predispositions are naturally selected to gradually form adaptive behavioural patterns, without the assistance of conscious mental processes. (In the last mentioned case, we need only think of the possibility that some species may have developed their behavioural patterns without ever developing any form of consciousness. For a discussion of the differences between the evolution of consciousness and unconscious cognition, see Århem and Liljenström 1997.) But it seems to me far more likely that consciousness has been preserved because of its usefulness and that part of its usefulness may consist in an ability to generate new behavioural patterns, that may sometimes pave the way for a natural selection of bodily structures and innate muscular-movement predispositions.

Notes

* I would like to thank Björn Forkman, Dugald Murdoch, Michael Ruse and Birgitta Tullberg for helpful comments on earlier versions of this paper. The paper was written within a project financially supported by The Bank of Sweden Tercentenary Foundation (No. 98–0215).

1. The name "organic selection" is problematic also because Baldwin used it for different things at different points of time. In his work *Mental Development in the Child and the Race* (1895: 174) he uses it to designate an organism's way of learning to react in an advantageous way: "how certain reactions of one single organism can be selected so as to adapt the organism better and give it a life-history" (for a discussion, see Richards 1987: 488). In Baldwin 1896b: 304, he uses "organic selection" for the selection of bodily movements in the "Circular Reaction" process (this process is described in the section "The evolution of innate behavioural patterns" below) . (When he later republishes this paper in *Development and Evolution* (1902: Chapter IX) he calls this form of selection instead "Functional Selection.") Baldwin's use of his old designation "organic selection" for the hypothesis discussed at the New York Academy of Sciences meeting on January 31st, 1896, seems to have been a part of his strategy in claiming priority for the development of this hypothesis (see Richards 1987: 398–404 and Chapter 10).

2. Alister Hardy (1965: 178) contends that the idea of "Organic Selection" was formulated already by the British geologist James Hutton (1726–97) in an unpublished work, *Principles of Agriculture.* Hardy bases this on a passage from Hutton's manuscript cited in Bailey (1950). This seems doubtful, however. Hutton's idea does not seem to include the crucial notions of plasticity and individual modification, but merely an influence of innate behavioural patterns ("instinctive arts") on the preservation of "forms" of the species. The passage

reads: "'To see this beautiful system of animal life (which is also applicable to vegetables) we are to consider, that in the infinite variation of the breed that form best adapted to the exercise of those instinctive arts, by which the species is to live, will be most certainly continued in the propagation of this animal, and will be always tending more and more to perfect itself by the natural variation which is continually taking place. Thus, for example where dogs are to live by the swiftness of their feet and the sharpness of their sight, the form best adapted to that end will be the most certain of remaining, while those forms that are least adapted to this manner of chase will be the first to perish; and, the same will hold with regard to all the other forms and faculties of the species, by which the instinctive arts of procuring its means of substance may be pursued'" (Bailey 1950: 361).

3. In our discussion of these questions I will not explicitly define the notions "consciousness" or "conscious mental processes." I believe that the examples I will give as the discussion proceeds will sufficiently clarify these notions. The examples include subjective phenomena such as states of awareness, emotions and sensations of pleasures and pains. Hence, the notions of consciousness and conscious mental processes, as I understand them, include what Steven Pinker (1997: 134–148) calls "sentience." See also my (1997).

4. In this connection it may be of interest to consider Tinbergen's (1951) very broad definition of "instinct." He states: "I will tentatively define an instinct as a hierarchically organized nervous mechanism which is susceptible to certain priming, releasing and directing impulses of internal as well as of external origin, and which responds to these impulses by coordinated movements that contribute to the maintenance of the individual and the species" (Tinbergen 1951: 112). Tinbergen's notion of instinctive behaviour includes a hierarchy of behavioural patterns, with various degrees of variability, each governed by a separate level of nerve centres. He explains: "The centres of the higher levels do control purposive behaviour which is adaptive with regard to the mechanisms it employs to attain the end. The lower levels, however, give rise to increasingly simple and more stereotyped movements, until at the level of the consummatory act we have to do with an entirely rigid component, the fixed pattern, and a more or less variable component, the taxis, the variability of which, however, is entirely dependent on changes in the outer world" (Tinbergen 1951: 110). Tinbergen emphasises that he views all these levels as instinctive. He contrasts this notion with that of Konrad Lorenz, which only includes the consummatory act.

5. Tinbergen (1951: 144) emphasises that the ability to learn by imitation is mainly restricted to man and higher mammals, with the possible exception of the song of some song-birds. Also Simpson (1953: 113) mentions the song of certain species of birds as behaviour learned by imitation and, he adds, in some instances possibly phylogenetically developed through "the Baldwin effect."

6. The lecture was not published until 1972, as Chapter 7 of *Objective Knowledge.* Popper's hypothesis, which he later called "the spearhead theory of behavioural mutations" (Popper 1979: 281), differs in some fundamental respects from both the MBO-hypothesis and the somewhat expanded hypothesis that Hardy developed. Popper's problem is also basically another.

Popper's problem is "the old problem of orthogenesis versus accidental and independent mutation" which arises from "the difficulty of understanding how a complicated organ, such as the eye, can ever result from the purely accidental co-operation of independent mutations" (Popper 1979: 273). And Popper's solution (hypothesis) is to distinguish between two parts of an animal, "a *behaviour-controlling part* like the central nervous system of the higher animals, and an *executive part* like the sense organs and the limbs, together with their sustaining structures," assuming that each part evolves in accordance with its own genetic programme, so that a change in one of the programmes will not affect the other, and that changes in the genetic programme determining the behaviour-controlling part may sometimes precede changes in the programme determining the executive part (Popper 1979: 273). This would make it possible, Popper reasons, for changes in the controlling part to pave the way for changes in the executive part, and for the evolution of the latter to appear goal-directed.

The perhaps most important difference between Popper's spearhead theory and the two discussed in the present paper, the MBO-hypothesis and Hardy's hypothesis, is that Popper's theory does not focus on distinguishing between congenitally definite dispositions in animals and their plastic abilities to modify their structures and behavioural patterns, nor does it explicitly shed any light on the question of the place of consciousness in the biological evolution. Popper's spearhead theory will therefore not be further discussed in the present paper. (For a discussion of Popper's theory, see Watkins 1995.)

7. That Hardy agrees with Morgan, Baldwin and Osborn on this point is clear from his discussion of instincts. In accordance with the MBO-hypothesis, Hardy (1965: 194) argues that "instinctive behaviour [...] must almost certainly have been derived from newly aquired habits [...]." He explains: "Surely it is more likely that genetical changes may have been selected to give, by new nerve-cell associations, a built-in inherited behaviour pattern to replace that of a learned habit, than that a chance change in the nervous mechanism (by mutation) may have produced a new form of behaviour which can be used with advantage by the animal" (Hardy 1965: 195–196).

8. Hardy (1965: 161) refers to his idea of how changes of habit may affect the course of evolution as a development of ideas originally put forward by Morgan and Baldwin, but acknowledges at the same time that "some people [...] insist that I am saying something rather different." He does not, however, further discuss wherein this difference may lie.

References

Århem, P. and H. Liljenström. 1997. "On the Coevolution of Cognition and Consciousness." *Journal of Theoretical Biology* 187: 601–612.

Bailey, E. B. 1950. "James Hutton, Founder of Modern Geology (1726–1797)." *Proceedings of the Royal Society of Edinburgh* B63: 357–368.

Baldwin, J. M. 1895. *Mental Development in the Child and the Race.* New York: Macmillan.

Baldwin, J. M. 1896a. "Heredity and Instinct." (I–II) *Science* 3: 438–441, 558–561.

Baldwin, J. M. 1896b. "Consciousness and Evolution." *The Psychological Review* 3: 300–309.

Baldwin, J. M. 1896c. "A New Factor in Evolution." *The American Naturalist* 30: 441–451, 536–553.

Baldwin, J. M. 1902. *Development and Evolution.* New York: Macmillan.

Broad, C. D. 1925. *The Mind and its Place in Nature.* London: Kegan Paul.
Bristol, C. L. 1896. "New York Academy of Sciences." *Science* 3: 529–530.
Burghardt, G. M. 1985. "Animal Awareness: Current Perceptions and Historical Perspective." *American Psychologist* 40: 905–919.
Darwin, C. 1859. *On the Origin of Species by Means of Natural Selection, or the Preservation of Favoured Races in the Struggle for Life.* London: John Murray.
Dennett, D. C. 1991. *Consciousness Explained.* Boston, MA: Little, Brown & Company.
Dennett, D. C. 1995. *Darwin's Dangerous Idea: Evolution and the Meanings of Life.* Harmondsworth: Allen Lane The Penguin Press.
Dohrn, A. 1875. *Der Ursprung der Wirbelthiere und das Princip des Functionswechsels.* Leipzig: Engelmann.
Dyar, H. G. 1896. "Stated Meeting. March 9th, 1896." *Transactions of the New York Academy of Sciences* 15: 137–143.
Ewer, R. F. 1960. "Natural Selection and Neoteny." *Acta Biotheoretica* 13: 161–184.
Gaukroger, S. 1995. *Descartes: An Intellectual Biography.* Oxford: Clarendon Press.
Griffin, D. R. 1976. *The Question of Animal Awareness: Evolutionary Continuity of Mental Experience.* New York: The Rockefeller University Press.
Griffin, D. R. 1992. *Animal Minds.* Chicago: The University of Chicago Press.
Griffin, D. R. 2001. *Animal Minds,* Second Edition. Chicago: The University of Chicago Press.
Hardy, A. 1965. *The Living Stream: A Restatement of Evolution Theory and Its Relation to the Spirit of Man.* London: Collins.
James, W. 1879. "Are We Automata?" *Mind* 4: 1–22.
James, W. 1890. *The Principles of Psychology,* Vol. 1. London: Macmillan.
Lack, D. 1947. *Darwin's Finches.* Cambridge: Cambridge University Press.
Lindahl, B. I. B. 1997. "Consciousness and Biological Evolution." *Journal of Theoretical Biology* 187: 613–629.
Mayr, E. 1960. "The Emergence of Evolutionary Novelties." In S. Tax (ed), *The Evolution of Life: Its Origin, History and Future.* Chicago: The University of Chicago Press: 349–380.
Mayr, E. 1963. *Animal Species and Evolution.* Cambridge, MA: The Belknap Press of Harvard University Press.
Mayr, E. 1982. *The Growth of Biological Thought: Diversity, Evolution, and Inheritance.* Cambridge, MA: The Belknap Press of Harvard University Press.
Mayr, E. 1997. *This is Biology: The Science of the Living World.* Cambridge, MA: The Belknap Press of Harvard University Press.
Morgan, C. L. 1894. *An Introduction to Comparative Psychology.* London: Walter Scott.
Morgan, C. L. 1896. "On Modification and Variation." *Science* 4: 733–740.
Pinker, S. 1997. *How the Mind Works.* New York: W. W. Norton & Company.
Popper, K. R. 1977. "Some Remarks on Panpsychism and Epiphenomenalism." *Dialectica* 31: 177–186.
Popper, K. 1978. "Natural Selection and the Emergence of Mind." *Dialectica* 32: 339–355.
Popper, K. R. 1979. *Objective Knowledge: An Evolutionary Approach.* Revised edition. Oxford: Clarendon Press.
Popper, K. R. and J. C. Eccles. 1977. *The Self and Its Brain: An Argument for Interactionism.* Berlin: Springer-Verlag.

Richards, R. J. 1987. *Darwin and the Emergence of Evolutionary Theories of Mind and Behavior.* Chicago: The University of Chicago Press.

Ristau, C. A., ed. 1991. *Cognitive Ethology: The Minds of Other Animals.* Hillsdale, NJ. : Lawrence Erlbaum Associates.

Rogers, L. J. 1997. *Minds of Their Own: Thinking and Awareness in Animals.* St Leonards: Allen & Unwin.

Simpson, G. G. 1953. "The Baldwin Effect." *Evolution* 7: 110–117.

Smythies, J. R. 1994. "Requiem for the Identity Theory." *Inquiry* 37: 311–329.

Svensson, G. 1994. "Reflections on the Problem of Identifying Mind and Brain." *Journal of Theoretical Biology* 171: 93–100.

Tinbergen, N. 1951. *The Study of Instinct.* Oxford: Clarendon Press.

Watkins, J. 1995. "Popper and Darwinism." In A. O'Hear (ed), *Karl Popper: Philosophy and Problems.* Cambridge: Cambridge University Press: 191–206.

Watkins, J. 1999. *Human Freedom After Darwin: A Critical Rationalist View.* Chicago: Open Court.

Imaging consciousness

Can cognitive neuroscience discover visual awareness in the brain?*

Antti Revonsuo
University of Turku

Introduction: Cognitive neuroscience as the science of consciousness

Cognitive neuroscience has declared itself "The Biology of the Mind" (Gazzaniga et al. 1998) and "the science of the explanatory gap" that resides between the mental realm and the biological or physical realm (Gazzaniga 1995). Thus, cognitive neuroscience undoubtedly plays a large part in the development of a science of consciousness, creating a firm link between consciousness studies and the natural sciences. Much of the scientific appeal and credibility of consciousness studies is due to the results coming from cognitive neuroscience on phenomena such as blindsight, 40-Hz synchronous neural activity correlated with perception, neural correlates of binocular rivalry, and functional brain imaging of conscious states. These studies are often reported in the world's leading science journals and widely discussed in the scientific community. One could even go so far as to say that without the contribution of cognitive neuroscience, the prospects for creating a genuine scientific research program on consciousness would look rather discouraging.

Like it or not, cognitive neuroscience is going to be highly significant for consciousness studies. Even if no such multidisciplinary field as consciousness studies existed, cognitive neuroscientists would probably just go on with their attempts to reveal the neural correlates of consciousness. In the light of these facts, it is surprising how little attention is paid in consciousness studies to the fundamental theoretical questions of cognitive neuroscience. No-one can deny that cognitive neuroscience produces research results that include significant implicit assumptions on what consciousness is, where it is to be found, and which methods can be used to reveal it (or at least its neural correlates) in the brain. However, few philosophers have critically analysed what the claims made in empirical cognitive neuroscience are really based on. How are the results generated? What exactly is measured or observed in the brain with the various methods of cognitive neuroscience? What can or cannot be concluded about consciousness on the basis of such results? I believe that a philosophy of cognitive neuroscience is called for: an empirically informed but philosophically critical analysis of the methods and claims of cognitive neuroscience. The present lack of a philosophy of cognitive neuroscience may be due to the fact that more often than not philosophers of mind are not particularly familiar with the concepts, theories and methods of brain research and neuroscience; some philosophers even regard knowledge of the empirical details of cognitive neuroscience as irrelevant for an understanding of the mind.

My aim in the present paper is, first of all, to briefly review some of the findings on visual awareness that have recently been made in cognitive neuroscience. Crick and Koch (1990) regarded visual awareness as a phenomenon which may be the first to reveal the secrets of consciousness to a systematic scientific approach. Consequently, visual awareness has been the royal road to the cognitive neuroscience of consciousness during the 1990's. After taking a look at the empirical studies on visual awareness, we will ask: What exactly are the phenomena that have been "observed" or "measured" in these studies? Should we expect to "discover" consciousness in the brain by looking into these results? In the final parts of this paper I suggest that we should analyse the methods and results of cognitive neuroscience studies by putting forward the question: Which levels of organization in the brain are revealed in the measurements? Furthermore I suggest that we should regard consciousness as a level of organization in the brain. But capturing that level of organization in a functional neuroimage is not a straightforward matter at all. I will close the paper by offering some speculations on whether the imaging of consciousness is ever going to be feasible even as our methods of functional brain imaging keep improving.

State-of-the-Art in the cognitive neuroscience of visual awareness

Binocular rivalry

Binocular rivalry refers to a condition in which two incongruous images are presented to the two eyes. For example, the image of a face may be presented to the left eye and the image of a banana to the right. Since these two images cannot be coherently fused together, they rival for access to visual awareness. During binocular rivalry only one of the images is seen at any given time (the dominant stimulus) while the other is being suppressed (sometimes also a mixture of the two stimuli can be momentarily seen). The dominance switches every now and then so that first one and then the other stimulus is in visual awareness. Thus, binocular rivalry is an ideal paradigm for studying the neural correlates of visual awareness: the content of awareness changes while the physical stimulus stays exactly the same.

In the study by Sheinberg and Logothetis (1997), single-cell activity of cortical neurons was recorded during binocular rivalry in the macaque monkey. The researchers first identified some single cells that selectively responded only to a certain visual image, e.g. a face, and others that selectively responded only to another image, say, a banana. The monkeys were trained to make specific behavioral responses to each stimulus. When the two stimuli were subsequently shown simultaneously in a rivalrous condition, the behavioral responses presumably reflected the content of the monkey's subjective visual awareness where the two stimuli were alternating although the physical stimulation remained identical all the time.

The researchers recorded the responses of single units in the monkey's temporal cortical areas. The activity of about 90% of the recorded cells in superior temporal sulcus and inferior temporal cortex covaried with and reliably predicted the behavioral response of the animal, and thus signified the content of the animal's visual awareness. However, in previous studies only a relatively small proportion (18–25%) of cells in the earlier visual areas V1, MT, and V4 had been found to correlate their activity with visual awareness (Logothetis & Schall 1989). These findings have been met with enthusiasm in consciousness studies: they have been taken to reveal the visual cortical areas whose activity directly correlates with subjective visual awareness. It has been suggested that the temporal cortical areas might be "a place where conscious visual information comes together" (Baars 1998: 59).

The findings reported by the Logothetis group were based on measurements of the firing rates of single units. A different view is provided by studies that, instead of firing rate, have measured the *synchronicity* of neural firing. Fries et al. (1997) recorded neuronal responses from cats in a binocular rivalry condition and found that although the firing rate of cells in areas 17 and 18 is not modulated by perceptual dominance, the synchronicity of firing nevertheless is strongly modulated: neurons representing the stimulus that is in visual awareness increase their synchrony, whereas cells representing the suppressed stimulus decrease the temporal correlation of their firing (for a review, see Engel et al. 1999). Thus, the question concerning the localization of the neural correlates of visual awareness now appears more complex than if only the firing rates reported by the Logothetis group were considered. We will return to these questions later.

Recently a binocular rivalry task has been applied in an fMRI study in humans. Tong et al. (1998) monitored activity in two cortical areas, one of which is known to be sensitive to face stimuli (the fusiform face area), the other to the layout of surrounding three-dimensional space (the parahippocampal place area). When images of faces and places were presented in a rivalry task, during face image dominance activity in the face area increased and in the place area decreased, and during place image dominance the opposite pattern emerged. Thus, activity in these areas in the human brain reflects the content of visual awareness rather than the physical or retinal stimulus per se.

We will return to the implications of these studies shortly, but for now it is useful to note that several different methods (single-cell firing rates, synchronicity of firing, fMRI) have been used to discover and localize the neural correlates of subjective visual awareness during binocular rivalry. The results show that, measured by these methods, neurons assumed to be actively involved in the construction of the present momentary content of visual awareness are more active or more organized than those that apparently code the stimulus only at a nonconscious level. But the question for consciousness studies to ponder is: What exactly do these results reveal about the ways in which consciousness is realized in the brain?

Visual awareness of coherent objects

We live in a world of objects. When we are visually aware of our surroundings, we see a multitude of coherent objects all around us. Even when we dream, the dream world that we are aware of is by and large a world of visually perceived objects. It is as if visual consciousness were specialized in generating a subjective phenomenal world of coherent objects. Therefore, the neural generation of coherent objects in visual awareness should be a very central task for the brain during visual perception. How and where is it accomplished?

Vanni et al. (1996) measured cortical magnetic responses (122-channel MEG) to visual awareness of objects in an object detection task. The subjects were shown pictures of coherent, meaningful objects and disorganized, meaningless nonobjects (one picture at a time) using very brief stimulus durations and a backward and forward mask. The subject's task was to detect the objects. Less than 50% of the objects were correctly detected at the shortest stimulus duration (30ms), but performance was very close to 100% correct detections at the longest stimulus duration (106ms). Source modeling of the evoked neuromagnetic signals was used in order to reveal the location of active brain areas. Although several different areas were more strongly activated by objects than nonobjects, the activation of only one area, the lateral occipital cortex (LO) in the right hemisphere, became stronger with increasing stimulus duration and directly correlated with the proportion of correct object detections (i.e. with subjective visual awareness of the objects). Thus, these results suggest that visual objects are represented and processed at multiple levels in the brain, but not all of these representations are directly reflected in visual awareness.

Recent functional imaging studies with PET and fMRI (Kanwisher et al. 1996, 1997; Grill-Spector et al. 1998) strongly support the view that the LO area participates in the construction and perception of coherent objects in the human brain. This area is only activated for visual stimuli with coherent shape, not for scrambled images. By contrast, earlier areas such as V1 are activated by coherent and scrambled images alike. Furthermore, the coherent shape of the stimulus can be defined by a number of completely different visual cues (luminance, texture, or movement): a shape defined by any of these cues activates the LO area all the same. The LO area thus seems to be involved in the overall binding together of the coherent form, or distinguishing the coherent figure from its background, no matter what the actual visual cues are that differentiate the figure from its background.

There is increasing evidence that gamma-frequency neural synchronization plays an important part in the generation of visual awareness of objects (for a review see Sauve 1999). Here I will mention one study in more detail. Revonsuo et al. (1997) measured scalp EEG in a task in which the subjects perceived the same physical stimulus (a random dot autostereogram) in one condition as an incoherent collection of random dots and in another condition as a coherent, symmetrical, three-dimensional Gestalt. The subjects free-fused the random-dot stereogram and pushed a button as soon as they saw the three-dimensional Gestalt clearly, i.e. when the illusory Gestalt had just emerged into visual awareness. In the control condition, they fused a stimulus from which no unified percept emerged and then pushed the button. Increase in 40-Hz power during the emergence of the coherent Gestalt (relative to the control condition) was observed at occipital and right posterior electrode sites in a time window 500–300 milliseconds before visual awareness of the coherent percept was reported. No corresponding changes in band power were observed at the lower frequencies that were analysed (8–13 Hz, 13–20 Hz).

This result suggests that the synchronous activity of large neural populations is involved in the construction of coherent visual percepts. Although it is not possible on the basis of scalp topography alone to say with any certainty *where* in the brain this activity was generated, it is interesting that the strongest increase occurred at occipito-temporal electrodes over the right hemisphere. This finding is at least consistent with the previous findings that the ventral occipito-temporal pathway in the right hemisphere is especially significant in the construction of the visual awareness of coherent objects.

Do these studies tell us how the visual awareness of objects is generated in the brain? At least they give us initial ideas about the localization of the areas likely to be critical for the task, and they hint at the neural mechanisms — synchronous activity — that may be necessary for the generation of the visual awareness of coherent objects.

Neural basis of visual hallucinations

In order to capture visual awareness in the brain, visual hallucinations would seem to be the ideal phenomena to study. Recently, a few studies have attempted to reveal what goes on in the brain during visual hallucinations. ffytche et al. (1998) used fMRI to detect the brain activation associated with visual hallucinations in patients with Charles Bonnet syndrome, a disorder associated with pathology in the visual system and characterized by visual hallucinations of people, animals, buildings and scenery. They found that hallucinations of e.g. colour, faces, and objects correlated with increased activity in the ventral visual stream, and the localization of the activity was associated with the content of the hallucination.

Braun et al. (1998) used positron emission tomography to measure brain activity during REM sleep and dreaming. They found that limbic regions and extrastriate visual cortices within the ventral visual stream were selectively activated, but in primary visual cortex (V1) and frontal association areas there was a decrease of activity. The authors suggested that extrastriate and limbic areas may operate as a closed system that is dissociated from brain regions that are more directly in interaction with the external world.

These studies show the important fact that activity in the ventral visual stream is closely associated with the generation of visual awareness even in the absence of any corresponding physical stimulation. The fundamental question still remains: what are these areas actually doing when visual awareness, be it hallucinatory or veridical, is generated?

Discovering visual awareness in the brain?

In the preceding section we briefly reviewed what are some of the most exciting new findings on the neural basis of visual awareness. But what exactly do these studies reveal about visual awareness? In what sense can we say that cognitive neuroscience has now "discovered" visual awareness (or its neural correlates) in the brain? What is the explanatory power of these findings: do we understand the brain basis of consciousness any better with these findings than without them? In order to answer questions like these, we need to analyse some fundamental questions in the philosophy of cognitive neuroscience. We need to understand, first: What is it that we are after when we try to capture consciousness with the methods of neuroscience? What is the phenomenon that we would like to observe or measure? And second, we need to be clear about what the actual phenomena are that have been measured or observed in the studies we reviewed above, and how exactly they are reflected in the reported measurements.

The key to analysing these issues is the notion of "levels of organization". I will here assume, without further argument, that consciousness is a biological phenomenon in the brain . Consciousness forms a specific phenomenal level of organization in the brain, which resembles a virtual reality simulation or a model of the world. When we study consciousness with the methods of cognitive neuroscience, we are at bottom trying to capture this level of organization in the brain (Revonsuo 2000).

Each research method in neuroscience, however, captures only a highly restricted set of biological phenomena, residing at some specific level of organization in the brain. The methods of cognitive neuroscience are extremely limited windows to the reality of the brain. So what do we actually see with the help of EEG, MEG, fMRI, PET and all the rest of the cognitive neuroscience arsenal?

Limitations of single-cell recordings

As we noted above, single-cell recordings in monkeys have been used to correlate neuronal firing rates with the content of visual awareness during binocular rivalry. Increased firing rates correlating with the content of awareness have been found, especially in temporal cortical areas. What exactly has been observed? And, perhaps more importantly, what has not been observed? Schiller (1996) reminds us of the limitations of single-cell recordings:

> Most cells can be studied only for brief periods of time before they disappear from the tip of the microelectrode; during this brief period, their responses can be examined for only a rather limited set of stimulus conditions and the

> stability of the response over time cannot be assessed at all. … During a typical vertical electrode penetration through the two millimeters of cortical gray matter, investigators are lucky to isolate 4 or 5 cells out of the more than 100 that the electrode encounters in its path. … We are limited to brief glimpses of a limited sample of neurons. (Schiller 1996: 28).

In the study of Sheinberg & Logothetis (1997), the researchers could access different sites within an 8x8mm^2 region. They isolated 159 visually responsive single cells, of which 50 were selective enough to be tested during binocular rivalry. Assuming that within the area they could reach there were about 10^7 cells (there are about 10^7 pyramidal cells per cm^2 of cortex), their sample was one out of every 200.000 potentially recordable cells. As the retinal images of even small objects will activate thousands of cells, we are gaining information from a very minor sample of cells. This limited sample is probably a heavily biased one at that: it consists of a subpopulation of particularly responsive cells which allowed clear isolation during the recording.

Thus, it is not clear what significance should be attached to these findings. However, one thing is clear: when we record firing rates from single cells, we are observing brain activity at a very low level of organization. What we can see are the isolated activities of the minuscule basic parts of the immensely complex biological system we are interested in. We have no idea how these isolated activities are supposed to add up to visual perception. Furthermore, we have no guarantee that we are observing the appropriate level of organization in the system. It may well be that isolated single cell activity is not anywhere near the level of description at which visual perception can be explained. We may be focusing on far too low a level of organization. The attempt may be as hopeless as trying to understand the three-dimensional structure of a complex protein molecule by looking at the isolated individual atoms of which the molecule is composed.

The studies on neural synchronization connected with binocular rivalry focus on a level of organization above the isolated single cell. Therefore it is no surprise that the results are different. Synchronization is a feature of not single neurons but of the temporal relationships of the activities between a multitude of neurons. A single neuron's activity can never be synchronized in isolation, but only in relation to the activity of other neurons. The rate of firing of an isolated neuron tells us nothing about the relationships of this firing to the activity of other cells. The modulation of synchronization and the modulation of firing rate can in principle take place independently of each other: one can change without affecting the other. Therefore, it is of interest that Fries et al.

(1997) found increased synchronization in early visual cortical areas for cells coding the dominant stimulus during binocular rivalry, although no change in firing rate was detected. This may be an indication that visual awareness is realized at higher levels of electrophysiological organization than the level of the single cell. In all likelihood we will need to discover and describe such higher levels of organization before it is possible to build a theory of the neural basis of visual awareness.

Limitations of extracranial electrical (EEG) and magnetic (MEG) recordings
Electroencephalography and magnetoencephalography are popular methods in cognitive neuroscience, and also in the search for the neural correlates of visual awareness. But what are the signals that we pick with EEG and MEG? What levels of organization in the brain do they reflect? Both of these methods detect certain electrophysiological phenomena in the brain with a temporal resolution of one millisecond: EEG detects the changes in electrical fields as reflected at the scalp, MEG detects the changes in the magnetic fields that accompany electrical phenomena in the brain.

These electrical potentials and magnetic fields detectable outside the skull are believed to be determined by the net current from postsynaptic potentials produced by pyramidal cell apical dendrites. For a typical detectable response to be generated, simultaneous activation of about 10^7 synapses in a cortical area of 1 cm^2, altogether containing about 10^{10} synapses, is sufficient. MEG, however, is only sensitive to tangentially oriented superficial sources located in sulci, for only those sources generate a magnetic field outside the head where the recording instrument resides. EEG is most sensitive to radially oriented sources in gyri, but not completely blind to tangential sources. EEG signals are spatially spread when they are conducted through tissues and skull onto the scalp surface, MEG signals do not suffer from such spatial blurring (Nunez 1995).

Unfortunately the electrical potentials or magnetic fields recorded outside the skull do not carry any definite information about their point of origin within the brain. Furthermore, it is impossible to determine mathematically the location of the actual electrical sources in the brain, if we only know the distribution of the electrical or magnetic field as it appears outside the skull. Any given field pattern outside the skull could have been brought about by an infinite variety of different current source generators, and there is no way to calculate from the observed pattern backwards to those ones that actually brought about the phenomenon. Consequently, the neural generators need to be *modeled.* A dipolar source is assigned to a certain location in a model of the head which then calculates the correspondence with actual observations of the modeled electrical or magnetic field. When the correspondence becomes good enough (i.e. the assigned source would create a closely similar field outside the head to the one that was actually observed), then the researcher *assumes* that the source was where the model shows it to be.

EEG and MEG thus detect fast changes in the gross synchronous activity of millions of synapses in selected areas on the cortical surface. If the sources are too small, or incoherently oriented, or asynchronously activated, they do not generate any signals detectable with EEG or MEG. Furthermore, we can never directly observe those changes actually taking place in a specific location in the cortex. Only an educated guess — a source model — can be constructed on the basis of the indirect observations.

When we evaluate results obtained with these methods, we should remember that we are at best seeing gross spatial averages of fast changes in the synchronous activity of millions of synapses whose location we cannot observe but only model. Lots of electrophysiological processes not detectable by these methods are simultaneously going on, but we have no conception of things we cannot by any means detect. Neither do we really know whether EEG and MEG signals reflect the activity of a certain functionally important level of organization in the brain, or perhaps only the grossly averaged humming electrical noise arising from lower levels of functional organization. Even if we assume that we are picking up true signals from a functionally relevant level of organization, we still have little idea what exactly is going on in the neural population where those millions of synapses were activated, generating the signal, and how that activity relates to activity elsewhere in the brain. How should we describe such a massively complex bioelectrical phenomenon? As a "computation", or a "stage of information processing", or a "neural correlate of phenomenal visual awareness"? In the absence of well-established theories of neural coding and of macro-level electrophysiological phenomena in large neural populations we have little idea how to interpret the measurements in ways that lead to genuine mechanistic explanations of cognitive phenomena.

Functional brain imaging with PET and f MRI

We found EEG and MEG to be relatively gross methods for detecting actual neural activity in the brain, and their ability for accurate localization of the origin of the signals was found to be poor. PET and fMRI are quite another story. They give relatively good spatial resolution: we can find out with reasonable accuracy where in the brain the signals that we detected were generated.

The bad news is that temporal resolution is disastrously poor: we need to collect signals for a PET image for several seconds or minutes; in fMRI the images can be generated somewhat faster.

However, and this is the worst part, neither of these methods detects signals that are directly generated by neural activity. Instead, PET detects gamma rays that were originated when a positron was annihilated in the brain; the positron was generated when a radioactive isotope in the tracer compound (e.g. labeled water or glucose analogue molecules) in the blood stream decayed. The idea is that the distribution of the radioactive tracer reflects where blood flow or glucose metabolism increases in the brain, relative to a control condition, and this distribution is supposed to give a general idea of "brain activation" in the experimental condition. In fMRI it is the relative amount of oxygenated vs. deoxygenated blood that is detected, for these have slightly differing magnetic properties.

Thus, PET and fMRI images are not images of *neurons* doing anything, but of what is going on in the *circulatory system* in the brain. The connection of haemodynamic changes with neural activity is indirect and not well understood. However, it is known that when neural activity increases in a location, there is a delay of several seconds before blood flow increases ("haemodynamic response function") (Turner et al. 1997). To put it bluntly, the colorful computer-generated images produced by these methods are certainly not "images of mind" (Posner & Raichle 1994) or, strictly speaking, even "neuroimages" but at best "images of blood flow" (or statistical color-coded maps of changes in blood flow). These maps are typically superimposed on structural MRI images, which mostly reflect proton densities of different tissues, and give good spatial resolution and contrast between different tissues. If we assume that increased blood flow actually reflects increased neuronal activity, then we can safely say that PET and fMRI images can be used to localize the activation of brain areas in relation to different tasks or contents of consciousness. After all, that is why they are widely used in cognitive neuroscience.

But the theoretical question that interests us in the present paper is whether these images reveal the levels of organization where consciousness is likely to be realized. The answer to this question is negative. Nobody believes that consciousness is realized in blood flow. We could in principle generate as detailed and accurate images of blood flow in the brain as could ever be imagined and never discover the levels of organization where consciousness is realized. If consciousness is a level of organization in the brain, it is closely related to higher levels of electrophysiological and bioelectrical phenomena. We have few theories of how those phenomena are organized at the levels of thousands or millions of interacting cells and populations of cells. We have no methods for imaging such electrophysiological activity with good temporal and spatial resolution. At the moment at least, imaging consciousness is impossible in practice, for technical reasons, and perhaps it will always remain impossible in principle, for theoretical reasons. But the latter claim is one whose truthfulness is far from established as yet.

Is the imaging of consciousness impossible in principle?

Our current methods of studying the brain are thus severely restricted as to their ability to reveal the levels of organization in the brain where consciousness might reside. But can we imagine theoretical and technical developments that could overcome these difficulties? Theoretical development in the biological sciences is often heavily dependent on the available research methods and techniques. New techniques have usually allowed the visualization of otherwise unobservable, microscopic biological phenomena (Bechtel & Richardson 1993; Sargent 1996). Biological knowledge is typically expressed not in general propositional laws but in *models* of biological systems. These models are often expressed in visualizable diagrams and figures.

Mechanistic explanation of macro-level phenomena in terms of lower level phenomena in biology thus has little to do with what philosophers of science call "theory reduction" (Bechtel & Richardson 1993). Biologists do not engage themselves in figuring out what the logical relationships of linguistic representations of biological knowledge might be. In fact, scientific knowledge in biology does not typically even consist of laws that are expressed in linguistic representations.

Explanation in neuroscience should be placed in the wider context of biological explanation. It is not difficult to see that neuroscientific models (e.g. models of the single neuron or models of neural connectivity in the cortex) and techniques (structural and functional imaging, brain mapping) heavily depend on the *visualization* of data, phenomena, and theoretical ideas. Indeed, Toga and Mazziotta (1996) in *Brain Mapping* state that maps can represent not only the spatial domain but virtually our complete understanding of an object. They argue that mapping or cartography and visualization go hand in hand: if a structure can be visualized, it can be mapped. But visualization is not a simple task:

> Choosing the most appropriate method of presentation requires a diverse skill set that includes artistic, psychophysical, and statistical considerations. Since the goal of display is to describe, summarize, and, in some instances, interact with the data, great care is necessary in its design.
> (Toga and Mazziotta 1996: 12).

However, when done properly, the visualization of data can be used not only to visualize phenomena already known but also to solve problems not yet completely solved, for the data may well make much more sense to the researcher once it is transformed into an appropriate spatial framework.

In the light of these considerations, I put forward the following claims: Insofar as we will ever understand consciousness as a biological phenomenon in the brain, development in both data acquisition and visualization is required. First, we need methods that directly tap the level of organization in the brain at which consciousness is realized. Our current methods are far from achieving this. Second, we need novel visualization techniques in order to present the data in an appropriate form. My guess is that "visualization" is too narrow a characterization of what will be required. Probably a full-scale virtual reality system that uses all sensory modalities will be necessary in order to present a "map" or "image" of the level of organization in the brain where consciousness resides.

Ron Chrisley (in this volume) seems to have something like this in mind when he discusses our ability to understand consciousness in terms of "maps" as " the view from anywhere" and of a person who could go into relevant experiential states in theoretically appropriate contexts for the understanding of the experience of some organism. In his talk he used the term "Virtual-Reality Content Specifier" of a system that might be used to communicate non-propositional knowledge of subjective states of consciousness. That sort of a system, I believe, will be needed also in order for us to get from the current methods of brain mapping to the imaging of consciousness and to an understanding of how the phenomenal level of organization is realized in the brain.

In conclusion, discovering consciousness in the brain is a challenge to future empirical research in cognitive neuroscience. Our ability to understand or explain consciousness is thus largely dependent on how empirical neuroscience will develop, not on how brilliant arguments can be put forward by philosophers. Nonetheless, a philosophy specializing in neuroscience would be much called for. Cognitive neuroscience includes all kinds of problematic theoretical and epistemological assumptions and uses quite different explanatory strategies from those in physics, the favourite (and only) branch of science for many a philosopher. The Philosophy of Neuroscience should explicate and clarify the theoretical assumptions of cognitive neuroscience and try to figure out how the explanation of mental phenomena, especially consciousness, is supposed to be carried out in the branch of science that has lately been boldly named the Biology of the Mind.

Notes

* The writing of this paper was supported by the Academy of Finland (project 36106).

References

Baars, B.J. 1998. "Metaphors of Consciousness and Attention in the Brain." *Trends in Neurosciences* 21: 58–62.

Bechtel, W. and Richardson R.C. 1993. *Discovering Complexity. Decomposition and Localization as Strategies in Scientific Research.* Princeton, NJ: Princeton University Press.

Braun, A.R., Balkin, T.J., Wesensten, N.J., Gwadry, F., Carson, R.E., Varga, M., Baldwin, P., Belenky, G. and Herschovitch, P. 1998. "Dissociated Pattern of Activity in Visual Cortices and their Projections During Human Rapid Eye Movement Sleep." *Science* 279: 91–95.

Crick, F. and Koch, C. 1990. "Towards a Neurobiological Theory of Consciousness." *Seminars in The Neurosciences* 2: 263–275.

Engel, A.K. Fries, P. König, P. Brecht, M. and Singer, W. 1999a. "Temporal Binding, Binocular Rivalry, and Consciousness." *Consciousness and Cognition* 8(2): 128–151.

ffytche, D.H. Howard, R.J. Brammer, M.J. David, A. Woodruff , P. and Williams, S. 1998. "The Anatomy of Conscious Vision: an fMRI Study of Visual Hallucinations." *Nature Neuroscience* 1: 738–742.

Fries, P. Roelfsema, P.R. Engel, A.K. König, P. and Singer, W. 1997. "Synchronization of Oscillatory Responses in Visual Cortex Correlates with Perception in Interocular Rivalry." *Proceedings of the National Academy of Sciences USA* 94: 12699–12704.

Gazzaniga, M.S. (ed.). 1995. *The Cognitive Neurosciences.* Cambridge, MA: MIT Press.

Gazzaniga, M.S. Ivry, R.B. and Mangun, G.R. 1998. *Cognitive Neuroscience: The Biology of the Mind.* New York: Norton.

Grill-Spector, K. Kushnir, T. Edelman, S. Itzchak, Y. and Malach, R. 1998. "Cue-invariant Activation in Object-related Areas of the Human Occipital Lobe." *Neuron* 21: 191–202.

Grill-Spector, K. Kushnir, T. Hendler, T. Edelman, S. Itzchak, Y. and Malach, R. 1998. "A Sequence of Object-processing Stages Revealed by fMRI in the Human Occipital Lobe." *Human Brain Mapping* 6: 316–328.

Kanwisher, N. Chun, M.M. McDermott, J. and Ledden, P.J. 1996. "Functional Imaging of Human Visual Recognition." *Cognitive Brain Research* 5: 55–67.

Kanwisher, N. Woods, R.P. Iacoboni, M. and Mazziotta, J.C. 1997. "A Locus in Human Extrastriate Cortex for Visual Shape Analysis." *Journal of Cognitive Neuroscience* 9: 133–142.

Logothetis, N.K. and Schall, J.D. 1989. "Neuronal Correlates of Subjective Visual Perception." *Science* 245: 761–763.

Nunez, P.L. 1995. *Neocortical Dynamics and Human EEG Rhythms.* New York: Oxford University Press.

Posner, M.I. and Raichle, M.E. 1994. *Images of Mind.* New York: Scientific American Library.

Revonsuo, A. Wilenius-Emet, M. Kuusela, J. and Lehto, M. 1997. "The Neural Generation of a Unified Illusion in Human Vision." *NeuroReport* 8 (18): 3867–3870.

Revonsuo, A. 2000. "Prospects for a Scientific Research Program on Consciousness." In Metzinger, T. (ed.) *Neural Correlates of Consciousness.* Cambridge, MA: MIT Press.

Sargent, P. 1996. "On the Use of Visualizations in the Practice of Science." *Philosophy of Science* 63 (Proceedings): S230-S238.

Saủvé, K. 1999. "Gamma-band Synchronous Oscillations: Recent Evidence Regarding their Functional Significance." *Consciousness and Cognition* 8(2): 213–224.

Schiller, P.H. 1996. "On the Specificity of Neurons and Visual Areas." *Behavioural Brain Research* 76: 21–35.

Sheinberg, D.L. and Logothetis, N.K. 1997. "The Role of Temporal Cortical Areas in Perceptual Organization." *Proceedings of the National Academy of Sciences USA* 94: 3408–3413.

Toga, A.W. and Mazziotta, J.C. 1996. *Brain Mapping.* San Diego: Academic Press.

Tong, F. Nakayama, K. Vaughan, J.T. and Kanwisher, N. 1998. "Binocular Rivalry and Visual Awareness in Human Extrastriate Cortex." *Neuron* 21: 753–759.

Turner, R. Howseman, A. Rees, G. and Josephs, O. 1997. "Functional Imaging with Magnetic Resonance." In R.S. Fracowiak K.J. Friston C.D. Frith R.J. Dolan and J.C. Mazziotta 1997 (eds.) *Human Brain Function.* San Diego: Academic Press, 467–486.

Vanni, S. Revonsuo, A. Saarinen, J. and Hari, R. 1996. "Visual Awareness of Objects Correlates with Activity of Right Occipital Cortex." *NeuroReport* 8:183–186.

Quantum Implications

Naturalizing the mind in a quantum framework

B. J. Hiley and Paavo Pylkkänen
University of London / University of Skövde

Introduction: The problem of naturalizing the mental

The problem of naturalizing the mental consists of the difficulties involved in seeing various mental phenomena as natural or more specifically, as physical phenomena. Among these difficulties one can mention the problem of naturalizing intentionality, the problem of mental causation, and the problems involved in naturalizing conscious experience.

What are these problems? Firstly, if the intentionality (i.e. meaningfulness, referentiality or directedness) of our mental states cannot be grounded in relations in the physical world, are we to postulate intentionality as a non-physical phenomenon, existing over and above physical phenomena, perhaps "supervenient" or dependent upon them? Secondly, if we cannot show that mental states *qua* mental play a role in determining our physical actions, how are we to account for the common sense view that our mental processes literally matter? Are we to deny the existence of the mental altogether as something superfluous, or to postulate some form of epiphenomenalist dualism? Thirdly, how is it possible to understand features of conscious experience, and more fundamentally the very existence of *experiencing* in relation to the physical world? Can subtle features such as the special unity of conscious experience be understood as arising from neural processes? And more fundamentally, why is there an experienced inner life *at all* accompanying physiological processes?

It is quite common in contemporary philosophical discussions of these issues to take for granted some common-sense notion of the physical domain and concentrate on making it intelligible how mental processes relate to this physical domain. One trouble with this approach is that the common-sense notion of the physical domain derives from classical physics and the mechanistic view of the physical universe. This was a simple and elegant characterization of the physical world which promises to explain complex phenomena in terms of some underlying level of elementary constituents and laws operating upon them. The general assumption is that in the end natural processes are simple and mechanical.

Developments in physics in the 20th century have shown that the mechanistic ideal, though seductive, is profoundly limited as a *general* characterization of nature. To be sure, natural systems have a mechanistic aspect, but contemporary physics makes it clear that they have other aspects as well — such as the wave properties of what were assumed to be just particles, or the apparently non-local, instantaneous connections between separated systems, and so on. Thus the contemporary physicist is aware — perhaps more so than other natural scientists — that nature has non-mechanistic aspects in it. This might also explain the different attitude that a physicist and a neuroscientist sometimes have towards mental phenomena and consciousness. The neuroscientist may think "consciousness *must* be explainable via some neural mechanism or else it is an illusion". The physicist may think "perhaps consciousness is a highly developed instance of the non-mechanistic aspects of matter which show up in an elementary form at the quantum level. Just as with quantum phenomena, we may be able to develop a theory of consciousness, but there is no *prima facie* reason to assume that the theory must be mechanistic, or expressed in terms of mechanically interacting particles and fields".

It would seem reasonable that when one is considering the general philosophical question about the place of mind in nature, one ought to consider also what physics says about nature at a general level. This is not to say that mental processes ought to be reduced, say, to the quantum level. The idea is rather that understanding physics helps to understand the nature of the physical context in which minds — in one way or another — have to find their place for the naturalist. Of course, it *may* be the case that mental processes can be explained at the currently studied neurophysiological level in terms of action potentials, neural network activations and the like, combined with certain functional structures realized at that level — we just don't yet see how. Yet a richer structure of levels may be involved. Nerve cells have a rich inner structure which may be involved in mental processes. Further, mental processes may constitute a relatively autonomous higher level emergent from neural and subneural processes. A better understanding of fundamental physical principles may thus well help us to understand which is (are) the right level(s) to explain consciousness in terms of (cf. Revonsuo, this volume). It is very common in science that higher level properties are explained in terms of the properties of the lower level ones. If we cannot account for consciousness in terms of the classically describable neurophysiological level, perhaps we have to take into account lower level properties. Of course, the explanation of consciousness may involve the operation and relation of many levels simultaneously (cf. Havel 2001) or even, to some extent at least, go beyond the concept of a hierarchy of levels altogether.

With the above types of considerations in mind we want in this paper to discuss some new ideas which arise from contemporary physics and which seem relevant to the general issue of naturalizing the mind. In particular, we will focus on David Bohm's ontological interpretation of the quantum theory (Bohm 1952; Bohm and Hiley 1993). One reason why it has been difficult to take into account quantum theory when discussing the mind-body problem is because whereas the mind-body problem is usually formulated as an ontological problem (the relation between mental and physical properties), quantum theory was traditionally interpreted in a way which said very little about an independent physical reality. In other words, the usual interpretation of quantum theory had no clear ontology which the philosophical mind-body discussion could have made use of. This makes ontological interpretations like Bohm's especially important for philosophers who work on the ontological mind-body problem (for a discussion of this problem, see e.g. Churchland 1988).

In the next section of this paper we thus introduce a developed version of the Bohm ontological interpretation in some detail. This interpretation implies that an additional potential affects processes at the quantum level. This "quantum potential" has some new properties, in particular the fact that it depends only upon the *form* of the quantum wave function. This suggests that it should be considered as an *information potential*–its role is to put form into the movement of quantum systems, rather than push and pull them mechanically like a classical potential typically does. It is this feature that we believe makes the Bohm interpretation at least potentially relevant to the wider philosophical issues about the place of mind in nature, for information can arguably be seen closely connected with mental and conscious states (cf. Dretske 1981; Chalmers 1996). We also discuss various analogies to the quantum potential with natural and artificial systems (in the section *The properties implied by the quantum potential*) and then move on to consider the extension of the ideas to quantum field theory. This latter is suggestive of a rich hierarchy of fields that seems particularly suitable when discussing what mental processes are and how they relate to the underlying manifest material activity in the brain and the body (see section *Extension to quantum field theory*).

The section *The Bohm interpretation and naturalizing the mental* offers a brief review of the possible relevance of the Bohm interpretation to some problems that arise when trying to naturalize the mind, problems related to mental causation, intentionality, unity of consciousness and the very existence of phenomenal properties in the first place.

In section *The need for a new physical theory* we point out that the Bohm ontological interpretation for both particles and fields has its limitations. In particular the way it presupposes the existence of space-time manifold is problematic in view of an important challenge physics faces, the problem of quantizing gravity. This leads us to consider some more general and fundamental ideas such as *prespace, non-locality* and *implicate order.* We do not fully develop the implications of these ideas to the naturalization of the mental here, but refer to earlier work and sketch our future challenges.

One might add here that we have in this paper adopted philosophically a rather naive attitude, ignoring for the most part fundamental epistemic issues (e.g. Kant 1991/1787; Strawson 1966). We have considered our approach (which is traditionally considered to be realist) in relation to antirealism and internal realism in other contexts (see Pylkkänen 1992; Hiley and Pylkkänen 1996), and aim to further develop this line in future research.

The Bohm ontological interpretation

Introduction

In order to provide the necessary background for our discussions it is useful to briefly outline some of the relevant features of the Bohm ontological interpretation (for more details see Bohm and Hiley 1993). We begin with the particle theory which, for example, accounts for the behaviour of electrons. At first sight the starting point for the ontological interpretation seems very unlikely to lead to anything remotely connected with mind. Its original purpose was to banish the observer from being a necessary component in the description of quantum phenomena. To this end we first substitute the expression $\psi(\mathbf{r},t) = R(\mathbf{r},t)$ $exp[iS(\mathbf{r},t)/\hbar]$ into the Schrödinger equation and then separating the real and imaginary parts of the resulting equation, we find that the real part gives

$$\frac{\partial S}{\partial t}+\frac{1}{2m}(\nabla S)^2+V+Q=0 \tag{1}$$

This equation would be identical to the single particle Hamilton-Jacobi equation provided $Q = 0$. In such a theory each particle has well defined position and momentum. But Q is a quantum mechanical term and takes the form

$$Q = -\frac{\hbar^2}{2m}\frac{\nabla^2 R}{R} \tag{2}$$

It is this term which produces a behaviour in the particle that distinguishes it from a classical particle. Those unfamiliar with the Hamilton-Jacobi theory will more easily recognise the following formula:

$$\frac{dp}{dt} = -\nabla[V+Q], \tag{3}$$

which is just Newton's equation of motion with an additional potential, Q, which we call the quantum potential.

Now it is well known that Newton's equation produces particle trajectories in the classical case as does the Hamilton-Jacobi equation. We argue that when Q is very small, but not zero, it is still possible to calculate trajectories from equation (3) and that these trajectories will hardly differ from the classical trajectories. As Q slowly increases, the trajectories will differ more and more from the classical trajectories, but at no point will we be able to say "At this point we must give up the notion of a trajectory". This implies that even in the quantum domain we can still regard every particle as having a well-defined position and momentum but in order to produce the quantum behaviour it must be accompanied by a new field $\psi(\mathbf{r},t)$ which satisfies the Schrödinger equation. Indeed these quantum trajectories can be (and have been) calculated for many different situations, including the classic two-slit interference experiment (see Bohm and Hiley 1993 for more details).

Quantum mechanics uses probability and in the Bohm approach the connection with probability emerges from the imaginary part of the Schrödinger equation. This is written as

$$\frac{\partial P}{\partial t} + \nabla(P^2\frac{\nabla S}{m}) = 0. \tag{4}$$

Here $P(\mathbf{r},t) = R(\mathbf{r},t)^2$ is interpreted as the probability of the particle to be at a particular point, $\mathbf{r}$, at time t. The statistics then arises simply from the contingent initial positions of the particle.

The properties implied by the quantum potential

It appears on the surface as if we have found a way to describe quantum phenomena in terms of classical concepts, and that we have surprisingly retained determinism. To achieve this all we have done is to rewrite the Schrödinger equation in a form that reveals a new potential, but if we probe deeper, we find that this new potential is totally different from any classical potential that has been used to date. This point is often missed by some supporters of this approach. This is because the potential appears alongside the classical potential in equation (3) and it looks as if an additional classical potential has been added to Newton's equation of motion. However the potential is derived from the quantum field $\psi(\mathbf{r},t)$ and it is from the properties of this field that the differences arise.

One feature that is of particular importance is that, unlike potentials derived from classical waves, the quantum potential is independent of the amplitude of the quantum wave. This means that a wave of very small amplitude can produce a large effect on the particle. In fact the force ultimately depends on the form of the wave profile.

We can give a useful analogy by recalling that in radio transmission the audio signal modulates the profile of the high frequency carrier wave. Here the audio energy can be quite small, but its form can be amplified to produce a large effect in the radio itself. By analogy the small energy in the quantum wave can be magnified by some as yet unknown internal process so as to produce a large effect on the particle.

By exploiting this analogy, we can begin to see how the quantum field with its very small energy could produce large effects on the particle. In the particle case, the energy must come from within the particle itself as there is no external source to provide any more energy. To see how this comes about, let us consider a stationary state for simplicity. Here the single particle Hamilton-Jacobi equation can be written in the form:

$$\text{Kinetic energy} + \text{classical PE} + \text{quantum PE} = \text{total energy.}$$

where PE stands for potential energy. Since the total energy is fixed, any change in the motion of the particle comes from a re-distribution of energy between the various kinds of energy. This redistribution can be regarded as a kind of self-organisation involved in the whole process.

The form dependence also helps us to understand why the quantum potential can produce significant effects over large distances. As a wave spreads out over a greater and greater distance, the amplitude of the wave decreases and any energy in the wave becomes more spread out. Had the force depended on the amplitude, then the force would necessarily decrease with distance, but since the quantum potential does not depend on the amplitude, the resultant force is not constrained in this way. Thus it is possible to have very long range quantum forces and even non-local forces of the type required to account for the situation described by Einstein-Podolsky-Rosen (1935) paradox.

We can take these arguments one stage further. If we consider the quantum potential in particular cases, for example, in the two-slit experiment, a detailed examination of the mathematical form of the quantum potential shows that it contains information about the momentum of the particle, the width of the slits and how far they are apart. That is, the potential carries information of the whole experimental arrangement. We can regard this information as being active in the sense that it modifies the behaviour of the particle. Bohr (1961a) came to a similar conclusion, but from a very different point of view. He saw the necessity of talking about the *wholeness of the quantum phenomena.* He writes (p.73):

> As a more appropriate way of expression I advocate the application of the word *phenomenon* exclusively to refer to the observations obtained under specified circumstances, including the *whole experimental arrangement.*

Wholeness implied that the quantum process could not be analysed even in principle, but the Bohm interpretation shows that analysis is possible and by carrying out this analysis, we can provide another way of understanding what is meant by *quantum wholeness,* a point we will discuss later.

It was this type of consideration that led us to the suggestion that the quantum potential should be considered as an *information potential.* Not only does the quantum potential carry information about the experimental set up, but, more importantly, it induces a change of form from within the system itself. It is in this more general sense that we can regard the quantum potential as an information potential. In making this suggestion, we were strongly influenced by the etymological roots of the word "information". In its simplest form to in-form literally means to form from within. As Miller (1987:21) writes:

> As with many words in the English language, the word "information" has both Greek and Latin roots. The Latin *informatio* bears direct and obvious structural similarities to our modern "information". The prefix (in) is equivalent to the English "in", "within", or "into"; the suffix (ito) denotes action or process and is used to construct nouns of action. The central stem (forma) carries the primary meaning of visible form, outward appearance, shape or outline. So *informo* (or *informare*) signifies the action of forming, fashioning or bringing

> a certain shape or order into something, and *informatio* is the noun from which signifies the "formation" thus arrived at.

In other words this information can be either active or passive.

The information carried by the quantum field is clearly not information for us, it is information for the electron and as such is objective. This information has meaning for the particle. Since meaning is involved, we are not using the word "information" in the sense of Shannon (1948). According to Shannon, the information content for the word "coming" as calculated using the expression $H = \Sigma p_i ln p_i$ is exactly the same as the word "gnmioc", but one is meaningful and the other is not. The quantum potential always has meaning for its particle, although it might not have meaning for other particles at the same location.

So far we have just considered the case of a single particle, but the notion of active information takes on a new and potentially more significant meaning in a many-body system. Consider a situation in which we have two sets of particles, A and B. Suppose system A is described by a non-product, or "entangled" wave function $\Psi_A(r_1,r_2,\ldots\mathrm{r}_n,t)$ which will produce a quantum potential $Q_A(r_1,r_2,\ldots\mathrm{r}_n,t)$ that couples all the particles of A into a coherent group, while the B group of particles are linked by a different quantum potential $Q_B(r'_1,r'_2,\ldots\mathrm{r}'_n,t)$ which arises from a different non-product wave function $\Psi_B(r'_1,r'_2,\ldots\mathrm{r}'_n,t)$. This implies that we have two independent groups of particles, each group being co-ordinated into some kind of coherent unit where each particle of the group responds *only* to the co-ordinated movement of the rest of the particles in its own group.

To help understand this co-ordinated movement we have likened the group behaviour to ballet dancers whose movements are co-ordinated, not by direct mechanical forces, but rather by each individual responding to a common theme. In the case of the ballet each dancer responds to the *meaning* provided by the musical score as it develops in time. Thus in the analogy the wave function provides the "score" to which the particles respond. The two independent wave functions correspond in the analogy to two sets of dancers following their own theme. Here the form of the movement in each group can be regarded as unfolding from within and the energy that is needed to bring about these changes is provided by the individuals themselves. Although the analogy has obvious weaknesses, it nevertheless highlights the radical difference between classical forces and the type of effect generated by the quantum potential.

One can see why attempts to continue to regard the quantum potential as producing another kind of mechanical force will fail by considering the two sets of particles discussed above. Members of the two groups can be in the same region of space and provided they have no classical forces between them, they will not experience the quantum potential of the other group. The quantum potential for each group is somehow a "private" experience for only that group. This is very different from typically classical phenomena. It is tempting — though perhaps a bit far-fetched — to see this privacy as a very rudimentary case of the sort of privacy we encounter in conscious experience and which is one of the philosophically problematic features of consciousness (see e.g. Churchland 1988).

Since the group behaviour is something that is intrinsic to that particular group of particles and to no others, it seems, once again, as if there were some kind of self-organisation involved, but a self-organisation that is shaped by the environment and mediated by the quantum potential. Thus the system behaves as a *whole* or a *totality* in such a way that the particles appear to be nonlocally linked.

This radical approach suggests that nature at its very fundamental level is more *organic* than expected. Indeed Bohm (1951) felt that a non-mechanical view is suggested even if quantum theory is looked at from the conventional point of view. In his book *Quantum Theory* he writes (p. 167):

> The entire universe must, on a very accurate level, be regarded as a single indivisible unit in which separate parts appear as idealisations permissible only on a classical level of accuracy of description. This means that the view of the world being analogous to a huge machine, the predominant view from the sixteenth to nineteenth centuries, is now shown to be only approximately correct. The underlying structure of matter, however, is not mechanical.

In a footnote he adds:

> This means that the term *quantum mechanics* is very much a misnomer. It should, perhaps, be called *quantum nonmechanics.*

Our use of the novel concept of *information potential* has, understandably, met with some scepticism. In order to try to counter this we will present some examples in which concepts like active and passive information have immediate use.

The first uses the analogy of the computer. Here information is carried in the chip and all of this information is passive until the appropriate software activates some of the information. Thus when the computer is working, some of this "passive" information becomes "active", modifying the input by giving it new form. Hence in the computer there is a continual interplay between passive and active information. It is interesting to note that Feynman once proposed that every point of space is like a computer processing incoming information and outputting new information (see Finkelstein 1969). For our approach to non-relativistic quantum mechanics, it is the particle that processes the information although in field theory (which we discuss later) our approach is very similar to the kind of structure Feynman had in mind. In the case of the computer, the significance of the information is decided by outside human activity both in terms of the software we use and the type of information that is stored in the chip.

It would be more convincing to have an example where there is no direct human intervention and here we have used DNA as an analogy. In this case, the genetic code can be regarded as the passive information that has accumulated over the years through the process of evolution. It was not put there by human beings (although this need no longer be the case.) Parts of this code can be accessed by RNA which carries the information to the appropriate part of the cell where the information can become active in the sense that the processes in the cell change to allow it to develop in a new and meaningful way. Here we see how passive information becomes active under appropriate conditions.

Notice that in all the examples above the additional energy does not come from the information carrier, but has some other source. In the case of the computer, it comes from the battery or external power point. In the case of the cell, it literally comes from within the cell itself.

The examples discussed above illustrate that the idea of active information applies quite naturally in a wide range of fields. Thus, although extending this notion to the quantum level may *prima facie* seem absurd, it is not naturalistically implausible as such. Another point that needs emphasizing is that although the various classical analogies (e.g. the ship) illustrate the operation of active information at the quantum level, the hypothesis is that quantum level active information has some radically non-classical, holistic properties, and that these properties open up new possibilities to discuss the relation between mind and matter.

Extension to quantum field theory

We have above discussed the way Bohm's ontological interpretation and the notion of active information can be used to make intelligible the behaviour of particles at the quantum level. It is important to realise that the Bohm model can easily be extended to fields (for more details see Bohm and Hiley 1993). The reason why this is important in the context of discussing the relation between the mental and the physical is that the field theory is suggestive of a natural extension into a hierarchy of levels. Because we find it implausible that mental properties can be reduced to the quantum level we think it is more likely that mental processes involve quantum-like but more subtle fields and the associated more subtle "information potentials". This is, of course, at present a piece of speculative metaphysics. But it is important to realize that it arises as a natural extension of a fundamental theory of physics. Let us therefore examine how the extension of the Bohm model to fields works.

The difference from the particle theory regarding beables is that the field, $\varphi(r,t)$ and its conjugate momentum, $\pi(r,t)$ replace the position and momentum of the particle theory as beables. (The term "beable" was introduced by John Bell; it refers to the things that are supposed to exist at the quantum level. Usual quantum theory emphasizes "observables" and is more silent about existence beyond observation.) These field quantities would then be the appropriate variables that are to be identified with the relevant fields — also fields functioning in the brain. These fields would be organised by a generalisation of the wave function, namely, the wave functional of the field, $\Psi(\varphi(r,t))$, which we call the superwave function. The time evolution of this superwave function is described by a super-Schrödinger wave equation

$$i\frac{\partial\psi(\phi(r,t))}{\partial t}=H(\phi(r,t),\pi(r,t))\psi(\phi(r,t)) \tag{5}$$

The correspondence between field theory and the particle theory is as follows:

$$r\leftrightarrow\phi(r,t) \qquad p\leftrightarrow\pi(r,t) \quad \left(=\frac{\partial L}{\partial\dot{\phi}}\right)$$

$$\varphi(r,t)\leftrightarrow\psi(\phi(r,t))$$

$$\frac{\partial S}{\partial t}+\frac{(\nabla S)^2}{2m}+V+Q=O)\leftrightarrow\frac{\partial S}{\partial t}+\frac{1}{2}\int[(\frac{\partial S}{\partial\phi})^2+(\nabla\phi)^2]d^3r+SQ=0 \tag{6}$$

$$Q=-\frac{1}{2m}\frac{\nabla^2 S}{R}\leftrightarrow SQ=-\frac{1}{2}\int\frac{\partial^2 R}{(\partial\phi)^2}d^3r$$

Here we find there is a super-quantum potential, SQ, that organises the field through a Hamilton-Jacobi field equation.

Since these equations have the same form as those describing particles, all the qualitative ideas discussed above for the particle model apply equally to quantum fields. However fields provide a much richer structure and is far more appropriate for discussing the mind/brain relationship.

One salient feature is the emergence of a hierarchy of levels which is of particular significance here. As far as these ideas have been applied to physical processes to date, only two levels are necessary (e.g. the level of the electromagnetic field and the level of the superquantum field which acts on the former). However our theory is suggestive of a third, fourth and yet higher levels, producing a rich hierarchy, each level generating subtle effects in the level below. Bohm (1990) indeed suggested that mental processes could be understood in terms of such hierarchy.

This structure frees us from all traces of the original mechanical starting point. For example, the Bosonic particles (e.g. photons) themselves are merely semi-autonomous manifestations of the fields which can be created and annihilated and are organised by a "pool of information" that is contained in the superwave function and mediated by the super-quantum potential. Thus even the Bosonic particles themselves are but discrete manifestations of the quantum fields. Various attempts to develop so called Fermi fields for the Bohm theory have also been made (see e.g. Bell 1987; Fermi fields describe in terms of the field concept particles, such as electrons, which obey Fermi statistics). If this can be done successfully, then even the particle theory discussed above (e.g. with electrons) can be directly incorporated to the hierarchical structure of fields currently present in the Bosonic field theory.

The Bohm versions of both the particle theory and the Bosonic field theory are very different from what we would expect from a physical theory. In the particle theory, for example, instead of giving rise to a mechanical model, the properties of the quantum field suggest that its main role is to organise groups of particles, atoms or molecules into co-ordinated movement which is shaped by the environment in which they find themselves. The appearance of nonlocality in such co-ordinated movements confirms that a mechanical interpretation of such movements is not adequate. Indeed the manifestation of nonlocality is to be expected since Bohr has already argued that some quantum phenomena exhibit a kind of wholeness that is not present in classical systems. This was the way he answered the Einstein-Podolsky-Rosen objection. If all of these points are taken together, the structure that begins to emerge is very reminiscent of the proposals of Whitehead (1927) who suggested that matter should be regarded as organic rather than mechanistic.

The Bohm interpretation and naturalizing the mental

David Bohm had throughout his work a strong interest philosophical questions and it is thus not surprising that he connected the idea of active information in the ontological interpretation with biological and mental processes (Bohm 1989; 1990). His suggestion (based on the Bosonic field theory) was that the quantum theory could be extended naturally to involve higher levels of active information, including the information contained in our consciousness. This way one could connect physical and mental processes naturally without introducing a break or cut between them. We have discussed Bohm's views in detail elsewhere (see Hiley and Pylkkänen 1997; Pylkkänen 1992). In what follows we shall give a brief review of the possible relevance of the Bohm interpretation to some problems involved with the naturalizing of the mind and make connections to some contemporary views.

Active information and mental causation

The problem of mental causation includes the following questions: "...how is it possible for the mind to cause a change in a material body? Through what mechanism or process does a mental event manage to initiate, or insert itself into, a causal chain of physical events?" (Kim 1996: 125) The way this question can be answered in the framework of Bohm's ontological interpretation was sketched by Bohm (1990); the issue was also discussed in more detail and in relation to the contemporary debate about mental causation by Pylkkänen (1992; 1995). Let us briefly summarize the idea here. The "bridge" between the physical and mental sides of reality is active information. Information is organized into a hierarchy of levels, and information at each level has always two aspects or sides, the mental and the physical. The mental aspect is *potentially active* information content, while the material aspect is an *actual activity* that operates to organize the less subtle levels. The ontological interpretation suggests that particles (from electrons to at least Bucky Balls or C60 molecules) and fields (e.g. the electromagnetic field) can be influenced at the fundamental level by a field of information (the quantum potential for particles and super-quantum potential for fields). Mental states involve essentially higher level fields of information that can influence and be influenced by lower level fields, all the way to the level of the quantum fields of the particles and fields of the brain. The Bohm interpretation provides one way of understanding — at present schematically — how the subtle information contained and experienced in our mental states can eventually determine the activity of more manifest matter in our body ("manifest matter" is that part of the brain/body approximately describable in terms of classical physics / standard neuroscience). In a reverse process, the state of the more manifest matter can, via the hierarchy of fields, influence the information content we experience. There is thus the possibility of a two-way traffic between the mental and the physical. The details of this scheme need to be worked out and possible quantum sites in the brain have to be specified etc. (see e.g. Beck and Eccles 1992; Beck 1996; Hameroff and Penrose 1996; for a quantum field theoretical approach see Jibu and Yasue 1995). But at this stage it is important to realize that the quantum potential is an example of an *entirely new kind of influence* upon "ordinary", manifest matter. Given the possibility that matter at the quantum level can be influenced by fields of information, the fact that information we experience in our mental states affects our body is not, as such, alien to fundamental physics.

Active information and intentionality

One issue to consider is whether the notion of active information introduced at the quantum level is relevant to the project of naturalising intentionality. Here one can ask whether the active information at the quantum level possesses some elementary kind of referentiality or meaningfulness to the electron or the Bucky Ball. If this could be made plausible, one could then further postulate that some primitive sort of intentionality is a fundamental property of the universe, perhaps as fundamental as the more usual physical properties such as mass, charge and spin, unlike what Fodor, for example, has emphasized (1987:xi, 97). The idea here is that because the information in the quantum field is assumed to be *information for the particle*, the sense in which the quantum field "represents" the environment to the particle is stronger than the sense in which, say, a thermostat represents the temperature of the surrounding air. One could say (as Fodor is happy to do) that thermostats represent only relative to our intention to keep the room warm. However, the idea in the Bohm ontological interpretation is that the quantum field represents (in a primitive sense) the environment to the particle regardless of our intentions and interests. The idea it that this "proto-intentionality" would then make the emergence of "full intentionality" in more complex systems more intelligible. Not everyone will find this strategy attractive — we are still left with the mystery of what is the origin of the "proto-intentionality" at the quantum level, can we really reasonably believe in it etc. But in our view it is better to have at least some naturalistically reasonable hypothesis about the origin and place of intentionality in the physical world, rather than no such hypothesis at all (for further discussion see Pylkkänen 1992; 1994).

Consciousness and its unity

For many researchers the debate about intentionality has to do with mental, as opposed to physical properties, but does not yet necessarily bring conscious experience into the picture. But it is today more and more widely recognised and admitted that the truly difficult problem in cognitive science and philosophy of mind is how to accommodate not only intentionality as a non-conscious mental feature, but also conscious awareness in the physical world.

There are a number of features of consciousness currently debated by philosophers and cognitive scientists, and we will here briefly consider only some for which quantum mechanics might be relevant. One of these is the unity of consciousness: how is phenomenal content integrated into the unified experience we experience at a particular moment? Or more neurally: how does the brain bind the sensory input into a unified information which provides the content for the multimodal "show" that is experienced in consciousness? (cf. Metzinger 1995: 30).

Note that the quantum potential can be seen as a *holistic organizing factor* for, say, a set of superconducting electrons. In trying to use "quantum ideas" in this context we could say as a starting point that underlying the unity of conscious experience is some new type of "organizing factor", analogous to but more subtle than the quantum potential. Of course, a great deal of the order of conscious experience can be explained in terms of classical physics and neuroscience. However, a full discussion of the synthesis of phenomenal content may well benefit from consideration of quantum principles, at least as a heuristic device. Kieseppä (1997: 97) has pointed out, as a criticism of our earlier suggestions (Hiley & Pylkkänen 1997), that the unity of consciousness is not the same type of unity as, say, the non-locality of quantum theory. By drawing attention to the role of the quantum potential as a holistic organizing factor which synthesizes the movement of elements, we hope to connect better with the problem of the unity of consciousness which is a problem of synthesizing elements of experience into a coherent whole.[1]

The hard problem of consciousness

There are other difficult aspects of the consciousness/mind/matter relation that deserve a brief mention here. There is the problem of experience vs. objective physical process. Why should an objective physical process, such as a neurophysiological process, give rise to or be accompanied by experience *at all*? This is what Chalmers (1996) calls the "hard problem of consciousness".

It is interesting to note that Chalmers himself has approached the hard problem by suggesting that information plays a key role. He argues for a kind of naturalistic dualism and suggests that a satisfactory theory of consciousness involves fundamental psychophysical laws, which will be cast at a level connecting basic properties of experience with simple features of the physical world. According to Chalmers, the level of physically realized information is the basic level at which the psychophysical laws apply to the physical world and as a result, experience arises from the physical (1996: 286).

The idea is that information has two aspects, the physical and the phenomenal and this way we can understand both the existence and lawful relationship between physical and phenomenal properties. By saying, in effect, that something phenomenal is fundamental in the universe, he hopes to make the appearance of conscious experience with physical processes more intelligible. In this regard the ontological interpretation provides a very concrete example of how information plays a fundamental role in physical processes, perhaps more so than Chalmers' discussion has been able to establish so far. If we now interpret active information in the spirit of Chalmers by assuming that it (at least in some circumstances) has both a phenomenal and a physical aspect, we have a concept of information which is both concrete and fundamental and also may help to approach the hard problem of consciousness in a more satisfactory way (see Pylkkänen 2000). There are, of course, differences between Chalmers' and our approaches — one of them is that he uses the Shannon notion of information which differs from Bohm's notion of active information (see section *The properties implied by the quantum potential* above).

The need for a new physical theory

We have above briefly discussed how ideas arising from the Bohm interpretation, such as active information, can be used when naturalizing the mental. Yet it is important to keep in mind that the Bohm interpretation has its limitations — Bohm himself was, of course, aware of this (see Bohm and Hiley 1993: ch 15). It is likely that radically new ideas are required before the basic theories of contemporary physics, especially quantum theory and general relativity can be reconciled — a project known as quantizing gravity. Physics is currently radically incomplete and thus any metaphysics based on it is likely to be similarly incomplete. This fact has given rise to a vigorous philosophical debate about the prospects of naturalizing the mental (see e.g. Montero 1999 and 2001 and the references therein). At the same time there are various ideas which try to enhance progress in these difficult matters. We will now consider some such deeper and more general ideas. We also briefly consider their relevance to the problem of naturalizing the mental. Going to the broader framework is not to say that the ideas dicussed above in connection with active information are wrong. It is more to say that they are incomplete and have a limited range of applicability.

Beyond the Cartesian order

The problem with the Bohm interpretation as it stands is that the fields and particles are regarded as existing in space-time, the space-time manifold being presupposed as a fundamental, absolute feature of the world. This is problematic when one moves on to consider a theory of quantum gravity. When any field (such as the electromagnetic field) is quantised, it is subjected to quantum fluctuations. If general relativity is a correct theory of gravity then we know from the theory that the metric of space-time plays the role of the gravitational potential. If the gravitational field fluctuates, the metric must fluctuate. But the metric is intimately related to the geometry of space-time. It enables us to define what is meant by angle, length, curvature, etc. In consequence if the metric fluctuates, all the geometric properties of space-time will also fluctuate. It is not clear to us what it means to have a fluctuating space-time.

Suppose at a deeper level, let us say at a sub-quantum level, space-time has no meaning, but that space-time emerges at some higher, semi-classical level. This could involve some form of statistical averaging in which the nonlocal effects average out to produce the local behaviour required at the classical level. Indeed we have already argued elsewhere that local relations and Lorentz invariance are statistical features and that underlying this is a structure that does not find a natural expression in the space-time continuum (Hiley 1991). The nonlocal features, which appear also in the standard approach to quantum theory, are then a macroscopic reflection of this deeper structure. In other words, this pre-space is not merely a curiosity manifesting itself at distances of the order of the Planck length ($\sim 10^{-33}$ cm). It has immediate consequences at the macroscopic level.

The actual nature of this pre-space is still being explored and we are a long way from understanding its essential features. As we have already stressed, one of the essential features exhibited by quantum processes is a kind of *wholeness* or *nonseparability* which cannot be reduced to a mechanical interaction of independent elements. The inseparability of the observer and the observing apparatus goes much deeper. It suggests a new order that requires nonseparability to be built in from the very start. It requires the notion of what we will call partial manifestation, as opposed to a complete manifestation of the physical domain implied by the Cartesian physical order. This new view must recognise that participation is a key element of the description. Participation is not merely a disturbance of the system because one is somehow "ham-fisted", but because the "disturbance" is actually necessary, fundamental and irreducible, exactly in the manner that Bohr has stressed. There is a kind of wholeness that denies the possibility of having a sharp separation between the observer and the observed system, and it is this wholeness that shows up as nonlocality when analysed in terms of the Cartesian order used in the Bohm approach.

In contrast, the Cartesian order depends upon the notion of absolute locality. In relativity we retain absolute locality even though space and time become relative. Is it possible to introduce a notion of relative locality? In other words, can we develop an order that does not take locality as basic and absolute? If we can do this, we are then forced to look at spacetime in an entirely different way. To add some support to this idea, recall that in the usual interpretation of quantum mechanics we must either use a spacetime description, or a description that works in the momentum-energy domain. We cannot use both together. In the latter, spacetime itself is not defined. This is just another way of looking at the consequences of the uncertainty principle. It is the essential lesson of Bohr's complementarity, namely, that in quantum mechanics we cannot use both descriptions together as you can in classical physics. This is to be contrasted with the Cartesian order which demands that we take spacetime to be basic and absolute, and all physical reality must be thought of as going on in space and time while energy and momentum remain sharply defined.

If spacetime is not be taken as basic as suggested in the previous paragraph then where does this leave the question of locality? Recall one of Einstein's major objections to quantum mechanics was that it seemed to contain "spooky action at a distance." He felt that it was necessary for physical processes to evolve through local interactions and this locality is something fundamental and basic in all physical processes. Indeed with the advent of relativity, causal local order is retained. Effects spread from neighbourhood to neighbourhood at the universally constant speed of light. It is as if locality were something absolute. Quantum processes involving entanglement seems to call the concept of an absolute neighbourhood into question. Is there anyway we can begin to understand this possibility?

The hologram involves a typical quantum transformation. Here, each local neighbourhood of an object is mapped onto the whole domain of the hologram. If this were not the case, we would not see the image of the whole object if, for example, only half of the hologram is illuminated. This means that local regions of the original object are mapped into every region of the hologram. Thus if we have a dynamical process evolving through time from neighbourhood to neighbourhood, we would see changes occurring at every point on the hologram. It would be as if changes were occurring everywhere at once. A local creature living in the hologram "world" would not see a local evolution of processes occurring in our world. Rather changes would occur at all regions simultaneously. All of this appears truly "spooky" until it is realised that transforming back into the spacetime representation there is a well defined local order in that representation.

One of the ideas that we can take from this example is that processes do not have to be displayed in spacetime, but nevertheless carry the spacetime properties implicitly within their structure. But we have something more radical appearing in quantum mechanics. Processes when represented in spacetime display a non-locality not present in the classical world. Could this imply that whatever is the basic underlying process it cannot be made manifest in a local way? If we follow the traditional view that physics is about particles or fields evolving in spacetime then this non-locality presents a severe problem. It suggests that the traditional starting point may not be correct. We need a very different approach and to this end we have proposed to take the notion of process as fundamental. In this sense we are following Whitehead (1926) who has warned us against the fallacy of misplaced concreteness! Electrons are not little rocks, nor are quarks. If they were we could not understand how particle and antiparticle annihilate each other leaving only electromagnetic radiation. Thus underlying all matter is not solid substance, but some sort of energy or, more generally, activity. This activity is not an activity of particles in motion, but the activity is some kind of primitive process or movement *per se*. It is this activity or movement, which is to be regarded as fundamental. Another key assumption in this view is that the vacuum is not empty, but is full of undifferentiated activity. The particles are then regarded as being mere "ripples" or invariant features sitting on top of this "holomovement": They are just the quasi-stable, semi-autonomous forms on the background activity. They depend on this background and are part of the whole process. So the particles do not constitute an ultimate separate reality they are only quasi-stable concentrations of energy which is assumed to be fundamental. Furthermore since all quasi-invariant forms can be seen as being connected through the background activity, we now have a possible way of understanding how nonlocality can arise. The particles are not separate entities in interaction but are distinguished forms arising from a common interconnected background.

In order to give some insight into how "particles" might appear, Bohm (1980) made use of a rather ingenious device called the unmixing device. This consists of two concentric cylinders with some glycerine between them (the glycerine and the cylinders are transparent). Suppose we put a spot of dye in the glycerine and then turn the outer cylinder relative to the inner. After n turns the spot disappears and no trace of it is evident. But when the cylinder is rewound, lo and behold the spot reappears! It looks as if what has disappeared actually returns and the glycerine contains, in some sense, a memory of the order of the past.

Suppose now a series of dots are put into the glycerine at different points. First we put one in at one point and turn the cylinder. Then put another spot in at another point and turn the inner cylinder again, and so on. If the sequence is run backwards, the spots will reappear and then disappear again, one spot following another. On seeing this sequence of dots, one may be tempted to infer that something had crossed your line of vision, but actually nothing of the kind has taken place. No particle actually crosses the screen. Rather there is a continuing process of condensing, evaporating, re-condensing, re-evaporating, and so on. Or in Bohm's words, there is a continual unfolding and enfolding of orders. The proposal, then, is that this may provide a richer picture of quantum processes. There is no continuity of substance, merely an unfolding of form. The more stable the form, the more persistent it is.

Suppose we apply this idea to the two-slit experiment. The slits will see this unfolding process and it will look as if a wave has gone through both slits, but the total process will manifest itself only when the energy is condensed to a small region, giving the appearance of a particle. There is no continuing particle, no continuity of substance, merely a continuity of form. Whether there is a periodic manifestation of the process or whether it only manifests in special physical processes which we call observing instruments is left open at this stage. The whole structure of notions that lie at the root of the new order is called the *implicate* order.

The implicate order

One of the key features of this new order is that everything cannot be made manifest together and it is this feature that destroys the Newtonian view of the material world in which it is assumed that everything can be made manifest together, all at the same time and displayed before us. We can again use the glycerine device described above to illustrate this idea.

Consider two of the dots enfolded into the glycerine. As one spot appears, the other is still enfolded and will not appear until the inner cylinder is further rotated during which time the first spot is enfolded again. Further enfoldment makes it disappear as well. If this applies at the level of elementary particles as well we can say that reality consists of a hierarchy of orders, in which typically only certain aspects of a certain order (e.g. an elementary particle) can be made manifest at any one time. It is these deeper orders that are contained in the implicate order. What can be made manifest together is called an explicate order which is only a partial order at the level of manifestation. But there may be many different explicate orders, each one giving rise to a unique appearance. Our participatory role as observers is then to make one explicate order manifest, rather than another, for example to make either position or momentum, but not both simultaneously manifest. It is only in the classical domain that participation can be neglected so that the whole classical order can be contained in one unique explicate order.

The new paradigm based on the implicate order, if correct, has deep implications for nature in general and offers the possibility of including a wider domain of phenomena (see Bohm 1980; ch 7). For example, in biological systems the notion of the unfolding form plays a central role and if non-biological systems also need to be described in terms of unfolding forms, then we have removed one distinction between organic and inorganic systems.

Furthermore the implicate order also seems to offer a way to encompass our thought processes. For example, if you try to hold an idea in the "working store" of your mind and attempt to keep it there, you know what inevitably happens, it disappears back into the general process of thought. Indeed in the mind, thought structures are continually appearing and dissolving. However there are relatively stable forms which can be re-captured easily and these are called "memories". But we know that on a longer time scale memories fade and become modified.

There is some similarity with ordinary matter to which we have already referred, namely, that particles are quasi-stable forms in an underlying process. One essential difference is that familiar matter is far more stable. It should not be forgotten that some elementary particles decay within 10^{-24} seconds after being created! In large scale matter, the stability is, of course, much stronger still, but even mountains move! This principle of stability is very important because without it, there would be no classical world. Thus as the particles begin to form out of the cosmic primordial Big Bang, the seeds of the classical world are sown and this world begins to dominate as more structures form and stabilise. But underlying these explicate features of matter and mind is the deeper order, namely, the implicate order.

The underlying idea of this section has been that successful future physics requires a radically new conceptual framework, where notions like pre-space, non-locality, implicate order, etc. are likely to play an important role. Some might see this as a breakdown of commonsense realism, thus giving support to the more antirealist approaches that have in recent years been proposed in the debate about naturalizing the mental (cf. Bilodeau 1996; Globus 1996; Hut and Shepard 1996; Pylkkö 1998; Varela et.al. 1991). But it is, of course, possible to be a realist about even such extraordinary and fundamental features as pre-space.

Conclusion: the new order and mind

In writing this paper we have been guided by the intuition that it seems impossible to understand the place of mind and consciousness in nature when staying within the framework of the mechanistic materialism of classical physics which, for example, dominates much of contemporary neuroscience. This apparent impossibility, we suggest, need not be that strange because we know from contemporary physics that mechanistic materialism is incomplete and radically mistaken as a general characterization of nature. The further question for the naturalist is whether it is possible to formulate an alternative general characterization of nature and if yes, whether it is possible to naturalize the mind in this new framework. This led us to first consider the Bohm ontological interpretation for particles and fields and especially the notion of active information, and to consider various aspects of the mental in relation to this framework. Knowing the limits of this framework we then moved on to discuss some more general features of fundamental physics, such as prespace, non-locality and their interpretation in terms of concepts such as the implicate order.

We will not discuss the naturalization of the mental in this more general framework at any detail in this paper, but refer the reader to Bohm's discussion in his 1980 book *Wholeness and the Implicate Order* (especially Chapter 7) and to B. J. Hiley's paper "Quantum mechanics and the relationship between mind and matter" (in Pylkkänen et. al. (eds) 1997). A challenge for our future research is to combine the active information approach with the implicate order approach, and thus attempt to provide a more coherent synthesis. We also need to consider more carefully the epistemic issues involved. No doubt many of our readers are likely to be sceptical towards the introduction of notions such as active information to the quantum level, and towards the rather metaphysical and even mystical ramifications of the implicate order approach. Is this just an other instance of pure reason indulging beyond what can be justifiably be known by it (cf. Kant 1991/1787)? No doubt we need to carry out a critique of our use of reason; and we need to watch out, in our search for intelligibility, not to end up offering explanations that are even more unintelligible than the troubles with mind and consciousness where we started from. But we emphasize that the notion of active information, for example, is offered as a means of "intelligibilizing" the puzzling features of quantum theory. Experiments in physics (as pure empirical raw data) mean not much if they are not interpreted; and our interpretations tend to reflect our scientific and philosophical upbringing which is historically and culturally contingent. In the current age of mechanistic materialism it is quite easy to dismiss unusual interpretations as unserious. Yet quantum theory clearly presents us with a number of experimental facts which radically differ from facts at the classical domain. Our challenge is to consider what these facts mean.

Note

1. We will here briefly comment on Kieseppä's (1997) reply to our earlier paper (Hiley and Pylkkänen 1997). Kieseppä concludes his carefully thought-out and clearly presented critique by saying that "*...the features of the ontological interpretation which seem to make it relevant for the mind-body problem are precisely the ones that are — in the sense of some methodological criteria that seem to be appropriate for evaluating other physical theories — ad hoc and unsatisfactory features in a fundamental physical theory*" (p. 96).

Our preliminary work on this issue suggests that Kieseppä's conclusion is based on rather weak premises. As Kieseppä himself points out, it is somewhat dubious here to appeal to "methodological criteria that seem to be appropriate for evaluating other physical theories" for one can be just inductively begging the question (pp. 95–6). Thus, Kieseppä leans towards *defining* "satisfactory explanation" as "mechanistic explanation". But nature at a more fundamental level may turn out to be non-mechanical, as the quantum experiments like the photo-electric effect, electron interference, Aspect experiments etc. all indicate. Kieseppä's intuition seems to be that in such a case we cannot have a good explanation or a good detailed account in physics. But alternatively, the proper explanation of the quantum domain may require the *modification* and *enrichment* of the mechanistic concepts of, say, particle and wave, which eventually can lead to revolutionary changes in the whole *conceptual structure* of physics (see Bohm's 1957 *Causality and Chance in Modern Physics*: 98). A notion like "holistic active information" (see Pylkkänen 1992) may — albeit in a developed form — find a natural and central place in such a new conceptual structure.

It may thus turn out that, quite opposite to what Kieseppä suggests, the features of the ontological interpretation which seem to make it relevant for the mind-body problem are precisely the ones that are also — in terms of some methodological criteria that will be seen as appropriate for evaluating physical theories of the quantum domain — among the essential features in a fundamental physical theory. We would argue that both the experimental evidence of contemporary physics and the concomitant theoretical development strongly point towards a holistic rather than a mechanistic framework. With this background we view Kieseppä's intuitions about the likely mechanicalness of successful future fundamental physical theories as an extrapolation of classical intuitions to a domain where current experiments and theories strongly suggest they will not be useful.

For a better appreciation of the debate between us and Kieseppä we refer the reader to our papers in Pylkkänen et. al. (eds) (1997).

References

Beck, F. 1996. "Can Quantum Processes Control Synaptic Emission?" *International Journal of Neural Systems,* 7: 343–353.

Beck, F. and Eccles, J.C. 1992. "Quantum Processes in the Brain: A Scientific Basis of Consciousness". *Proceedings of the National Academy of Sciences USA* 89: 11357–11361.

Bell, J. 1987. *Speakable and unspeakable in quantum mechanics: Collected papers on quantum philosophy.* Cambridge: Cambridge University Press.

Bilodeau, D.J. 1996. "Physics, Machines and the Hard Problem." *Journal of Consciousness Studies,* 3: 386–401.

Bohm, D. 1951. *Quantum Theory,* New Jersey: Prentice Hall.

Bohm, D. 1952. "A Suggested Interpretation of the Quantum Theory in Terms of Hidden Variables". *Physical Review,* 85: 166–179, 180–193.

Bohm, D. 1957/1984. *Causality and Chance in Modern Physics.* London: Routledge.

Bohm, D. 1980. *Wholeness and the Implicate Order,* London: Routledge.

Bohm, D. 1989. "Meaning and Information". In P.Pylkkänen (ed.) 1989.

Bohm, D. 1990. "A New Theory of the Relationship of Mind and Matter", *Philosophical Psychology,* 3: 271–286.

Bohm, D. and Hiley, B.J. 1993. *The Undivided Universe: an Ontological Interpretation of Quantum Theory.* London: Routledge.

Bohr, N. 1961. *Atomic Physics and Human Knowledge,* New York, Science Editions.

Chalmers, D.J. 1996. *The Conscious Mind: In Search of a Fundamental Theory.* Oxford: Oxford University Press.

Churchland, P.M. 1988. *Matter and Consciousness. 2nd edition.* Cambridge, Mass.: MIT Press.

Dennett, D.C. 1991. *Consciousness Explained.* London: Little, Brown and Co.

Dretske, F. 1981. *Knowledge and the Flow of Information.* Cambridge, Mass.: MIT Press.

Dyson, F. 1979. *Disturbing the Universe.* New York: Harper and Row.

Eccles, J.C. 1994. *How the Brain Controls Itself.* Berlin: Springer-Verlag.

Edelman, G. 1992. *Bright Air, Brilliant Fire: On Mind and Matter.* London: Penguin.
Einstein, A., Podolsky, B. and Rosen, N. 1935. "Can Quantum-mechanical Description of Physical Reality be Considered Complete?" *Physical Review* 47: 777–80.
Finkelstein, D. 1969. "Space-time Code." *Physical Review* 184: 1261.
Fodor, J. 1987. *Psychosemantics.* Cambridge, Mass.: MIT Press.
Fodor, J. 1990. *A Theory of Content.* Cambridge, Mass.: MIT Press.
Globus, G. 1995. *Postmodern Brain,* Amsterdam: John Benjamins.
Hameroff, S. and Penrose, R. 1996. "Conscious Events as Orchestrated Space-time Selections". *Journal of Consciousness Studies* 3: 36–53.
Havel, I. 2001. "Causal Domains and Emergent Rationality". Preprint.
Hiley, B.J. 1991. "Vacuum or Holomovement", in *The Philosophy of Vacuum,* ed. by S. Saunders and H. Brown. Cambridge: Cambridge Univ. Press: 217–249
Hiley, B.J. and Pylkkänen, P. 1996. "Representation and Interpretation in Quantum Physics". In D.Peterson ed. *Forms of Representation — An interdisciplinary Theme for Cognitive Science.* Exeter: Intellect books.
Hiley, B.J. and Pylkkänen, P. 1997. "Active Information and Cognitive Science: A Reply to Kieseppä". In P.Pylkkänen et.al. (eds.) 1997.
Hut, P. and Shepard, R. 1996. "Turning the Hard Problem Upside Down and Sideways", *Journal of Consciousness Studies* 3: 313–29.
Jibu, M. and Yasue, K. 1995. *Quantum Brain Dynamics and Consciousness.* Amsterdam: John Benjamins.
Kant, I. 1991. *Critique of Pure Reason.* London: J.M. Dent & Sons Ltd. 2nd edition, originally published in German in 1787.
Kieseppä, I.A. 1997. "On the Difference between Quantum and Classical Potentials — A Reply to Hiley and Pylkkänen", in P. Pylkkänen et.al. (eds.) 1997.
Kim, J. 1998. *Mind in a Physical World. An Essay on the Mind-Body Problem and Mental Causation.* Cambridge, Mass.: MIT Press.
MacLennan, B. 1996. "The Elements of Consciousness and Their Neurodynamical Correlates." *Journal of Consciousness Studies* 3: 409–24.
Metzinger, T. 1995. "The Problem of Consciousness." In T. Metzinger (ed.) *Conscious Experience.* Schönigh: Imprint Academic.
Miller, G.L. 1987. *Resonance, Information and the Primacy of Process: Ancient Light on Modern Information and Communication Theory and Technology.* Doctoral Thesis, Rutgers. University Microfilms International, Michigan.
Montero, B. 1999. "The Body Problem". *Nous* 33: 183–200.
Montero, B. 2001. "Post-Physicalism." *Journal of Consciousness Studies,* 8: 61–80.
Pribram, K.H. 1991. *Brain and Perception: Holonomy and the Structure in Figural Processing.* New Jersey: Lawrence Erlbaum Associates.
Pylkkänen, P. ed. 1989. *The Search for Meaning.* Thorsons, Wellingborough.
Pylkkänen, P. 1992. *Mind, Matter and Active Information: The Relevance of David Bohm's Interpretation of Quantum Theory to Cognitive Science.* Reports from the Department of Philosophy, University of Helsinki.
Pylkkänen, P. 1994 "Merkityksen naturalisointi ja kvanttiontologia" ["The Naturalization of Meaning and Quantum Ontology"]. In S. Heinämaa ed. *Merkitys* [*Meaning*]. Philosophical studies from the University of Tampere, 45. [in Finnish]

Pylkkänen, P. 1995. "Mental Causation and Quantum Ontology". In L. Haaparanta and S. Heinämaa (eds.) *Mind and Cognition: Philosophical Perspectives into Cognitive Science and AI, Acta Philosophica Fennica* 58. Helsinki: The Philosopical Society of Finland.

Pylkkänen, P. 2000. "The Problem of Consciousness, Natural and Artificial". In H.Hyötyniemi ed. *SteP 2000–Millenium of Artificial Intelligence.* Helsinki: Publications of the Finnish Artificial Intelligence Society.

Pylkkänen, P., Pylkkö, P. and Hautamäki, A. (eds.) 1997. *Brain, Mind and Physics.* Amsterdam: IOS Press.

Pylkkö, P. 1998. *The Aconceptual Mind.* Amsterdam: John Benjamins.

Searle, J. R. 1992. *The Rediscovery of the Mind.* Cambridge, Mass.: MIT Press.

Shannon, C. E. 1948. "A Mathematical Theory of Communication." *Bell System Technical Journal* 27: 379.

Stapp, H. P. 1993. *Mind, Matter and Quantum Mechanics,* Berlin: Springer.

Stapp, H. P. 1995. "Why Classical Mechanics Cannot Naturally Accommodate Consciousness but Quantum Mechanics Can." *Psyche* 2, May.

Strawson, P. F. 1966. *The Bounds of Sense. An Essay on Kant's Critique of Pure Reason.* London: Routledge.

Stuart, C. I. J. M., Takahashi Y. and Umezawa H. 1978. "On the Stability and Non-local Properties of Memory." *Journal of Theorertical Biology* 71: 605–18.

Varela, F., et. al. 1991. *The Embodied Mind.* Cambridge, Mass.: MIT Press.

Whitehead, A. N. 1957. *Process and Reality,* New York: Harper and Row.

Whitehead, A. N. 1926. *Science in the Modern World,* Cambridge: Cambridge University Press.

Postmodern implications of quantum brain dynamics

Gordon Globus and Elena Bezzubova
University of California, Irvine / Russian State Medical College, Moscow

Introduction

Quantum brain dynamics (QBD) offers new resources for philosophical discussion. QBD is applied here to Heideggerian concepts of being, time, and situatedness; QBD and postmodernism, conventionally strange bedfellows, are "thought together."

Brain science has made spectacular advances in recent decades, and surely there is no sense of crisis in brain science. Yet a faint cry of "revolution" is in the air, the claim that there is a hitherto unrecognized quantum level of brain functioning. Brain science, however, is unable to recognize a crisis in the murk of philosophical discussion about consciousness, and goes sanguinely about its highly successful business. But the consciousness problem is truly a scandal hidden in a clamor. If quantum brain dynamics (QBD) might open up new postmodern conceptions to deal with the consciousness problem, then why not consider it? Perhaps science and consciousness can be brought amicably together, if quantum degrees of freedom are admitted to brain functioning.

Of course, the postmodern interest is unlikely to be attracted by either quantum brain science (which is seen as just more science-technology) or consciousness (which is seen as just more modernity). From the postmodern perspective, QBD, even if successful, is just the cutting edge of the techno-scientific Gestell of our times, a metaphysical framework which postmodernists sniff at.

A fundamental mistake is made by this attitude, however, which is properly directed toward classical physics and quantum mechanics. Yes, classical physics and quantum statistical mechanics will never fully satisfy postmodernism, but quantum statistical mechanics is really the classical phase of quantum physics which has been succeeded by quantum field theory (QFT). Perhaps QFT has better prospects for being relevant to postmodernism and deserves consideration, especially in its QBD application to brain functioning. There are profound differences in conception across the classical and QBD models of how the brain works, as we should only expect, given the profound differences between classical physics and QFT. So a fresh look at quantum brain science by postmodernists is appropriate.

However another move is required for the rapprochement between quantum brain science and postmodernism to develop: the concept of consciousness must be relinquished. There has been such an excited resurgence of modernistic interest in consciousness that it has been difficult to see its deficiencies. A questioning of consciousness is easily mistaken as crassly materialistic in intent. But "consciousness" is a very ambiguous term (Natsoulas 1978); literally it means to know together and thus is a social term.

Jibu and Yasue (1995: 218), in their introduction to QBD, tell us that "consciousness is a term indicating the totality of mental phenomena a human being experiences." But what does "mental phenomena" mean? What does "experience" mean? (The original meaning of experience is to try out, as in experiment, and only later is it connected to consciousness.) Penrose (1989: 406 and following) wants "to be as straightforward as we can about what we mean by 'consciousness'." He thinks it unwise to attempt a precise definition, but is confident that "we can rely, to good measure, on our subjective impressions and intuitive common sense as to what the term means." Lets focus on how confusing Penrose's subjective impressions and intuitions really are.

"To be conscious, I seem to have to be conscious of something" … so intentionality is part of Penrose's meaning of consciousness. But he also brings in the non-technical meaning of intention as bringing about an action ("or I may be consciously intending to speak or to take some other action such as get up from my seat"). But consciousness on Penrose's ecumenical intuition is also reflection ("or I may even just be conscious of my own consciousness"). Penrose (1994: 39) adds that "active" consciousness has the *feeling* of free will and "passive" consciousness is related to "the perception of the colour red …the sensation of pain or the appreciation of a melody" (that is, qualia). To build a science of consciousness on such an amorphous mess seems a dubious endeavor!

But the ambiguity of the concept of consciousness is not a postmodern concern; what is bothersome is the duality introduced between consciousness and the brain, the mental and the physical, alongside of many other metaphysical dualities, such as subject/object, immanent/transcendent, spirit/matter, inside/outside, sensible/intelligible, origin/end, center/periphery. Thus to admit consciousness is to embrace modernity.

What quantum degrees of freedom provide

In the quantum conception there is provision for a *fullness* in the form of superposed (interpenetrated) possibilities (which are eigenstates of the quantum system). The various possibilities are all entangled in an unbroken whole. This is no Pandora's box filled with individual butterfly possibilities; instead various possibilities are all enfolded to an unbroken whole. Possibilities are nonlocal. The quantum conception thus provides a nonclassical *plenum* in which all possibilities are entangled as one (Globus 1997, 1998).

The interpenetrated possibilities of this quantum plenum have varying probabilities of actualization and these probabilities are adjustable, tunable (Globus 1998). Infinite possibilities are interpenetrated in the plenum but only certain of them are at all likely to be actualized, and the probabilities change fluidly with tuning. So the plenum of interpenetrated possibilities is a dynamical attunement. Interpenetration of possibilities makes the effect of tuning *instantaneous;* local changes are felt instantaneously globally.

How different this is from classical conceptions of information processing! In computer computation, representations consist of local individuals, each at their own memory address. Neural networks have superposed representations, it is true, but without the property of nonlocality. Change a connection weight somewhere, under constant input, and the entire network is roused to work, to minimize the computational energy of the net, and *after a duration of time,* the network settles into a low energy state, until input or connection weights change, and the whole Sysiphean process starts up again. No one could be more local than Sysiphus laboring up the hill! In quantum systems, in contrast, change is instantaneously global, yes like Superman, faster than the speed of light, because of quantum entanglement over macroscopic distances. The dynamical fullness of interpenetrated possibilities whose probabilities are under nonlocal cognitive control, is nothing like the local memory in computers or the durations of local frenzy by the nodes of neural nets.

These tuned possibilities provide conditions of satisfaction on an interaction with re-presentatives of the surrounding reality. What is offered to the interaction with reality is possibilities whose conditions might be satisfied in the interaction. The possibilities whose conditions might be satisfied comprise a global attunement that situates the brain for its interaction with reality's representatives. Such a situatedness cannot be described by a set of rules. This shifting attunement is "holonomic" (Bohm 1980), under the law of the whole.

There is yet another profound difference that admitting quantum degrees of freedom introduces. In information processing conceptions, something is "put-in," some logical operations are performed on it, and something is "put-out," as in a deterministic sausage factory. The potter at the wheel, the *Demiurgous* whose hands are filled with shapeless chaos, the Cartesian subject of modernity, and now, at the forefront of the technological Gestell, the computer engineers and programmers — all these stand outside the process, they dominate it under the banner of modernity.

In the quantum conception, dominance is replaced by participation in a dynamical interaction, mutuality, accommodation, global resonance (Globus 1998). This is of cardinal importance: the domination so characteristic of modernity is replaced by a flowing participation. Nothing deterministically rules the evolution (though there is a Hamilton-like least action principle under which the evolution proceeds so as to minimize a certain energy). In that evolution symmetry (invariance over time) is conserved. There is no steady dominance of logic, instead what happens is unpredictably decided on the fly — which by the way sounds like us, since in the moment we can be rather unpredictable spontaneous creatures.

Being and time

So what's so Heideggerian about this, other than situatedness? Recall that for Heidegger "Being" means presence. Dasein is an entity, an entity that importantly has a human brain, the entity that discloses the world. But there is a real problem here, how the entity Dasein is able to always find itself already thrown amidst the world, when all Dasein's brain has to go on is neural re-presentations of the world. After all, anesthetize the brain and the *Lichtung* (the clearing, a lighted place) goes dark and Dasein's world will disappear. Dasein's brain must have something to do with world-thrownness, with *Existenz* itself, and so there must be an interface somehow, even in the Heideggerian frame. So long as the brain is thought of as a wet computational device, the interface shuts down, but with QBD the brain-Existenz interface opens up, and in a way that hopefully avoids duality.

It is curious that the same kind of problem arises in quantum physics, where world presence is constricted to measuring apparatus, and the problem goes by the name of the "measurement problem." Quantum systems are typically represented mathematically by wave functions. Because of their imaginary terms, wave functions do not represent observables. To get real numbers associated with observables, you have to somehow "collapse" the wave function, with statistical results. Penrose (1994) thinks that gravity collapses wave functions in living neural tissue. Von Neumann, Wigner, and Stapp think that consciousness is doing it, collapsing the wave function onto one or another eigenstate (Stapp 1993).

Now mathematically the collapse is straight-forward enough, according to the Born postulate. Multiply the wave function by its complex conjugate so that it becomes a real number, and then interpret this number as the probability of making a certain observation. A wave of probability collapses into a certain actuality. But this is a very ad hoc move, this procedure of bringing in a complex conjugate, motivated by the need to get out real numbers. The justification is that it works, has always been confirmed experimentally.

In living neural tissue, however, a novel situation arises: a complex reality confronts its conjugate image. Here wave functions are made to interact. One participating wave function is the global attunement and the other represents the surrounding reality, representing it by means of symmetry conservation (that is, retaining invariant relationships over time). And in this interaction, there are conjugate matchings between the attunement and reality's re-presentatives, and the conjugately matching wave functions collapse together. Which match happens to be made is probabilistic.

So in living neural tissue, observables presence in the conjugate match between quantum attunement and quantum re-presentatives of the surrounding quantum reality. Indeed Dasein provides the *Lichtung* where the world is dis-closed, and most everywhere else, at least in the absence of life, there is utter quantum darkness. Dasein has this capacity because Dasein's brain is a place where a conjugate match can be arranged, so that interacting wave functions collapse as one onto world presence.

It has been argued that Dasein has a brain which cannot be ignored, that the brain has a quantum level of functioning, and that situatedness and world presence can be comprehended in quantum brain dynamical terms. Time is next considered, which Vitiello (1995) has discussed in QBD terms.

There is no time without memory. More carefully put, Dasein has no time without the *presence of* memory (and secondarily, the presence *of* an anticipated future). That capability for presenting memory sounds like a case for Dasein's brain.

Now Umezawa (1993) included thermodynamics in his quantum field theory, and called it "thermofield dynamics." Thermofield dynamics depends on the assumption of a tilde domain, which is a special kind of mirror image of the real domain, but which can never be observed. The tilde is a time-reversed mirror image of the nontilde. The ordinary quantum domain is nontilde. When the nontilde image goes into the tilde image, holes are left in the ordinary domain, which are unobservable. Vitiello shows that memories can be stored in vacuum states without overwriting of memories on top of each other, while associative properties are retained. Recovery of the memory to presence depends on the tilde-conjugate match with incoming nontilde energies. (Because associated memories are mutually entangled, the original input for one memory can also recover a previously associated memory. Similarly, a memory part recovers the whole.) So presencing of world and memories arise from a tilde-conjugate match, a balanced exchange in the vacuum states upheld by living neural tissue. Situatedness is a nonlocal attunement.

Water and light ... and love

There is lots of detail that could be added to the QBD story but what it really boils down to is water and light... The theory can be intuited without equations. Picture tiny, tiny tubules at the nanolevel of 10^{-9} m whose walls consist of ultrarapidly oscillating proteins, called tubulins. Tubulins pass patterns of energy to the tubule interior, which consists mainly of water molecules, whose physical properties are such that they naturally form a loose lattice structure, a quasi-crystal whose nodes are spinning dipoles. Under these conditions, a quantum field, the water dipole field, forms. In such a field, quanta can become coherent over macroscopic regions, which is called "Bose-Einstein condensation." The water dipole field interacts with the electromagnetic field. The microtubules are in effect nanolevel water lasers (Jibu et al 1994; Jibu, Pribram and Yasue 1996; Jibu and Yasue 1997). It is water and light, down there at the nanolevel (no surprise to poets and old hippies), where the fabulous quantum stuff is happening.

There is a western philosophical tradition that emphasizes flow. In pre-Socratic times, Heraclitus conceived the importance of unceasing flow, which surfaces in the 20th century as Heidegger's *Ereignis* and Derrida's *Differance*

(Globus 1995). *Es gibt Sein. Es gibt Zeit.,* Heidegger says, in a dynamical movement he calls *Ereignis.* There is a continual gift of Being and Time in this eruption *(Ursprung).* It is important to see the ontological point that this gift does not have the self-sustaining continuity of Heraclitus' river. There may be an illusion of continuously sustained flow but in fact each phase of the flow is generated by a more fundamental movement. Derrida's *Differance* conceives an unruly aconceptual textual flow that characterizes discourse.

David Bohm (1980) added the powerful idea that the flow is indivisible. He called it the holomovement, in which implicate order is continually explicated to presence. Here again world presence is not the continuity of something but is each moment generated anew in seamless fashion. The presence of the world is an achievement of the holomovement.

Heraclitus also had a vision of a dynamical balance of polar opposites. Vitiello (1995), building on Umezawa's (1993) thermofield dynamics, succeeds polar opposition with the opposition between nontilde and tilde. Here dynamical balance is a match in which memory presences and time made possible. The present suggestion, which builds on Jibu and Yasue's (1995; 1997) quantum brain dynamics, succeeds Heraclitean polar opposition with the opposition between complex and complex conjugate. Here dynamical balance is a match in which the world presences. There are nonlocal cybernetics which guide the direction of flow.

There is something rather terrifying in the attempt to think together postmodernism and quantum brain dynamics. Each brain unfolds its own world thrownness; there is no homey world-in-common, but parallel worlds. Brains that have more or less the same attunements because of culture, and represent more or less the same realities, will support the presence of more or less the same worlds. The illusion of a world-in-common is accordingly sustained, but in the quantum framework we see this to be a mere show of *maya* put on by water and light.

It seems quite scary and definitely *unheimlich* to relinquish the world in common. As much as anyone likes being alone, to be thrown irretrievably all-by-oneself-in-one's-own-little-world? Borgesian vertigo overcomes us! Scattered bubbles of perception (Castaneda 1972) in the roiling quantum darkness? Perhaps … perhaps at times this condition might be transcended, in love that participates in a more all-embracing holonomic dynamic that mutes the terror of our profound isolation.

Appendix

Paavo Pylkkänen has raised a question in discussion which can be formulated as follows. It seems to be a category mistake to relate the brain to consciousness or existence. Giving the brain quantum degrees of freedom doesn't change the category mistake ... there is still no fit of brain with consciousness or existence. Our intuition balks at the relationship...

First answer: Yes, if we are looking in the mirror at our own brain through a window in our forehead, the mushy brain tissue seems entirely incompatible with existence. But properly, it is *being* that brain which is compatible with existence. *What it is to BE the brain is to exist.* What the brain looks like to an observer, even ourselves as observer of our own brain, is irrelevant. (This is just Russell's (1948) distinction between knowledge by acquaintance and knowledge by description.)

Second answer: We have to be very wary in talking about the "brain." The perceived brain is a product of someone's brain activity *ex hypothesi.* That's not the one we are talking about being. There is a real brain which is an object under quantum description and accordingly unobservable. The perceived brain conserves the real brain's symmetry. The present claim is that what it is to be the real brain is to exist.

There are real stones, real computers, real cabbages, real livers and real brains, all unobservable objects (which Umezawa (1993) succeeds in giving a macroscopic description in quantum field theoretical terms by Bogliubov transformation of the quantized field). What it is to be a real stone or a real computer is nothing, and what it is to be a real living cabbage is, at best, hardly anything, and being a liver is not that much more. But what it is to be a real brain ... that is something, because the real brain arranges for interactions between nontilde complex and tilde complex conjugate realities (and isolates this interaction from interaction with the environment, which would otherwise quickly bring about decoherence (Zurek 1991)) and so the otherwise ineluctable quantum darkness lights up in the conjugate match.

Note that one's intuitions are irrelevant to this thesis. We cannot claim respectable intuitions about an unobservable object under quantum field description! This undermines the putative category mistake.

References

Bohm, D. 1980. *Wholeness and the Implicate Order.* Boston: Routledge and Kegan Paul.

Castaneda, C. 1972. *Journey to Ixtlan.* New York: Simon and Schuster.

Globus, G. 1995. *The Postmodern Brain* Amsterdam and Philadelphia: John Benjamins.

Globus, G. 1997. "Nonlinear Brain Systems with Nonlocal Degrees of Freedom." *Journal of Mind And Behavior* 18: 195–204.

Globus, G. 1998. "Self, Cognition, Qualia and World in Quantum Brain Dynamics." *Journal of Consciousness Studies* 5: 34–52.

Jibu M., Hagan, S., Hameroff, S.R., Pribram, K.H. and Yasue, K. 1994. "Quantum Optical Coherence in Cytoskeletal Microtubules: Implications for Brain Function." *Biosystems* 32: 195–209.

Jibu, M. and Yasue, K. 1995. *Quantum Brain Dynamics and Consciousness.* Amsterdam and Philadelphia: John Benjamins.

Jibu, M., Pribram, K., Yasue, K. 1996. "From Conscious Experience to Memory Storage and Retrieval: The Role of Quantum Brain Dynamics and Boson Condensation of Evanescent Photons." *International. Journal of Modern Physics B* 10: 1735–1754.

Jibu and Yasue 1997. "Magic without Magic: Meaning of Quantum Brain Dynamics." *Journal of Mind and Behavior* 18: 205–228.

Natsoulas, T. 1978. "Consciousness." *American Psychologist* 33: 906–14.

Penrose, R. 1994. *Shadows of the Mind.* New York: Oxford U. Press.

Russell, B. 1948. *Human Knowledge: Its Scope and Limits.* New York: Simon & Shuster.

Stapp, H. 1993. *Mind, Matter, and Quantum Mechanics.* Berlin, Heidelberg and New York: Springer Verlag.

Umezawa, H. 1993. *Advanced Field Theory: Micro, Macro, and Thermal Physics.* New York: American Institute of Physics.

Vitiello, G. 1995. "Dissipation and Memory in the Quantum Brain Model." *International Journal of Modern Physics B* 9: 973–989.

Zurek, W.H. 1991. "Decoherence and the Transition from Quantum to Classical." *Physics Today* 44: 3644.

Experiential Dimensions

Where's the poetry?

Consciousness as the flight of three blackbirds

John Briggs
Western Connecticut State University, Danburg

Introduction

Perhaps the most striking feature of many current recipes for consciousness is their hubris. Every month authors of books and papers confidently announce their solutions to "the problem" of consciousness. In a 1997 issue of the *Journal of Consciousness Studies*, one prominent biophysicist claimed to have located the "mechanism of consciousness" in what he calls the "master module" or "core circuitry of consciousness" (Cotterill 1997). Scores of other authors believe that a full-blown artificial mind will relatively soon emerge out of computer programming imitations of the brain's processing schemes. It's tempting to lampoon some of the positions, such as the one in which a world-class theorist has been able to solve the "hard problem" of consciousness — and incidentally expand his own self-importance — by declaring that the self (and therefore the problem) doesn't exist.

One would like to think of such pronouncements as no more than what Wallace Stevens called in his poem, "The Sense of the Slight-of-Hand man," "one's grand flights, one's Sunday baths,/ One's tootings at the weddings of the soul" (1954: 222). But they do have an ominous ring about them. They seem to foreshadow our intention to do to consciousness what we have so determinedly done to our environment by chopping it to bits and cleverly reassembling it for a profit. Will our hubris now lead us to a kind of environmental crisis of the human mind?

Perhaps not if we can still allow poetry to influence us.

Poetry, painting, music and other arts embody an appreciation of the mind's creative mysteries. I believe they tell us something valuable about why we should not be so glib about reducing consciousness to a code and why we should probably not be in such a hurry to try.

To hear what poetry has to say on this subject I suggest we think about consciousness in terms of three "orders," or, more properly, three "ordering processes" — the flight of three blackbirds. The first blackbird represents much of our everyday awareness; the second represents an apparently paradoxical conscious activity; the third represents poetry. This third order — or third blackbird — I call "the order of this*other-ness." I will also call it by other names. It relies on the other two orders in dynamically circular ways.

(A caveat: In discussing these three orders I don't mean to suggest that the brain contains distinct neurological structures, neurotransmitters, feedback mechanisms or other apparatus that generate them. In fact, it's possible that, to some degree, one or even all of the orders operates *through* the brain rather than being generated *by* it. As Forman puts it, "Brain cells may receive, guide, arbitrate, or canalize an awareness which is somehow transcendental to them" (1998: 197). But that is not the issue I'd like to concentrate on in the next pages.)

The primary order

The order within consciousness most researched by brain scientists and most discussed by consciousness theorists (remembering, again, that the word order refers to the activity of order*ing*) I propose to call, with just a small touch of irony, the "primary order."

The primary order seems to dominate our Western awareness and probably dominates the reader's awareness reading these sentences.

Crudely put, this order involves consciousness organizing the organism's experience of the world into knowledge. The general principle of the primary order is quite simple, though its realization in cytoplasm, protein, neurotransmitters, quantum particles and whatever else, is incredibly complex: The primary order "abstracts" out of the constant flow of energy impinging on the organism's senses and emerging from its own interior processes certain "relatively invariant" features, to use physicist David Bohm's phrase (1965: 185). These abstractions are then structured into maps which, in turn, abstract further features. Many of the "filters", categories, schema, or maps that do the abstracting appear to be built *into* the anatomical processes of the nervous system. But many are acquired or built *up* through the individual's interaction with the physical and social environment. Both the built-*in* and built-*up* types of filters organize into networked layers of interacting categories and maps within consciousness and perception.

Perhaps the most famous example in modern neuroscience of a built-in abstraction device is the system discovered by David Hubel and Torsten Wiesel in the 1950s. They demonstrated that a cell in the lateral geniculate nucleus of a cat responds with wild excitation when a line of light in a specific orientation is shone on a screen in front of the cat's eye. The researchers determined that different cells in this area respond to very specific orientations of light. In effect, the cells appear to be hard wired to abstract (analyze or filter) out of the flood-tide of input from the cat's environment relatively invariant information about the orientation of the light (Zeki 1993:76–81). Such hard-wired abstractions combine with other abstractions to generate interacting maps or representations in consciousness of the organism's experience.

Examples of built-up maps, as opposed to built-in ones, abound. Prejudices, ideas, paradigms, emotional reactions, linguistic categories. We can construe all of these as networked layers of abstraction and mapping. In *The Essential Tension*, Kuhn neatly illustrates how such mapping can occur. He asks us to imagine Johnny and his father walking in a zoological garden:

> Johnny's education proceeds as follows. Father points to a bird, saying, "Look, Johnny, there's a swan." A short time later Johnny himself points to a bird, saying, "Daddy, another swan." He has not yet, however, learned what swans are and must be corrected: "No, Johnny, that's a goose." Johnny's next identification of a swan proves to be correct, but his next "goose" is, in fact, a duck, and he is again set straight. After a few more such encounters, however, each with its appropriate correction or reinforcement, Johnny's ability to identify these waterfowl is as great as his father's. Instruction has been quickly completed.
>
> I ask now what has happened to Johnny, and I urge the plausibility of the following answer. During the afternoon, part of the neural mechanism by which he processes visual stimuli has been reprogrammed, and the data he receives from stimuli which would all earlier have evoked "bird" have changed. When he began his walk, the neural program highlighted the differences between individual swans as much as those between swans and geese. By the end of the walk, features like the length and curvature of the swan's neck have been highlighted [i.e., abstracted and mapped] and others have been suppressed [for example, a goose style of preening may be quite similar to that of a swan; but such a nuance is suppressed in learning this paradigm, though it might not be suppressed in a culture other than Johnny's where the paradigm is different] so that swan data match each other and differ from goose and duck data as they had not before. Birds that had previously all

> looked alike (and also different) are now grouped in discrete clusters in perceptual space (1977: 309–310).

Johnny is also, of course, having his emotional space mapped by the tone in which his father conducts this lesson.[1] The ideational-emotional content of any individual's consciousness undulates with maps composed of abstractions drawn out and then linked by the many forces of conditioning (i.e., family, society, the physical environment).[2] As Bohm says, "Very soon immediate perception takes on the structure of these "maps" and, after this, one is no longer aware that the map only represents what has been found to be invariant. Rather, the map begins to interpenetrate what is perceived in such a way that it seems to be an inevitable and necessary feature of the whole of experience" (1965: 196).

Over the past few decades many types of abstracting, categorizing and mapping processes have been discovered in consciousness and the details of how much and which of them are built-in or built-up continues to be the subject of heated debate.

A popular approach follows from the logic of Chomsky suggesting that the brain contains a wired-in universal grammar module. According to the theory, the particular language environment into which the brain is born sculpts these universal schema creating a semantic map of the individual's native language. Other inbuilt modules have been proposed, such as one for visually identifying physical objects, and one for abstracting the features of faces.

Extensive research indicates that the blackbird I've called the primary order exists in the brain. However, the materialist attempt to make the whole of consciousness out of such a primary order has resulted in the ludicrous image of the human mind as a bootstrapped perceptual, emotional and cognitive automaton.

The primordial order

To extend the irony, I call the second general order of consciousness — our second blackbird — the "primordial order." It reveals itself in the following story:

> Gutei raised his finger, whenever he was asked a question about Zen. A boy attendant began to imitate him in this way. When anyone asked the boy what his master had preached about, the boy would raise his finger.

> Gutei heard about the boy's mischief. He seized him and cut off his finger. The boy cried and ran away. Gutei called and stopped him. When the boy turned his head to Gutei, Gutei raised up his own finger. In that instant the boy was enlightened (Sohl and Carr 1970:54).

If the primary order abstracts out elements from the flux, creates categories and formulates our responses, the primordial order *de-abstracts* abstractions to generate (at least momentarily) an unmapped, unabstracted state.

An example from the ancient Taoist sage Chuang Tzu provides a particularly clear picture of the primordial order in action.

Chuang's passage begins with the statement, "Heaven and earth were born at the same time I was, and the ten thousand things are one with me." The sage's initial assertion is logically absurd. It unabstracts the boundary lines we use to divide time and space. But then, apparently aware of the ability of the primary order consciousness to make maps out of anything, Chuang Tzu doesn't let his statement rest; instead, he ratchets it back upon itself. "We have already become one," he says, "so how can I say anything? But I have just *said* that we are one, so how can I not be saying something? The one and what I said about it make two, and two and the original one make three, If we go on this way, then even the cleverest mathematician can't tell where we'll end…" (Watson 1968:43). Maps come undone, abstractions fly apart.

The primordial order has not been extensively researched by scientists, though throughout the human record it flowers into consciousness, often with great import.

"Jesus said to them: When you make the two one, and make the inside like the outside, and the outside like the inside, and the upper side like the under side, and in such a way that you make the man with the woman a single one, in order that the man is not the man and the woman is not woman;… then you will go into the kingdom" (Sohl and Carr 1970:71).

Heraclitus: "The bones connected to the joints are at once a unitary whole and not a unitary whole. To be in agreement is to differ; the concordant is the discordant. From out of all the many particulars comes oneness, and out of oneness come all the many particulars" (Wheelwright 1968:90).

Nicholas of Cusa appeared to undermine the mind by describing God as the "*De Li Non Aliud*," the "Not-Other" (Hopkins 1979). Meister Eckhart observed, "The eye by which I see God is the same as the eye by which God sees me. My eye and God's eye are one and the same — one in seeing, one in knowing, and one in loving." And he advised, "Who is Jesus? He has no name" (Sohl and Carr 1970:90–92). The Hindu tradition makes the primordial observation that: *Tut vum asi* (You are that, that is you) and insists that the Atman, or individual soul, is the same as Brahman, the world soul.

In sum, the primordial order operates in the mind to break down the primary order separations, distinctions and maps of knowledge and perception. Western traditions have weighed in heavily on the side of primary order consciousness, while Eastern and indigenous shamanic traditions have emphasized the primordial.

In indigenous storytelling one of the great embodiments of the primordial, unabstracting activity of mind, is Trickster — a figure found the world over:

> Two farmers who owned adjoining fields were one day enjoying each other's company when Trickster appeared, walking the boundary between lands. He wore his hat backwards, fastened his tobacco pipe to the nape of his neck and wore his staff across his back instead of his chest. When he had passed, the two friends began to argue about which direction he'd been traveling in. When Trickster repeated his passage along the boundary between fields, the argument between the two so-called friends grew even hotter, to the point where they came to blows. Finally, the two were separated by others and brought before the chief. Trickster, observing all this, entered the village while everyone was distracted by the commotion and set fire to the houses. Seeing the smoke and flames, the villagers ran to their homes and began to pull the possessions out of their houses; chaos ensued as everyone's belongings became mixed up with everyone else's. As he ran from the scene of disorder he had caused, Trickster boasted that everyone had played his game well (Pelton 1980: 141).

Holland and Combs remark, "Here we see Trickster disrupting the assumptions about good friendship held by the two farmers and about the coherence of their community and the autonomy of individuals within it held by the villagers." Trickster brings the audience for this story to a boundary and points across it to a reality shorn of maps. Trickster produces chaos — at least chaos from the point of view of the villagers. But he himself is not chaotic. In simplest terms, he represents a kind of mirror order, reversing and therefore undoing the known world. When we imagine that we've got everything tied up and accounted for, Trickster appears, so even accounting for him as a mirror figure won't work. He'll only trick us again.

In the ancient Tarot deck, Trickster shows up in the form of the Fool, the figure with the cap and bells. According to tradition, the Fool is foolishness or madness, but he is also spirit. He is the perfected spirit of man approaching the undifferentiated One, the 0 which contains all things but itself is no-thing (Cavandish 1968: 114). As a book on the Tarot says under its description for the image, the Fool is the character "whose Divine *un*wisdom uncouples the chains of time and space" (Matthews 1990). Consider the primordial role taken by Fools in great literature like *King Lear*. The Fool tells the Truth, which is that all the "normal" folk, including the royal elite, have become enmeshed in illusory certitudes of their primary order.

Though the primordial order (or *un*ordering) appears destructive and Dionysian — as we heard with the West African trickster story — it isn't. If we pay attention to what happens when an unabstracting process takes place in our own consciousness, we observe that the movement feels creative, more like a flowering than a destruction. What appears to be destructive from the perspective of the primary order, from the perspective consciousness as a whole, is freedom.

In the wonderful Winnebago story cycle, the trickster, Wakdjunkaga, experiences his life as "something of a wild phantasmagoria" (Radin 1972: 138). He carries his penis around on his back; he burns his anus; he tricks mothers into leaving their children with him so he can eat them; he violates and satirizes deeply important Winnebago beliefs and rituals. He sets his listeners free of their assumptions so that they may accommodate themselves to the vicissitudes of the human condition and appreciate their own involvement in making reality.

Below are a few of the many places where I think the primordial order (or order*ing*) of consciousness is at work.

Mystical experience. Forman discriminates two classes of mystical states. The first involves the "cessation of sensation and conceptualization… meditation without content…" He believes this shows a consciousness exists "even when one has *no* perception, thought or evaluation" (1998: 190–91). St. Teresa of Avila, referring to her self in the third person, said of this state that "even if she would, she could not think of any single thing.... She is utterly dead to the things of the world.... She neither sees, hears, nor understands" (1998: 189). And Eckhart: "In this case … memory no longer functioned, nor understanding, nor the senses, nor the powers that should function so as to govern and grace the body… In this way a man should flee his senses, turn his powers inward and sink into an oblivion of all things and himself" (1998: 189). He added; "The tablet is never so suitable for writing as when absolutely nothing is written on it" (1998: 195).

In Forman's analysis, a second, more profound, type of mystical state occurs when the individual consciousness experiences itself as merging or merged with the whole of existence outside itself. For example, Bernadette

Roberts, ex-nun, mother, housewife and author of *The Experience of No-Self*, described standing on a hillside overlooking the ocean watching a seagull and realizing, "What I am *is* the seagull, and what the seagull is, *I* am."

In both of the mystical states delineated by Forman, the primordial order suddenly saturates awareness in the way that the primary order usually does.

I don't at all mean to suggest that mystical experience is reducible to the primordial order. Who knows if it might not be closer to reality to say that mystical consciousness uses the primordial order as a means to express itself.

Alchemy. Primordial awareness riddles the rhetoric of Medieval alchemists. They asserted that it was only through the force of contraries that the elixir of life could be coaxed into the open. They described the philosopher's stone as paradoxically the highest and yet most primitive state of matter. They called it the *prima materia.* In some texts the alchemist was portrayed as distilling the *prima materia* from dung.

Shamanism. According to many accounts, during initiation a shaman has his body — that is, his/her primary structure and order of sensations, perceptions and thoughts — torn apart, cleaned, and reassembled. Shamans testify that at various times during their careers they have changed sex — gender being presumably one of our most basic certainties of primary order. This overturning of gender categories in the shamanic context apparently releases deep insight and healing power (Halifax 1991).

Humor. In his classic treatise, *Le Rire*, Bergson postulates that humor occurs with the undercutting of some "stiffness" or *raideur.* We laugh when the *grande dame* or fastidious prig gets a pie in the face or slips on a banana peel. John Cleese's absurdly rigid character Basil in the television show *Fawlty Towers* is a contemporary example. The stiffness of a self-image or an unquestioned assumption (both rooted in primary order consciousness) set up potential fall guys for humor.

Humor seems vital, possibly even central, to human consciousness. Years ago I read about holocaust survivor who reportedly told a joke he said went around his camp. As I recall, it went something like this: Two men are on their way to the gas chamber. One turns to the other and says, "Well, Jacob, next time we'll have a chance to be next to each other like this, we'll be two bars of soap on a shelf in a Budapest shop." Here we see the primordial order within humor providing a measure of freedom from the grip of a totalized and deadly primary order.

But not all humor is primordial. Humor that targets a particular group or individual, relying on stereotypes, actually serves to reinforce the relatively invariant categories and maps of the primary order.

Dreams. In REM sleep the brain makes juxtapositions which, at least at some levels, undo the established abstractions of conscious awareness. Dreams appear to partake of the primordial order, but they also serve as handmaidens for creating, elaborating and reinforcing the primary abstractions of consciousness.

The woman who experienced the following dream was clearly having the schema of her memory and emotions unraveled by seeing them placed in bizarre juxtapositions:

> I was walking in a rocky place, almost mountainous. Out of the blue I met a girl from school (she had never been a close friend) called L. L., (very slim, bony prominent nose, attractive, dark-eyed, thin hair). She was carrying a body under her arm. She had a machine around her neck, like a box on her chest, and tubes went into the body, connected in, like a life-support system.
>
> I asked, "Why are you carrying this person?" She replied, "Oh, it's my mother, I must keep her going." I said , "If you go on the rocks, the mountains will support her." The body was naked, but there was no hair; it was a clothlike body, but I knew it was alive and female (Ullman and Limmer 1987: 39).

On the one hand, the dream imagery unabstracts abstractions. (For example here, the body is a doll's body, yet it's alive.) But, on the other hand, the dream easily yields to an interpretation which fits with the maps of the primary order: This dreamer was anticipating the arrival of her aging, unwell mother for their annual holiday.

Interestingly, the *un*abstractions of dream metaphor appear to serve the mind's primary abstracting and mapping process in a way that is not well understood. Perhaps dreams operate as our own personal tricksters, undermining the ossifying structures of our primary order so as to keep daily consciousness reasonably flexible and sane. It may even be (paradoxically) that drawing our maps requires the input of our ability to erase them.

Metaphors. Language is filled with metaphors, most of them dead. But the live ones, have a primordial effect, momentarily overturning primary abstractions. For instance, suppose you overheard someone in a conversation say, "Oh, right. This guy's brain is a stone." For a quick moment the metaphor disassembles the categories which define what a mind and a person are. But the metaphors of everyday discourse quickly resolve into the primary order, reconnecting to our system of classifications and categories. In the case of this metaphor, the context of the discussion would immediately convert the metaphor into some primary order judgment or description about the man in question — for example, a classification that the man's mind is impenetrable. Poetic metaphors, however, don't resolve in this way (as we'll see when we come to our third blackbird).

Psychoactive drugs. Some drugs can disrupt the categorical mechanisms of the brain, scrambling maps and map-making abilities. To an extent, they may imitate the effect of the primordial order. Or, (as in peyote rituals) they may facilitate the primordial ordering's rise into conscious awareness. Often, however, drugs simply seem to *derange* the abstractions of the primary order without really unabstracting them.[3]

Deconstruction. Post-structuralist theory can be viewed as a philosophical formalization of an unabstracting process. Terry Eagleton characterizes the deconstructive maneuver as an "unsettling venture into the inner world of the text which lays bare the illusoriness of meaning, the impossibility of truth and the deceitful guiles of all discourse" (Eagleton 1996: 126). The problem is that deconstruction as an abstract nihilistic theory is subject to the same "takeover" by the primary order as the statement about Oneness that Chuang Tzu addressed. Unless a tricksterist spirit of primordial order is brought to bear during the deconstruction, the post-structuralist strategy turns into another sort of map, a mental structure of categorical opinions cleverly disguising themselves as non-categories and non-opinions.

Double-think. Orwellian-type double-think goes on in society all the time. During the 2000 U. S. presidental election, republican George W. Bush declared himself a "compassionate conservative." This oxymoron was Bush's attempt to maintain his traditional conservatism while adding a facade liberalism.

Quite possibly the primordial order animates many deceptions, self-deceptions and perversities of human nature and human thought. Perhaps it operates behind the scene when we vow we won't eat any more fatty foods and then right away feel obliged to gorge on them. Clearly there is a movement of consciousness which is constantly subversive to its own structures. (But as the mystical experience suggests, this is not merely a destructive impulse.)

The primordial order may be lurking behind the scenes in much of ordinary discourse. When I try to describe a complex scene, an emotionally moving or unusual sight, a subtle idea or insight, some part of my consciousness seems to be unabstracting my description even as I make it. Something causes both mind and physiology to hesitate and veer. I feel afflicted by some fleeting awareness of the ambiguity of words, of the contradictions lurking in the signals of inflection and body language, and of the terrible insufficiency of categories and even of perception and sensation to capture what is here. We tacitly observe this fundamental ambiguity going on all the time in discourse. Someone says he had a wonderful time at the beach but other signals he gives out subtly negate his assertion. We're aware of a hole in the communication, a space in which there's something we can't put our finger on (presumably what the boy with the chopped-off finger understood). We ignore this sort of subliminal mental activity, for the most part. The primary order dominates. Artists, however, bring the primordial order to the foreground. The playwright Harold Pinter, for example, shows us that the day-to-day banalities of our conversations contain abysses. We all know that it's often what someone is failing to communicate that communicates to us most powerfully. Virginia Woolf exploited the unabstracting aspect of ordinary thought and speech by generously crafting ellipses into unfinished sentences and phrases that suggest the collapse of abstractions at crucial moments.

In its most basic form, the primordial order expresses our ability to actively seek and recognize the contradictions within our primary constructions. Thus, it is an essential part of the creative activity that goes into the construction and remodeling of each perception and conceptualization that consciousness undertakes. But the primordial, I believe, also does much more. It functions sometimes simply to negate the primary abstractions in a way that keeps us open to the fact that no construction of reality is adequate.

Our awareness of our own death provides a deep experience of the primordial order's presence. In this awareness, we glimpse that nature continuously abstracts elements out itself in order to generate new structures and "categories" of beings, both living and inanimate, and also continuously "unabstracts" these structures through erosion and death. For humans, of course, even the contemplation of that unabstracted state from which no traveler returns puzzles our will, profoundly unmaps us. One imagines that if death were abolished tomorrow, our very humanity would be destroyed along with it. We might be drawn, even more than we are now, to live solely in our primary order constructions, in the relative shallowness of our knowledge, avoiding even more than now the experience of anything that might lie beyond our abstractions. Death provides a healthy balance for the mind by opening up what moves beyond the mind's superstructure, revealing what isn't abstract-able and categorize-able (despite all our efforts), bringing to us, as God tells Isaiah, "the treasures of darkness."

The primordial order in nature (as distinguished from the primordial order in consciousness) also shows itself in other ways than cessation and death — tricksterish ways often disguised by our primary maps. Marie Louise von Franz tells the following story in *Alchemical Imagination*:

> I once lectured at the CERN, the nuclear center in Geneva, Switzerland. When I mentioned synchronicity there were roars of laughter and these famous physicists said: "Oh, we know that very, very well: our computer absolutely always answers as we expect it to answer. If we believe in a wrong theory… the computer just performs according to what we expect; and then a colleague, who does not believe it, uses the computer for a few hours and gets a completely different result." They roared with laughter. But when I tried to pin them down and say, "Well Gentlemen, then please take that experience seriously," Weiskopf said, "Oh, that's all nonsense, synchronicity is all nonsense," but with a mad affect (quoted in Holland and Combs 1995).

It seems reasonable to imagine that in its primary and primordial movements human consciousness reflects the primary and primordial movement of the universe in general — movements out of which our consciousness itself is born.

Perhaps you could argue a survival advantage for a conscious organism possessing an explicit ability to unconstruct its own constructions — perhaps a necessary ability if you want to keep from getting stuck in your schema. However, I don't readily subscribe to such a materialist approach. The scientific conviction that the universe is essentially, or perhaps entirely, material and that subjective mental phenomena emerge out of a material substrate constitutes a primary order "take" on reality. Thus, from the scientific perspective, the primordial, unabstracted, order described by mystics, shamans and poets seems to be nothing more than an illusion. However, from vantage point of the primordial order the universe takes on a radically different look. The Hindu sages proposed that from the perspective of *Maya*, the world of the primary order is actually the illusion. This illusion contains an unabstract-able emptiness, a primordial no-thing-ness at its core.

So, does that mean the primary and primordial orders are merely another grand set of dualities in conflict? I suggest they aren't.

I can very primitively represent why with a little diagram. Imagine that the background field on which this network, or organic grid, is drawn is the field of "Truth" in the sense of the Latin word, *veritas*, meaning "that which is", and implying "all of that which is," the whole of things. Imagine it as also Truth in

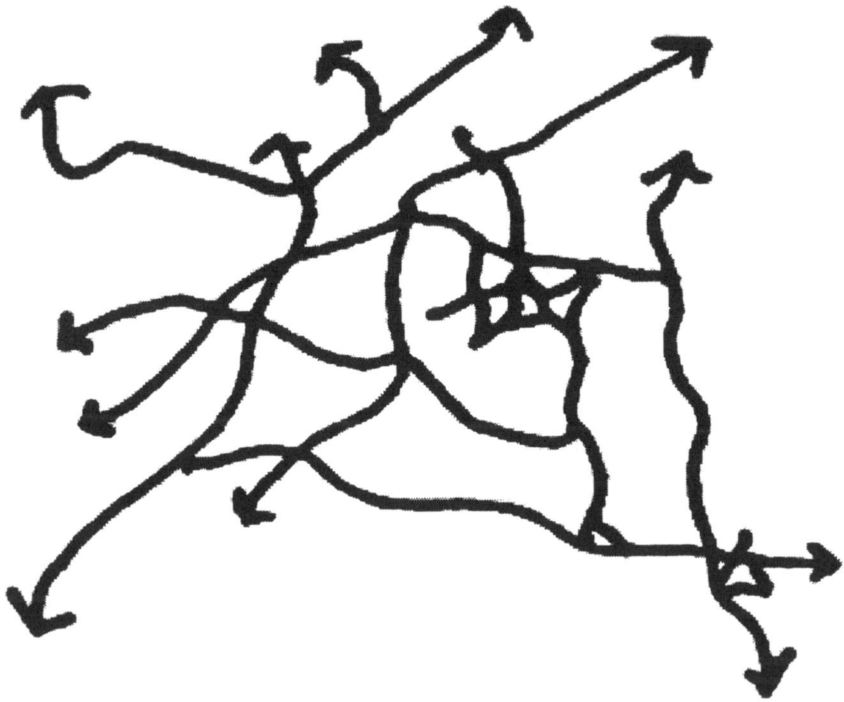

Figure 1. Primary/Primordial Grid

the sense of *aletheia* — the Truth that both reveals and conceals — not relative truth or absolute truth but Truth as a kind of living, organic, holistic movement of things. The lines on this grid represent the primary order, which is to say they represent the intricate network of abstractions, categories and maps, including those which constitute what we call our subjective and objective experience. The spaces between the lines are the primordial order which is *neither* subjective *nor* objective. Of course, the grid here is static while knowledge and abstracting constantly move and change in their relationship to the total field of Truth. But there will always be spaces in knowledge, and these unabstracted spaces continuously transmogrify, just as knowledge does. To glimpse the grid and its space as a whole, requires art.

The order of this*other-ness, the third blackbird

Herman Melville's novel *Moby Dick* provides a clear example of the proposed third order, the "order of this*other-ness," at work in the mind. The great white whale pursued by Ahab and the crew of the Pequod presents itself to us, on the one hand, as an actual animal (and Melville constantly assaults us with scientific facts about whales and a wealth of technical detail about whaling in order to keep us in mind of this actuality). On the other hand, the whale represents a god or demon, an indifferent force of nature, or a malevolent exemplar of karma. The work compels us into a dynamic whirlpool where the whale breaches the surface as both "*this*," real primary thing, and also something vastly "*other*" than this, a mysterious primordial maw.

The dynamic of works of art is a dynamic of this*other-ness. The * of my made-up word indicates that the dynamic continuously folds back on itself. Whenever we imagine that the work is *this* (merely a whale), we are faced with the fact that it is *other* (god-like, devil-like, etc.); but if we conclude that it's *other* (Oh, you mean it's God), then we encounter that it's *this* (it's a sperm whale). Perhaps it is easiest to understand the dynamic of the order of this*other-ness by watching more closely how it functions in literary or artistic metaphors, which I've sometimes called "reflectaphors" or "metaprimes" in order to distinguish them from the everyday, common use variety of metaphor mentioned earlier. My word metaprime (the term I'll prefer here) indicates that this type of metaphor mediates between the primary and primordial orders even as it transforms them. "Meta" means between, and among and expresses change or alteration. With the word metaprime I mean to suggest that there are vital metaphor-like strategies at work in all the arts, from painting to music to film. These metaphor-like strategies are central to the emergence of the order of this*other-ness within a creative work.

A classic literary metaphor (reflectaphor or metaprime) asserts an identity between two terms which are categorically dissimilar. Relating terms in this way has an unabstracting, primordial effect. But the impact also goes beyond the primordial, as in this a literary metaphor from Homer's *Iliad*.

> So he [Agamemnon] spoke, and the Argives shouted aloud, as surf crashing against a sheerness, driven by the south wind descending, some cliff out-jutting, left never alone by the waves from all the winds that blow, as they rise one place and another, they stood up scattering and made for the ships… (Lattimore 1951: 86).

The metaphor (metaprime of literature) creates an identity between the Argives responding to Agamemnon and the surf crashing against a cliff. The Greeks appear to us as a *this* (they're the Argive army) but also as *other* than this (the sea). The metaphor "works" on us because, from one angle, (the angle of the primary order) an army and the surf are categorically different types of things, while, from another angle the metaphor makes us perceive they're the same. The clash and merging, and the merging and clash of the two terms unabstracts them and the maps they're connected to, and opens up rich ambiguities.

But "ambiguities" here doesn't imply "unclear"; in fact this metaphor seems starkly clear. Unlike the mostly dead and dying metaphors we use every day, the literary metaprime does not move to resolve itself into a primary order abstraction we could map into knowledge. In order to see this, simply reflect: "Does the human army in this metaphor appear to you as powerful and mighty as the sea or does it seem the helpless victim of circumstance blown and shattered like surf against a rock?" By forcing us to experience these two entirely contradictory, entirely unresolved perceptions (and others) simultaneously, Homer takes us into the paradoxical movement of Truth where man 1) is helplessly driven by circumstances (fate) and 2) willfully drives and creates his own fate. This sort of thing is what literary metaphors, metaprimes and reflectaphors do to create a sense of this*other-ness in the work.

These lines have something in common with ones written almost 3,000 years later by Stevens in his "Thirteen Ways of Looking at a Blackbird":

> The blackbird whirled in the autumn winds.
> It was a small part of the pantomime (1954: 93).

Here we can reflect whether the blackbird whirls of its own volition or is being spun by the wind. The whirling appears as both "this" (the bird is doing the action) and "other than this" (the wind is doing it). Within the context of the line, the single term "whirled" functions as if it were composed of two contradictory terms whirling around each other.

Puns, irony, poetic images, all these have a similar dynamic. Woolf called her art a process of working to "attain similarity by means of infinite discords." (Gordon 1984: 108)

Homer's and Stevens' metaprimes affirm the primary order by giving us armies, surf, blackbirds and autumn winds to perceive. These categories seem "real" to us — as both objective and subjective representations within consciousness. But at the same time the metaprimal juxtaposition unravels the network containing these categories. As a result of this, an awareness emerges of a dimension of things not quite real, not quite unreal, neither entirely existent nor yet just non-existent, neither objective nor subjective. Imbued with a sense of this*other-ness, reality seems both familiar and uncanny, known and unknown, dreamlike and solid. Woolf called the experiences of this*other-ness "moments of being," and said they are not always pleasant.

An awareness of the strange and familiar this*other-ness of life is the gift of a great work of art.

Melville reportedly became enraged when someone suggested that his story about the giant white whale was an allegory. In this context we can understand his pique. An allegory is a one-to-one correspondence, a primary order. An allegorical whale converts into the category of Satan (or God) and nothing more. An allegory lacks the folding-back this*other-ness dynamic that embraces the force of the primordial order as it folds and unfolds through our primary order.

That dynamic is thoroughly apparent in the Winnebego Trickster cycle mentioned earlier. In one story Wakjunkaga is a victim, in the next a victimizer; he metamorphoses from an apparent exemplar of undifferentiated consciousness into a satirist of the onerous aspects of community life. A literary metaphor, Wakjunkaga dances and spins primordially, always other than our attempts to fit him into a primary order. At the same time, however, he reaffirms that the stage he spins on *is* the primary order. He returns us to the this-ness of life even as he reveals that it is always other than we believe it to be. Like two mirrors facing each other, their reflections hurled back and forth at the speed of light, Wakjunkaga's movement shows us something right before our eyes that is beyond our vision.

The dynamic order of this*other-ness also unfolds in great works of music. Beethoven's Fifth Symphony provides a simple example. Recall the opening four notes and the dramatic effect that follows when the composer repeats the first three and then changes the next (note 8). Those first four notes are the first term of a metaprime. The notes 5 through 8 are the second term. The metaprime asserts, in effect, that the two terms are identical and then leaves us shocked by their difference. As the symphony progresses, Beethoven orchestrates chains and nests of metaprimal figures echoing this initial metaprime everywhere in the piece and creating a reverberation of this*other-ness throughout.

In his Harvard Lectures, Leonard Bernstein employed Chomsky's theory of transformational grammar and an idea of literary metaphor to describe how musical figures evolve in a work through a kind of simultaneous comparison-contrast. Slight changes in a figure or theme create opportunities to compare the figure to its transformation. Each time the figure reappears it is perceived as simultaneously similar and different because it has been inverted or transposed or diminished or run through a different section of the orchestra. In referring to the repetition with variation he found in Beethoven's Sixth Symphony, Bernstein said:

> First, not one of those repeats is an exact or literal repeat. Each one contains some slight variation or other — a slight elaboration, or an added voice, or a structural ambiguity, or a change in the dynamics of loud and soft. And second, what is variation, anyway? It's always, in one way or another, a manifestation of the mighty dramatic principle known as the Violation of Expectation. What is expected is, of course, repetition — either literal or in the form of an answer, a counterstatement, or whatever; and when those expectations are violated, you've got variation. The violation is the variation
> (Bernstein 1976: 162).

The order within the musical composition is peculiar. On one side, the musical form allows us to discern a relatively invariant pattern, an accomodation of our primary order consciousness. But on the other side, the compositional pattern always violates and subverts our expectation, evoking our primordial awareness. The result is that the composition seems always to extend beyond itself and beyond our ability to comprehend it or even apprehend it in its immediate presence. Even as it is right before us in our primary awareness, it slips from our grasp.

In her novel *The Bluest Eye* Nobel Laureate Tony Morrison portrays the random events that shaped the life of one of her characters, Cholly Breedlove. The scenes of these events contain strong images: a watermellon, asefetida bag, images of being humiliated in the sexual act by a white man with a flashlight. Morrison captures the unifying order of this*other-ness when she writes:

> The pieces of Cholly's life could become coherent only in the head of a musician. Only those who talk their talk through the gold of curved metal, or in the touch of black-and-white rectangles and taut skins and strings echoing from wooden corridors, could give true form to his life. Only they would know how to connect the heart of a red watermelon to the asafetida bag to the muscadine to the flashlight on his behind to the fists of money to the lemonade in a Mason jar to a man called Blue and come up with what all of that meant in joy, in pain, in anger, in love, and give it its final and pervading ache of freedom (Morrison 1994: 129).

In the order of this*other-ness, the contradictions and fragments of the life come together and create a whole which is immediate and familiar — yet also dreamlike and beyond the network of knowledge or explanation. The emotion created by or expressed in the order of this*other-ness is unlike those emotions arising from our genetics or conditioning. Though deep and passionate, the aesthetic emotion contains an "aesthetic distance," a quality of impersonality. The emotion is both intensely subjective and objective at the same time.

I seriously doubt that a mechanism or algorithm can explain the origin or function of the order of this*other-ness as an order of consciousness. I've read at least one consciousness theorist who has taken note of the mind's capacity for making analogy and metaphor and tried to incorporate it into his depiction of conscious mechanism. But the problem is that an algorithmic theory can't account for a simple fact implicit in what I've just described about artistic order. Every artist knows that some metaprimes "work" — that is they actualize this*other-ness — and some don't and that sometimes the metaprimes which fail to work seem far more colorful and dramatic than the ones that succeed. Success is measured by a sense of Truth in the metaprime, a sense of being. In other words, the metaprime provides a glimpse of both the lines of the grid and its spaces. A metaprime that evokes a sense of Truth or being requires that the terms composing it be similar to each other and dissimilar from each other in precisely the right balance for the context. If that balance isn't achieved (one that creates the proper "violation of expectation" as Bernstein called it and sets off a this*other-ness dynamic), the metaprime falls flat. In that case, the juxtaposition of terms seems either a primary order "this" (a colorful description of something), a primary order "other than this" (an idea or allegory), or nonsense (the two terms don't seem to fit together at all). Certainly computer could be programmed to randomly equate dissimilar terms. Undoubtedly it would generate nonsense, banalities and some occasional striking metaphors. However, only a human mind could tell which of those metaphors rang true and which were merely striking or nonsense. To create an entire work that has the ring of truth means the artist must continually subvert her own abstractions, her own expectations, her own algorithms and her own nonsense. Poet John Keats described the truth or sense of being that results from this activity as a state of "uncertainties, mysteries and doubts" (Page 1945). It is hard to imagine how any computer algorithm could accomplish such a state.

In a 1988 *Scientific American* article on art and the visual system, Margaret Livingstone pointed out how great visual artists exploit the feature detection, contrast detection and other systems in the vision system to create illusions. For example, according to Livingstone, in the so called "color-selective blob" part of the visual system which abstracts "lower acuity" visual information, "two colors can have entirely opposite effects on each other depending on their spatial arrangement. When two different colors are juxtaposed, they normally oppose each other, so that each appears less like the other (that is, each tends toward the complement of the other). On the other hand, when the two colors are interdigitated in a fine pattern, there is an opposite effect: they come to look more like each other, that is, they blend or 'bleed'" (1988:84). Seurat and Monet, among others, exploited this system to produce striking effects of this*other-ness. Figures and terrain appear both solid and diffused, as if dissolving or materializing, or as if we were peering through the apparent solidity of the world into the quantum level. Seurat had to make dots of paint large enough to be seen by the form system, but too fine for the color system. Seurat's use of this technique wasn't programmatic, however, because he applies the technique to a greater or lesser extent in different areas of a piece. The result is that the kind of violation of expectation Bernstein referred to appears throughout a painting and makes it seem organismic.

I believe the ability to create and appreciate the order of this*other-ness proceeds from the deepest movements of nature. As an order of consciousness, this*other-ness may be *analogous* to the natural order discovered by quantum mechanics. Perhaps the relationship of the primary and primordial operating within the metaprimes of artworks is analogous to the relationship of wave to particle in quantum reality — an irreducible paradox from the perspective of the primary order. Perhaps, too, an ironclad uncertainty principle governs artistic order so that we can never entirely pin down its movements with an algorithm. No one can tell us how to make a metaprime that is not reducible to an idea, a category, a judgment or an abstraction. No one can tell us how to craft one that is open and true. Artists and poets testify that the true metaprime — the one inculcating this*other-ness and being — remains something that happens to us, or through us, sometimes in spite of us.

Creators' often report that a work of art and, for that matter, a creative career, begins with an acute, irresistible awareness of this*other-ness. Henry James said that the "germ" which touched off a piece for him might be an odd phrase or stray thought, paradoxically both trivial and portentous. It was an "infection" which grew. Poet Jorge Luis Borges described both the initial feeling and the unfolding poetic process as the keen sense of an "imminence of revelation which is never fulfilled." (Alifano 1983) Perhaps not surprisingly, unfolding the germ into a pattern, or web, of metaprimes results in an organic structure that mirrors in virtually every dimension this imminence of revelation never fulfilled — an organic ordering of this*other-ness, in other words.

Conclusion

This*other-ness seems to provide a window into the primordial order, into that movement of consciousness that propels us beyond our abstractions. But at the same time it seems to affirm the very primary order act of making abstractions. In its antinomous dynamic, I suspect that this*other-ness is really much closer to the real nature of consciousness than the sorts of primary order awareness Western science has tended to research.

I suspect that at various levels we experience the this*other-ness of the world all the time. We experience that the things we identify as categories of thought and perception are also not those categories; we are aware that the lines on our grids have no meaning without the spaces which make the lines, like a spider's strands, appear a little dreamlike and frail. It is possible that such tacit awareness infuses all of our consciousness.

In a strictly materialist universe I can't imagine that what I've called the order of this*other-ness would offer a survival advantage. The main function of this order seems to be to encounter and represent in the mind the truth about being (a glimpse of both lines and space). It's not clear why this would be necessary to a Darwinian animal, though I'm sure resourceful adaptationists would be able to think up a reason and thus bring even this dimension of consciousness into the orbit of the reductionist program. Personally, I would prefer that this order in art and mind remain a mystery because that is what I think it ontologically is. But maybe you can't fight progress or city hall. Except by poetry.

So I'll conclude by lodging my protest against a merely primary explanation with some lines from a poem. Again, Wallace Stevens:

> I was of three minds,
> Like a tree
> In which there are three blackbirds

Notes

1. Antonio Damasio has shown that the idea of built-in and built-up mapping also applies to the domain of emotions. He divides emotions into two types. An example of the first type is fear. "We are wired," says Damasio "to respond with an emotion, in preorganized fashion, when certain [relatively invariant] features of stimuli in the world or in our bodies are perceived, alone or in combination. Examples of such features include size (as in large animals); large span (as in flying eagles); type of motion (as in reptiles); certain sounds (such

as growling); certain configurations of body state (as in the pain felt during a heart attack). Such features, individually or conjunctively, would be processed and then detected by a component of the brain's limbic system, say, the amygdala..." (1994: 131).

A second class of emotions, such as melancholy and shyness, is composed, according to Damasio, of built-up nuances or permutations of the hard-wired emotional schema, new abstractions constructed out of memories, perceptual objects and situations.

2. Even the sense of embodiment involves a process of mapping. Edelman comments that the domain of abstracting processes discussed by Lakoff provides "a basis for linguistic meaning" within consciousness. Lakoff argues that consciousness possesses "*container schemas* (defining a boundary, or "in and out"), a *part-whole* schema, a *link* schema (one thing connected to another, as by a string), a *center-periphery* schema (as in body center versus arms and legs, and a *source-path-goal* schema (starting point, directional path, midpoint) including *up-down* and *front-back* schemas" (1992: 249).

3. Psychopathologies may also derange the primary order. In a psychotic episode an individual may imagine himself as an atomic bomb, understand a coke can left on a subway as the sign of a vast conspiracy against him, or speak in a "word salad" of ideas. Though such behavior appears to unabstract the primary order, it is really a deformed, often especially rigid, form of mapping. For the most part I would not include psychiatric maladies as examples of the primordial order at work, though it may well be that the prevalence of mental illness in the west is a sign of our almost total reliance on primary order consciousness and it may suggest that derangement may result from such an extensive reliance.

References

Alifano, Roberto. 1983. "Jorges Luis Borges: A Conversation with Roberto Alifano." Aváuz, Nichomedes Suárez and Willis Barnstone. (trs.). *The American Poetry Review*: November-December.

Bernstein, Leonard. 1976. *The Unanswered Question. Six talks at Harvard.* Cambridge, Mass: Harvard U. Press.

Bohm, David. 1965. *The Special Theory of Relativity.* New York: W.A. Benjamin.

Cavandish, Richard. 1968. *The Black Arts.* New York: Capricorn.

Cotterill, Rodney M.J. 1997. "On the Mechanism of Consciousness." *Journal of Consciousness Studies* 4(3): 231–47.

Damasio, Antonio R. 1994. *Descartes' Error. Emotion, reason and the human brain.* New York: Gosset/Putnam.

Eagleton, Terry. 1996. *Literary Theory: An Introduction.* 2nd ed. Minneapolis: U. of Minn. Press.

Edelman, Gerald M. 1992. *Bright Air, Brilliant Fire.* New York: BasicBooks.

Forman, Robert K.C. 1998. "What Does Mysticism Have to Teach Us About Consciousness?" *Journal of Consciousness Studies* 5(2): 185–201.

Gordon, Lyndall. 1984. *Virginia Woolf. A Writer's Life.* New York: W.W. Norton.

Halifax, Joan. 1991. *Shamanic Voices. A Survey of Visionary Narratives.* New York: Arkana, Penguin.

Holland, Mark and Allan Combs. "Following the Trickster: A Model of Consciousness." Presented at the 1995 International Conference on Consciousness, Tuscon. Arizona.

Hopkins, Jasper. (tr.) 1979. *Nicholas of Cusa and God as Not-Other.* Minneapolis: U. of Minn. Press.

Kuhn, Thomas. 1977. *The Essential Tension.* Chicago: University of Chicago Press.

Lattimore, Richard. (tr.) 1951. *The Iliad of Homer.* Chicago: University of Chicago Press.

Livingston, Margaret. 1988. "Art, Illusion and the Visual System." *Scientific American* 258(1): 78–85.

Matthews, Caitlin and John. 1990. *The Arthurian Tarot.* New York: HarperCollins.

Morrison, Tony. 1994. *The Bluest Eye.* New York: Penguin.

Page, Frederick. (ed.) 1945. *Letters of John Keats.* London: Oxford U. Press.

Pelton, Robert. 1980. *The Trickster in West Africa. A study of mythic irony and sacred delight.* Berkeley: U. of Calif. Press.

Radin, Paul. 1972. *The Trickster. A study in American Indian mythology.* New York: Schocken.

Stevens, Wallace. 1954. *Wallace Stevens, The Collected Poems.* New York: Vintage.

Sohl, Robert and Audrey Carr. (eds.) 1970. *The Gospel According to Zen.* New York: New American Library.

Ullman, Montague and Claire Limmer. (eds.) 1987. *The Variety of Dream Experience.* New York: Continuum.

Watson, Burton. (tr.) 1968. *The Complete Works of Chuang Tzu.* New York: Columbia U. Press.

Wheelwright, Philip. (tr.) 1968. *Heraclitus.* New York: Atheneum.

Zeki, Semir. 1993. *A Vision of the Brain.* London: Blackwell Scientific.

Consciousness, art and media

Reflections on mediated experience

Susanne Ackers
University of Skövde

There are a number of art historians who separate the history of art from the history of technology strictly. Herbert Read is one of them. In his book *Icon and Idea — The Function of Art in the Development of Human Consciousness* he suggests to interpret art as a materialization of consciousness — based on the Platonic concept of beauty and harmony. He claims that mankind perceives, e.g., symmetry because it is an integral of the human body — this moment in history he calls "consciousness of symmetry" — after which artists can make a "conscious use of symmetry". His example for this early stage of a materialized consciousness is paleolithic sculpture. The next step in the materialization of consciousness, according to Read, is the addition of "a third dimension, of space in depth." Read claims that "all the laws of geometrical composition were first made evident in art; the first science was a notation of the discoveries of the artist; mathematics arose as a notation on artifacts."

I am intrigued by Read's suggestion that art is a "materialization of consciousness" but I want to oppose his separation of the history of art from the history of technology and rather suggest the contrary: that art history can be read as media history — claiming that architecture, painting, sculpture are media as music and language and computers are.

The decision to start my paper with a negative result is based in the interdisciplinarity of this book. My background in classical art history and aesthetics and my research during recent years within the field of what I used to call "electronic art" brought me to a point where I need to reconfigure the main stream definition or idea of "art". To mediate this experience to you, I will try to perform the effect of Read's assumption on the interpretation of a recent art work which was produced some years ago. An art historical attempt to analyse this work without accepting the compatibility of art and technology would look as follows.

My paper is based on the art work *Osmose*, a virtual reality installation created and developed by a team headed by Charlotte Davies, including John Harrison for the virtual reality software, Georges Mauro for the graphics, Rick Bidlack for the music, and Dorota Blaszczak for the design and sound programming. *Osmose* is an immersive virtual space, based on virtual reality technology, where goggles provide visuals, and a device dependant on breathing navigates the user through the space. The work was shown for the first time in 1995 in Montréal at the 6th International Symposium on Electronic Arts (ISEA 95).

Char Davies, the artist, the concept of the art work

I could describe the artist and her background and mention that Char Davies has absolved a classical education as a painter. Her interest in photorealism led her to the insight that painting as a medium could not perform her contemporary needs. Being involved in the development of software for moving images, she helped establish one of the best known software companies (Softimage) that merged with Microsoft in 1994.

Looking at her paintings, I could describe them as photorealistic with a growing interest in a complexity of light reflections and shadows of objects onto object surfaces that fragment the objects in a cubistic way. Focussing more and more on light effects and not on the solidity of the objects or surfaces, her last paintings resemble early impressionistic paintings such as those by William Turner.

I could bring up more biographical information about Char Davies' experiences with scuba diving, that led to the development of an interface that allowed her to enter the visual world she had in her mind. If I were to do this, I would prove the correctness of my results with citations out of the exhibition catalogue:

> It was the first time in my life that I entered a space where there was nothing to see, no separations between inside and outside. If you saw a little tiny speck, you didn't know whether it was the glint in a barracuda's eye, or a little jellyfish, or a misfiring of a rod in your retina. I guess I started accessing endorphins or something, because I really got into a trance. (Eric Davies' article)

For Davies, *Osmose* is trying to create an environment of being still and just being — allowing things to come to you — rather than always doing, getting, conquering and moving forward. That stasis is so antithetical to our culture of doing. (Francis Dyson's article)

> Philosophically, Davies says, *Osmose* is about "being-in-the-world" in its most profound sense. It's about our subjective experience as sentient, embodied, incarnate, living beings embedded in enveloping, flowing space. (Margaret Wertheim's article)
>
> … filled with passages from philosophical works that have inspired Davies. Selections from Heidegger, Rilke, Huxley, Joseph Campbell, and Gaston Bachelard explore issues of nature, the body, and technology itself. Interspersed with these texts are some of Davies' own writings about *Osmose*. (Margaret Wertheim's article)
>
> Above all, by "reminding people of the extraordinariness of simply being alive in the world", Davies hopes that *Osmose* and its successor can act as "arenas in which we can perhaps relearn how to "be". (Margaret Wertheim's article)

This would enlighten the "concept" of the art work *Osmose*.

John Harrison, programmer of *Osmose*, the making of the art work

I would have to continue this analysis by describing the making or the production of the concept or the idea. So I would have to talk about John Harrison, the person who developed the necessary software which is an invention in itself because of the visualization of transparency in a real time environment. I could talk about his background and his experiences of being a programmer at the Banff Center, near Seattle where he started to program within an art context. I could continue by examining the works he has already realised and compare the aesthetics within these works and look for similarities. And although the "artistic partners" were different ones, I could start to look for his personal style in programming and so on and so on.

Much more interesting is the cooperation between Char Davies and John Harrison. In untaped interviews that I recall from memory here, the latter told me that the early paintings of Char were a tool of visual communication between them.

> Programming VR software means that I had to imagine the negative of what the "immersant" is getting as visual inputs. While I was working on that, I remembered a short story by Ursula LeGuinn, in which a tree is telling the story of its life. The tree is the fix point in the story in form of the story teller, in a similar way, the program has to act like this: whereever the "immersant" is heading to, the program has to create the counter part that is moving towards the position of the immersant, not the other way around. Although

> the immersant of course gets the illusion to move forwards actively. (untaped interview between John Harrison and Susanne Ackers during the exhibition of *Osmose* in Newcastle upon Tyne, November 1996)

The imagery of *Osmose*, the visual content described in works of literature, the art work

Another methodological tool is to focus on the reception of an art work. This method has its roots within disciplines that are based in literature studies.

> The first image the immersant discovers is a kind of large clearing where a stream flows and in the center sits a hieratic tree with bare branches. When one comes closer and enters into the tangling of its branches, there appears a dense folliage that will disappear from the eyes of the spectator going away. The space of the forest around is a dense underwood inviting one to get lost. The spectator can also get closer to the stream, crossed by little lights which turned out to be fish-fireflies constituted by several dot of light like constellations. By sinking into the water, different life forms manifest themselves and it is possible to slip into other contiguous spaces like the one of computer code which is in fact the scripts of the *Osmose* application. At the far end of the dive, a huge waving bubble appears, welcoming a visit. In penetrating it, the spectator finds him or herself back in the beginnning scene with the tree and the stream looping the universe on itself. All the spaces show a high formal coherence, playing with transparencies and blue-gray tones. The semi-darkness, shadowy light, and lonely ambiance have a very strong poetic power and the desire for dreamily strolling never gives out in one session. (Florent Aziosmanoff's article)

This would have to be the end of my analysis if I would deny a merging between technology and art in such a dogmatic way as Read does, and not only him.

What I did until now, was to describe the art work in a traditional way: the artist and her concept of the art work, the programmer and the production of the art work and the immersant and his reception or perception of the art work.

I would like to use this paper to present two versions of art history to you: (1) The history of two dimensional visuals using perspectival laws to create three dimensional spaces on two dimensional surfaces is a short one — it started around 1500 and broke within the context of art from 1800 onwards but has been continued until today through the invention and widespread use of photography, film and TV. (2) The history of the different media that were combined at different times into art works, e.g. gothic architecture — and the fact that it was relations between numbers that created the aesthetical bridge between the different media.

My thesis in the context of this book (and I am stressing this because I will be drifting into fields that do not provide me with a solid ground knowledge, so I am asking for guidance by the specialists) on consciousness is that the history of art could be read as a history that merged the two abstract systems of communication — mathematics and philosophy — into materialized products that are mediating knowledge.

A short history of visual art

Perspective as symbolic form

In his article "Perspective as Symbolic Form" Erwin Panofsky (1892–1968) reconstructs the interpretation of Greek sources on the subject of perspective in the Renaissance, proving that the revival of Euclid's publication "Optica" was not done without contemporary adjustments.

Euclid had differentiated the subject of perspective into *perspectiva naturalis* and *perspectiva artificialis.* In other words, Euclid was aware of the difference between the perception of the human eye with its concave background serving as a projection screen and the "artificial" effort to project this impression onto a two dimensional surface. While the Greek mathematician respected this contradiction, his Renaissance translators and interpretators did not. Panofsky gives several examples in which this, Euclid's 8th theorem, was either incorrectly translated or completely neglected.

The projection onto a two-dimensional surface is an abstract procedure and it can be seen as a loss of the psychophysiological space[1], but Panofsky points out that instead the loss was balanced by a bondage between bodies and space. Distances became measurable and through the tool "perspective" visualizable.

The use of "Perspective as Symbolic Form" or PASF did not only influence the history of art but also the history of visualization for scientific purposes. Along with the emerging natural sciences such as botanics and mineralogy, astronomy and geology, scientists were eager to visualize their objects and results. Plants and stones — being objects that did not move — were easy to visualize. These objects were static, with clear outlines and could be drawn in what is later known as an objective, scientific way.

The objects of interest for artists and scientists changed throughout time: from a plant and a stone, to astronomical objects like the moon, to geological phenomena such as erupting volcanos, to products of the early industrial age such as steam trains. We notice a rising perception and production of velocity.

And, to mention it explicitly, until the middle of the 19th century, all these objects were represented visually with the use of PASF and a flat surface.

The breakdown of Perspective as Symbolic Form or PASF
As scientists became more acute in their observations of natural processes, a new system of visualization became necessary. It is no wonder then, that photography, also based on the principles of PASF became an important medium for scientific observation and documentation.

At the end of the 18th century, PASF split into two factions and within the context of art, lost much of its power. If scientists paid artists to produce visuals of the Vesuvius in a way that would serve an objective documentation, what would happen to the artistic process of visualizing this sublime performance of nature?

"Impressionism" can be described as a creative field of experimenting with the denial of the rules of *perspectiva artificialis.* Above all, it was the genre of landscape painting that allowed to develop new painterly approaches during the 19th century. Instead of the focussed central perspective, or PASF, multiple view points served as a pattern for visualization. But nevertheless, the medium of painting is still static and the viewer is fixed in front of the painting. In other words, viewers still have to visit, say, the Tate Gallery in London and position themselves in front of a two-dimensional surface.

Joseph Mallord William Turner (1775–1851) painted light effects and avoided linear outlines and perspective laws. In his paintings, time as a process becomes an authorized subject of painting allowing him to represent a moving train in a static medium.

As such, the visual aesthetics of *Osmose* which offer multiple viewpoints can be understood within a continuing tradition of visual art. The two-dimensional static surface has changed into a two-dimensional projection screen that generates picture elements. Taking into account the restrictions of the human eye, the velocity of the picture is not being perceived consciously. Instead, *Osmose* takes into account the perception of individual time.

Examples of real time experiences in literature

Literature was the medium to provide experiences of individual time but not in real time. 24 hours in the life of the reader are not 24 hours in the life of let's say James Joyce's *Ulysses.* Without being competent enough to interpret the following two text passages, I nevertheless would like you to read them and claim that there have been developments in the area of literature that prepared "real time experiences" of the sort they are visualized in *Osmose.*

My first example is taken from a short story by Ursula Le Guin from 1975, the second example is a passage from Carlos Castaneda's *A Separate Reality. Further Conversations with Don Juan* (1972).

> We watched the tiny lights come and go around us, and doing so, we gained a sense of space and of direction — near and far, at least, and higher and lower. It was that sense of space that allowed us to become aware of the currents. Space was no longer entirely still around us, suppressed by the enormous pressure of its own weight. Very dimly we were aware that the cold darkness moved, slowly, softly, pressing against us a little for a long time, then ceasing, in a vast oscillation. The empty darkness flowed slowly along our unmoving unseen bodies; along them, past them; perhaps through them; we could not tell.
>
> Where did they come from, those dim, slow, vast tides? What pressure or attraction stirred the depths to these slow drifting movements? We could not understand that; we could only feel their touch against us, but in straining our sense to guess their origin or end, we became aware of something else: something out there in the darkness of the great currents: sounds. We listened. We heard. So our sense of space sharpened and localised to a sense of place. For sound is local, as sight is not. (Le Guin 1975)

> I tried to focus my gaze on the water but its movement distracted me. My mind and my eyes began to wander onto other features of the immediate surroundings. [...] Finally I noticed that my mind and my eyes were focusing on the water; in spite of its movement I was becoming immersed in my view of its liquidness. The water became slightly different. It seemed to be heavier and uniformly grayish green. I could notice the ripples it made as it moved. The ripples were extremely sharp. And then, suddenly, I had the sensation that I was not looking at a mass of moving water but at a picture of water; what I had in front of my eyes was a frozen segment of the running water. The ripples were immobile. I could look at every one of them. Then they began to acquire a green phosphorescence and a sort of green fog oozed out of them. The fog expanded in ripples and as it moved, its greenness became more brilliant until it was a dazzling radiance that covered everything.
> [...]
> I became immersed in the mist again and noticed that it was not fog at all, or at least it was not what I conceive fog to be like. The foglike phenomenon was composed of tiny bubbles, round objects that came into my field of "vision" and moved out of it with a floating quality. I watched their movement for a while, then a loud, distant noise jolted my attention and I lost my capacity to

> focus and could no longer perceive the tiny bubbles. All I was aware of then was a green, amorphous, foglike glow. I heard the loud noise again and the jolt it gave dispelled the fog at once and I found myself looking at the water of the irrigation ditch. Then I heard it again much closer; it was don Juan's voice. (Castaneda 1972)

Within the last decades of our century, developments such as land art, performance art, concept art, and video installations have been developed, all of which urge the viewer or visitor to move in space. The motion of the participant consequently touches more than the visual sense within the viewer.

Perception of individual time in *Osmose*

In many ways, the jump from the use of perspective in painting to impressionistic techniques is comparable to the leap made by the techniques of the visuals in *Osmose.* The visuals in *Osmose* are created by algorithms. As such, they are no longer dependent on visual images that are taken from real life such as photography or film, but rather are generated by the computer. While the visuals do not continue the PASF tradition, they do continue the concurrent Perception of Individual Time (PIT) form — realized through the cooperation of specialists in the different fields.

Indeed, the virtual reality environment stands as a technological development within the scientific line of PASF and thus is not a simulation of *perspectiva naturalis* but rather a continuation of *perspectiva artificialis.* VR technology which was developed for architectural and engineering simulations serves as a mirror of what visual reality looks like after a history of 500 years of PASF — and in a recent use for big investment architecture such as the Potsdamer Platz in Berlin, they even invade our actual space and materialize in every-day-life.

To my knowledge, *Osmose* is the first work based on virtual reality technology, which offers a visual aesthetic that contrasts the Cartesian grid that is visible in the very beginning and that is used to focus the immersants sight individually. I am not saying, that *Osmose* is negating the tradition of PASF, but it is irritating the immersant through the difference in visuals that lead off the usual pathces in VR or in the urban spaces of Western civilization.[2]

Since the 1960s, most concept art or installation art created or used spaces that the viewer enters with his/her body, whereas with VR technology the spaces are only created and perceived by the immersant through visual and audio input. This is accomplished through the use of screens attached to the eyes of the viewer. In this respect, the process of visual perception has not changed.

What has changed then, is the fact that the viewer's visual position within the constructed space has been detached from its fixed position. Although in reality, the body of the viewer is not moving outside of a radius of half a meter, (s)he is travelling through a larger immersive virtual space — perceiving movement visually.

As long as the position of the viewer was or is fixed in front of a painting, a photography, or a film screen, we can speak of a fore-, middle-, and background — even describe the deconstruction of these forms. In an immersive space like *Osmose*, these descriptions are inappropriate. The viewer moves within a complex space which is nothing more or less than moving points of light created by a programme generating algorithms. The points of light are in motion because the immersant responds to his/her perceptions.

In *Osmose*, "perspective" is perceivable as individual time. A constant need for (re)positioning within the dimensions of "time and space" creates an aesthetic experience which irritates our common sense ideas of space and time, ideas that are (still) influenced and shaped by PASF through photography and film. The viewer is immersed in *Osmose* and spends his/her own "real time". Through the interface (s)he responds in an intuitive way — reacting to visual and acoustic input. There are no concrete objects, no defined boundaries, no visuals that are drawn from the tradition of PASF. Our trained patterns of orientation which take us along a wall, towards defined places are no longer useable. Apart from reconfiguring our perception of space and time, the parameters of light and velocity in *Osmose* are the only means to relate to. Even without any active input other than breathing, the immersant sinks down through the worlds of *Osmose* – experiencing time passing by.

The introduction of Perception of Individual Time or PIT

Before painting gained priority in art history in the early 15th century, we find a conglomeration of different media that offered unique experiences for contemporaries. The correspondence of proportions within music and architecture in Gothic churches is a recent field of research, based e.g. on the research into acoustic reverberation and the composition of music for certain architecture.

The use of mathematical knowledge within architecture and music is based on the medieval educational structure which is known under the name of "the Seven Liberal Arts". While the trivium: rhetorics, dialectics and grammar were based on language, the quadrivium: music, geometry, arithmethics and astronomy can be summarized under the reign of numbers. It is this complex interaction that was made perceivable in a Gothic cathedral. The "artist" had the knowledge about numbers and sciences, the "craftsmen" developed practical skills that would turn theory into reality.

Can an aesthetic experience be explained by relating it back to the use of proportions? If aesthetics is the science that describes patterns of "art works" and if we consider the dome of Florence and the Motet by Dufay as art works, can we then understand the experience of both (sitting in the cathedral and listening to music) as an art work in and of itself?

Closing the circle back to Herbert Read's suggestion that consciousness materializes in art, has a contemporary form of consciousness materialized in *Osmose*? What exactly is its materialization? The digital programming? The digital visuals? What about the hardware and the interface? What about the real time experience of the immersant and the activities within his brain while being immersed? Is *Osmose* an art work? What is its content? Maybe a materialization of consciousness itself — as it was defined by William James in 1884?

The theory that time is a flux and not a sum of discrete units is linked with the theory that human consciousness is a stream and not a conglomeration of separate faculties or ideas. The first reference to the mind as a "stream of thought" appears in an essay by William James in 1884, which criticized David Hume's view of the mind as an "aglutination in various shapes of separate entities called ideas" and Johann Herbart's representation of it as the result of "mutual repugnancies of separate entities called Vorstellungen. […]"

In 1890 James repeated these arguments in a popular textbook of psychology and added a formulation that subsequently became famous. "Consciousness does not appear to itself chopped up in bits. Such words as 'chain' or 'train' do not describe it fitly … It is nothing jointed; it flows. A 'river' or a 'stream' are the metaphors by which it is most naturally described. In talking of it hereafter, let us call it the stream of thought, of consciousness." (quoted in Kern 1983:24).

Notes

1. Panofsky (1927) is relating to Ernst Cassirer's *Philosophie der symbolischen Formen.*

2. Margarete Wertheim is currently working on a cultural history of space. In this upcoming publication, *Osmose* will be discussed. Her recent book *Pythagoras' Trousers. God, Physics,*

and the Gender Wars (1997) throws an inspiring light on 2500 years of the history of physics and its compatibility to the history of catholicism.

References

Castaneda, Carlos 1972. *A Separate Reality. Further Conversations with Don Juan.* New York: Pocket Book.

Kern, Stephen 1983. *The culture of time and space. 1880–1918.* Cambridge, Ma.: Harvard University Press.

Le Guin, Ursula K. 1975. "The New Atlantis." in Silverberg R. (ed.) *The New Atlantis.* London: Hawthorn Books.

Panonfsky, Erwin, 1927. *Perspective as Symbolic Form.* New York: Zone Books.

Read, Herbert 1945/1965. *Icon and Idea — The Function of Art in the Development of Human Consciousness.* New York: Faber & Faber.

Wertheim, Margarete 1997. *Pythagoras' Trousers. God, Physics, and the Gender Wars.* London: Fourth Estate.

Do dreams work?

Tere Vadén
University of Skövde

> "people are starting to behave as though it was nothing at all, as though nothing had happened, as though taking into account the event of psychoanalysis, a logic of the unconscious, of 'unconscious concepts', even, were no longer *de rigueur*, no longer even had a place in something like the history of reason: as if one could calmly continue the good old discourse of the Enlightenment, return to Kant, call us back to the ethical or juridical or political responsibility of the subject by restoring the authority of consciousness, of the ego, of the reflexive cogito, of an 'I think' without pain or paradox; as if, in this moment of philosophical restoration that is in the air — for what is on the agenda, the agenda's moral agenda, is a sort of shameful, botched restoration — as if it were a matter of flattening supposed demands of reason into a discourse that is purely communicative, informational, smooth; as though, finally, it were again legitimate to accuse of obscurity or irrationalism anyone who complicates things a little by wondering about the reason of reason, about the history of the principle of reason or about the event — perhaps a traumatic one — constituted by something like psychoanalysis in reason's relation to itself."
>
> (Jacques Derrida "Let Us Not Forget — Psychoanalysis." *Oxford Literary Review* 12: 4).

Metaphysics of subjectivity

It is well known that while realism and other forms of metaphysics of subjectivity rely on clear-cut dualities — like that between subject and object or truth and falsity — so-called postmodern discussions often end at dissoluting or undermining these dualities by way of deconstructing them. Another example of such duality is the polarity between dream and waking. For the metaphysical realist the waking life, at least in some of its ideal or normal mode, gives the subject a more or less reliable access to objective (subject-independent or intersubjective) reality, while dreams are "subjective" in the sense of being detached from objective reality. The role of the terms "subject" and "subjective" in this context is of utmost importance. An examination of what is involved in the use of those terms will also lead to the topic of dream/waking-duality.

The metaphysics of subjectivity can be briefly characterised as a view in which human subjectivity is held central. For instance, the subject is seen as a system of representation or information processing that gathers beliefs and knowledge concerning an objective reality independent and outside of itself. This kind of subject is thought to have a more or less defined structure that is common to all subjects. On this view, subjects might have some peripheral individual or idiosyncratic differences, but the defining essential structure does not vary from one subject to the next. On the contrary, what makes a subject a subject is some universal and essential characteristic, such as rationality, representational structure, a definite functional or neural mechanism, soul, or whatever. For example, Husserl's theory of the intentionality of mind in terms of a transcendental ego can be seen as a paradigm case of such universal and essential subjectivity. This meaning of the term "subject" (subject as a universal structure) is through its use to an extent opposite to the term "subjective" as used in connection to different points of view, or "perspectivity", as for example when referring to the "subjective" or non-universal particularity of dreams. In the metaphysical sense, however, everything that is subjective, must be available to all subjects that share the defining structure and thus what is "subjective" can not in any genuine sense be idiosyncratic or unique. The whole philosophical point in supposing some universal subject-structure is precisely the predictability and repeatability that such structure makes possible. The structure in question has had many interpretations in the philosophical tradition, such as Kant's reason, Husserl's intentionality or the more modern functionalist-representational picture of the mind, but the basic constraint of some structure with universal and lasting identity has withstood all these different interpretations. This means that the term "subjective" as alluding to a common structure that defines or constitutes a transcendental condition for "humanity", "rationality", "cognition" or the like, is highly metaphysical in the sense that it serves as a guarantee and basis for the non-empirical yearning for identity, calculability and predictability that are removed from the instability encountered in the experienced world. Therefore it is this sense of the term "subject" that is most readily recognisable as the target of attack when postphenomenological or postmodern philosophers argue against "a metaphysics of subjectivity."

However, when we take a closer look, the term "subjective" in the second sense, as alluding to the perspective of a person, is no less metaphysical than the term "subject". To see this, we may take as an example the "subjective" nature of art or of dreams. It is often said, for instance, that modern art is characterised by its lack of objectivity or intersubjectivity (this claim is often heard as a negative criticism from both a high-modernist enlightenment-rationalist conservative camp and a romatical-utopian radicalist camp). What is characteristic of artistic creation is rather "subjectivity" in the sense of perspectivity and idiosyncrasy. What is celebrated is the subjective genius of individuals like Picasso, Dali or Warhol. Their greatness lies in their power to create perspectives that are somehow immediately recognisable as great, at least by those with the proper training and background. However, the greatness of a great artist or work of art is thought to be something universal, something that every subject can or even should, in principle, entertain. For instance, the traditions of museums of fine arts and art history emphasise art as a continual movement with a direction, or at least as a related series of stages that react to previous stages. This means that there is a common denominator to art and especially to great or good art, even though there might be different interpretations of what is the criterion for "good". Such a common denominator is inevitably tied to the idea that there is some core that all humans share ("humanism") and through which art can enter and influence us. Thus the universality of metaphysical subjectivity is only emphasised by this seemingly different use of the term "subjective". The same goes for most modern accounts of dreams and dreaming. Even in the case of dreams, the subjective element is thought to rise on account of some features of the subject's history or structure, particularly on account of the interaction between the subject and its environment, and in a realist-metaphysical view both the subject and the outside world do have a definite nature even if that nature may be partly unknown. Therefore the subjective, genial or idiosyncratic aspects of dreams or of art can in principle be intersubjectively corrected and controlled, and used in enriching and enlightening the common subjectual universality. Such is the case, for instance, in the Freudian psychoanalytic tradition.

Another characteristic feature of the metaphysics of subjectivity — a feature that has been emphasised in the surrealist critique — is the servility included in the notion of subject. To see this we first have to observe how the subject arises out of something that is not the subject. For the surrealists, the discovery of the genesis of the subject was not only a result of paying attention to certain poets and writers, but also the import of Freud's scientific psychology. Freud's theory of the unconscious was understood as showing how subjectivity, reason, and logic float on an ocean of asubjectivity, unreason, and illogic, and how the psyche is driven by certain irresistible energetic flows. Similarly, some forms of what may be called postphenomenological philosophy have arrived at asubjective views of the mind that attempt to hear the subject and object as relatively late and parasitic effects of a more primordial asubjective and aobjective process. In these kind of broadly energetic-Freudian or asubjectivistic views, the subject is seen as a control structure repressing and covering-up other possible elements of experience. Moreover, the subject is felt as a structure of servile work, of serving some universal structural principles or constraints of subjectivity. To work in this sense means to satisfy the demands of some principles or categories in a productive, useful and computable manner. In this sense work and consumption are not direct opposites but rather the expression of the same subjectivistic urge for utility and identity. Thus working and consuming and the metaphysical constitution of the subject are intimately tied in servility, and find their ametaphysical release in the freedom of useless waste or expenditure. Subjectual servitude seals the unholy trinity of usefulness, survival and "good", so that asubjective thinking has to deny that the subject with its servitude is coterminous with survival or life. In philosophy, Foucault's work has been outstanding in its attempt to show how these constraints of subjectivity are created. For the surrealists, this creation was self-evident and they concentrated in identifying and destroying the link these constraints have to the ever expanding and all-eating petit-bourgeoisie life form of the West. The subject as a metaphysical structure is universal and can not but serve the constraints of its own structure in order to remain a subject. Anything asubjective is either foreign or threatening from the viewpoint of the subject; this, in general, is the root for the horror and laughter evoked by the unconscious or surrealist art.

Of course, Freud himself might not have taken as revolutionary steps as some of his followers did on the basis of his theories. After all, as a psychotherapist Freud was explicitly taking the side of love and work, of sanity and order, which quite easily — but not necessarily — tips the balance towards subjectual notions. In fact, the unbalance leads to subjectual notions only if the unholy trinity of servitude is accepted; love and sanity do not necessarily have anything to do with utility or survival. In Freud there is also a characteristic insistence on the universality of the structures (ego, id, symbolic structures in dreams, etc.) that are postulated in the theory. This universality may work directly in the hands of metaphysics and humanism by giving a lively and sophisticated account of what all human subjects are. The surrealist genius-cult invented and upheld by Dali and others paid more or less ironical heed to this kind of scientific-mythical humanism. Thus, far from being the enemies of metaphysics of subjectivity, Freudian and modernist artistic schools of thought might enforce the belief in universal subjectual structures and the universal acceptance of certain values that go with these structures. Not surprisingly then, this kind of falling into metaphysics and servility was what Breton suggested had happened to Dali, and both Bataille and Dali suggested had happened to Breton (for one side of the issue see Bataille 1994). This characteristic holier-than-thou skirmish does not, however, show that all surrealism was necessarily ineffectual in its criticism and that it in the end played in the hands of the bourgeoisie metaphysics. All told, there is a crucial difference between the Freudian undermining of reason and the surrealistic active destruction of reason. In this connection it might be good to remember that the metaphysics of subjectivity finds its most modern counterpart in objectivist science (as Freud's idea of "scientific psychology" already illustrates.) In objectivist science humans are treated as neural objects, and the alleged universality is found not in any "inner" subjectivity, but rather in the "outer" or "real" object that we supposedly are. This "metaphysics of objectivity" has all the characteristics of metaphysics of subjectivity, even in a more sinister manner, as neuroscience undermines the possibility of freedom by explaining the subject away as a more or less mechanical object. It is easy to see why this naturalistic or biologistic kind of undermining of reason and subjectivity does not pave the way for asubjective or surrealistic notions, but rather for ultra-objectivistic and servile forms of life.

Dreamwork

The unbalance in favour of reason, i.e., the idea that health equals reason, and against asubjective and irrational forms of experience can be discerned from the Freudian idea of "dreamwork".[1] The idea is that dreams are seen as an attempt to work through the residual or left-over meanings of waking life encounters with subject-independent reality. The dream gives the left-over meanings new symbolic guises that help the dreamer to attain given goals of his/her particular psychodynamic situation. In this sense the manifest dream is a second-hand version of the primary goals set in waking consciousness, even if the dream might have ways of its own — subjective ways — in accessing these goals. So despite its wildness, smoothness and "idiosyncrasy" the dream can be seen as an impoverished form of waking life meanings mutated by the symbolic transformations of the dreamwork. (This is, of course, a caricature. But a glance at the literature of consciousness studies and contemporary studies of dreams confirms the ubiquity of this realistic-metaphysical view; for an overview see Globus 1987.)

The realistic interpretation implies that the dream "works", i.e., that the dream is servile to the subjectual conflicts, meanings and goals of waking life. The dream works in the purpose of benefiting the primary waking consciousness, its task are implicated in the tasks of the waking consciousness and in the relation that the waking consciousness has to the consciousness-independent world. Secondly, the dream works through symbolic transformations of meanings. All of this happens under the hold of the psychodynamical harmony-constraint of the subject (or an "objective" neural mechanism, or whatever). In order for the interpretation of the dream to help the subject, the symbolic language of the dream has to be re-transformed so that its meaning is disclosed to the conscious and rational part of the subject. In this way the dream may submit a message from one part of the experiencing self to another part. The partition itself, however, does not radically undermine the fundamental unity or centrality of the wakeful conscious subject, because the dreamwork can be used to serve its purposes (such as unity and centrality), at least under careful psychoanalytical or scientific interpretation.

These two characteristics of dreams, namely that they work and that they are symbolic (contain symbols or symbolise waking-life meanings), are the ones that an asubjective story of the mind or consciousness has to view with suspicion. The connection between dream and work is by no means innocent or accidental. The connecting link is precisely a metaphysical notion of a permanent subject or self. Work is a means of production, of producing as stable and secure conditions for the permanence of the self as possible (or for the biological-objective survival of the brain and the body, as modern theories would have it). Now, if dreams along with the unconscious are seen as threats to the structural and permanent identity of the self and its rational rule, then what better way to domesticate the dream than to put it to work?

The idea that the dream works may take different forms in current theoretical pictures of the mind. One form is the thought that dreams are the idlings of a computational system when it is deprived of input. The system works, and as it has nothing (nothing sensory, nothing "outer", that is) to chew on, it produces fantastic and irrelevant side-effects. Here dreamwork is about the same as the afterglow of a heated owen. Another view holds that the noise produced in the idling computation system during dreams is somehow healthy for the system. Here the dream works by increasing the vitality and eventually survival ability of the organism as an object — and as a subject. The latter idea has a myriad variations, of which the Freudian caricature presented above is one. What is common to these views is a downgrading of the dream. In the extreme this downgrading is seen in the view that the dream is nothing but an uninteresting epiphenomenon of the idle running of the representational system or that the dream is a virtual training-venue where past or future scenes may be exercised (while the idling or training may serve some, e.g., survivalistic purpose, the dream content as such does not). The situation is not much better in the views that along the Freudian ones see the dream as a secondary helping hand of the conscious waking ego serving the tasks that waking consciousness has set for itself, the main one being the establishment of a "healthy relationship" to the outside world.

This downgrading view of the dream can be challenged in at least two different ways. First, we may introduce reasons for believing that the distinction between dream and waking is not that sharp, after all. If the distinction can not be maintained, the non-neutral attitude taken towards the dream in these metaphysical-humanistic views is seen in a new perspective: it is a device of socio-economic control. Second, we can start from an account of human experience that does not favour the underlying humanistic subject-object distinction and which in this manner promises a genuine (primary) existence for the dream.

Scepticism with regard to the realist-metaphysical distinction

From the radical methodological scepticism of René Descartes we learned that the dream may be so convincing that telling it apart form the waking consciousness is extremely hard if not impossible. Several criteria for making out the distinction have been proposed. Often and quite typically for realist-metaphysical arguments many of the suggested criteria are circular by already presupposing a subject-independent reality in terms of which waking contact with that world is distinguished from the supposedly mind-dependent dream. The idea in all these distinctions is that there is some reliable part in waking consciousness — such as sensation, reflection, or common sense — that can be trusted while telling waking apart from dreaming. Freud's idea of unconscious motives behind conscious thoughts of course puts the reliability of all such reliabilities into question (compare also the famous experiments on unconscious initiative of action in Libet 1985 and the research on so-called false memories). So the deconstruction of the dream/waking-duality can proceed also from discrediting any putative beyond-doubt reliable part of the conscious subject. What could such reliability be, if its is not of the metaphysical kind already introduced by Descartes in terms of an ego or subject (or the more contemporary one in terms of a scientific object)?

One naive criteria for the distinction is that in waking we are in contact with an outside world through the senses whereas in the dream we encounter a world which is of our own making. This is a typically circular criterion. We presuppose the subject and the object, the mind and the world, and presuppose a link of sensation between them. It helps, of course, with regard to subjectivistic criteria: but what about asubjective experience, in which there is no such distinction? Furthermore, the criterion of sensation is not able to make a clear-cut distinction, only a gradual transition from acute sensation to less acute. The same goes for reflection, or the idea that in waking we can reflect on our mental states. Reflection also leaks from both ends: weak and lazy reflection as well as extremely intensive reflection are inseparable from dreaming. Same goes for "objective" criteria of neuroscience: in the absence of metaphysics (the subject-object distinction) they do not suggest a clear distinction between the state or function of waking and dreaming (see Llinas and Paré 1991). These criteria are, then, matters of degree, of gradually creating the distinction between subject and object, mind and world, dream and waking. They are not criteria of absolute boundaries, which was what the surrealists were suspecting from the start. It is not the case that dream and waking consciousness are sharply separate modes of contact with the world. They are rather different poles of an inseparable and antirealist experience, out of which "the world" as well as "the subject" are under some conditions thematised, whether that be in "dreaming" or in "waking". (Incidentally, it might even be the case that the subjectivity of the subject is best experienced and thematised in dreams, namely in so-called lucid dreams.)

There is furthermore a general cause for doubting all of these criteria. It can be claimed that it is not the case that as human beings we encounter a ready-made outside world with objects. Rather, we are constructors of that world, of how it appears to us. This antirealist line of thinking is exhibited for instance in the phenomenological-existential tradition, where the basic starting point is the way in which human being existentially opens up the world in which we live, so that the constitution of the world is made up by the way in which we exist. In this view, the dream can be seen as a primordial way of existing, of world-building, in the absence of the immediate intersubjective field (see Foucault 1993). If we along this phenomenological idea think that both the waking world as well as the dreaming world are existential ways of being, then a possibility for a first-hand account of the dream as experience opens up. We can dispense with the dualistic assumption that dreams are something that happen to us (as objects of neuroscience), or something that we as subjects see. It is rather the case that we are our dreams, that our dreams are us, which implicates a dissolution of the subject-object distinction.

Asubjectivity and aobjectivity

The term asubjective is intended to describe forms of experience in which a distinction between the subject and objects does not exist — not yet or not anymore. If we strongly believe in the metaphysical-realist view of the human mind, then it might seem impossible that there are forms of experience which are not "subjective" in either of the senses of the word. Actually, this might be a genuine experiential possibility: it may be possible that in some cases the experiental centre called the subject is so well defined and so well in control that indeed any other form of experience is strictly impossible or at least disregarded as something less than experience. The experience of the subject is purified in the sense that anything not subjectually controlled is removed away, sterilised, homogenised. If this is the case, then the possibility of asubjective experience is based on the (temporary) dissolution of the subjectual borders and control-mechanisms and becomes quite an extreme experience: anxiety, panic, nearness of death. In some cases where the subject is less defined and more diffuse it is possible to imagine less extreme and less subject-threatening forms of asubjective experience, e.g., in the case of quite young or very old people, in experiences of love, in intense reflection, meditation or physical exercise, in hunting, and so on. These experiences are characterised not only by the absence of a clear subject-object distinction but also by their uselessness and irrationality.

Servitude to the utilitarian principles of reason and the subject is something that is under threat in asubjective modes of experience. Whereas the subject is characterised by useful servitude — meaning production in the service of reason (=usefulness=survival) — asubjective modes develop a form of useless waste or expenditure. The uselessness with regard to reason (though a "rational" justification might after the fact be invented in order to domesticate these experiences) can be seen from such modes of conscious experience as religion, war, the enrapture in art or nature, a practice of eroticism, or, indeed, dreaming. These serve no rational utility, but rather waste or expend the subjectual self in order to give way to asubjectivistic experience. The possibility of work is based on the allocation of temporal and spatial resources to principled and reasonable aims that serve the calculative interests of the subject. These interest are non-neutral in the sense that they strongly favour the metaphysical tendency to attain the One and the Same through the eternal preservation of the Subject. The expenditure in asubjective experiences is based on the irrational, unproductive and irreversible (and thus unique) waste of the resources. The waste is typically intensified by the fact that in asubjective experience — as in dreams — temporality and spatiality assume forms that are different compared to the realistically accepted ones.

This notion of expenditure can be given an energetic-economical-mythical interpretation along the lines of the surrealist thinker Georges Bataille (see, e.g., Bataille 1994). Life on earth is based on the useless expenditure of energy that the sun makes of itself. Life-forms are temporary basins of energy, pools dammed out of the ever entropifying energy-flow. Now the subject is one such pool-and-dam, in fact one that tries to make the dam not only certain and everlasting, but also through useful work to ever enlarge the pool and not to waste any of it. In these subjectual terms also the outside world becomes to be seen as a standing reserve or resource well (Heidegger's *Bestand*) for the needs of useful work or technology. In precisely this sense the subject is co-terminous with one understanding of the Judaeo-Christian God, who promises eternal life that will not go to waste if it is used in the service of Him. This attempt at eternal Oneness and Sameness also produces the need for clear-cut distinctions such as life-death, subject-object, dreaming-wakeful. What goes wrong with this damming-work of the subject is the idea that life and utility are completely moved to the side of calculation and certainty. This is also the reason why asubjective forms of experience are virtually forced near death and sickness. The subject becomes the machine. It is only through asubjective experience that does not allow a distinction between the subject and the object that we are parts of the continuity of the energy-flow. In this sense asubjective experience is continuous with the experience of other centres of experience, whereas the subject is always closed inside the walls of its dams and lives in a state of constant nostalgia and yearning.

In the asubjective experience the distinction between dream and waking is as secondary and artificial as that between the subject and object (Foucault writes, for instance, that in dreaming the subject of the dream is the whole dream, 1993:59). If we allow for the genuinely unpredictable asubjectivistic experience, then certainty and control are not anymore synonymous with life and health. This also means that not only those functions that serve the calculative rationality of the subject are able to promote survival or enrich life, but also those functions that the subject would term "death" or "sickness" have their ineliminable role in engendering pleasure; if not else then at least through the destruction of the subject that is a necessary condition for the possibility of asubjective experience. Similarly, the dream is a genuine form of experience that does not stand in need for any "external" support or role in a working scheme of the waking consciousness. The health promised through the dream is not one of hygienic or explanatory relief for the subject, but an existential mode of being in itself. The existential world engendered in the dream is not a distorted or fanciful copy of the "real" world, but rather a sovereign experiental actuality in itself. The dream is not a second hand or auxiliary tool of calculative survival, it is rather a door out of calculative survival. Moreover, if the subject-object distinction is dissoluted, then the dream can not work as a *via regia* to any knowledge about the subject or its psychological condition.

In sum, then, if we set out from an anti-realist and asubjective view of experience, then there is no need to downgrade dream as a second-hand mode of experience. The second-handness emerges only from the subjectivist-metaphysical viewpoint. There is a double-strategy involved in the subjectivistic idea of dreamwork. From the point of view of the subject, any form and amount of asubjective experience is threatening. The subject is a supposedly universal structure of control and prediction, of calculation and utility, and thus the genuine unpredictability and holism of asubjective experience is threatening to the subject. Dreams, in particular, are forms of experience where many of the subjectual strategies are undermined. In dreams we may experience the loss of subjectivity and the connected holism of asubjective experience in a convincing and lasting way. In view of this threat, the subject employs the double strategy. First, the dream is termed second-hand, deprived of its originality, so that its role in the general economy of the subject may be belittled and eventually covered-up or forgotten. Second, the dream is harnessed by a role in the work of the subject, a role of servitude, of enslavement to the subjectual waking consciousness. This double-strategy serves to domesticate the impact that dreams have on the purified, reasonable and useful waking consciousness. There is maybe no good reason to attribute this domesticative attempt to the historical figure "Freud", for his theory is, as we saw, open to and suggestive of an energetic interpretation. In contrast, the domestication attempt is glaringly evident in the scientific-objective accounts on dreams.

Conclusion

From the asubjective and antirealist perspective, then, it is not the case that dreams are a derivative second-hand ways of symbolically working through the meanings and experiences of the waking consciousness. If in dreams there is the possibility of sovereign asubjective experience, then it seems that rather the opposite is the case. The impoverished and purified waking consciousness of the identity-preserving subject dealing with objects is a derivative second-hand way of servile toiling that receives most of its energy and intensity out of the asubjective dream experience. We must add the words "possibility of" in front of the expression "sovereign asubjective experience", because if there is no clear-cut boundary between dream and waking, then there is no reason why the subject could not in principle corrupt dream experience into a subjective workforce, too. Similarly, if there is no absolute boundary, then there is no a priori reason why waking life could not be saturated by asubjective experience. However, this saturation is harder to achieve, because the notion of self-identical consciousness as technology-in-us supports and reproduces a metaphysical understanding of experience. Only through a metaphysical understanding can dreaming be seen as the subject fulfilling its dreams (this wish-fulfilling dreaming is the case for which Foucault reserves the word "imagination", to be distinguished from the existential mode of "dreaming", see Foucault 1993). The corruption of dreaming into imagination is indeed possible, but there are reasons for doubting that the corruption will be total, the main reason being that dreams are wonderfully resistant to the servitude assigned to them. The nature of dreams like the nature of memories is to betray the subject. Both are based on a form of selective presence, presenting something on the cost of absenting or withdrawing something else. From an ultra-rational subjective perspective this kind of selective truth or trace is identical with lies.

So we can in conclusion suspect that the idea of dreamwork is doubly wrong. First, the dream does not necessarily work, but does just the opposite, namely it wastes and expends uselessly. Second, the dream is not a symbolic and subjective second hand version of the world of the waking subject, but rather asubjective dreaming as experience is the energetic ground out of which the subject as well as the objective world are built up in a process of purification and enslavement. It is said that if blindness develops late in life, one still dreams with vivid visual imagery, but returns to blindness while awake (Llinas and Paré 1991:525). Analogously, it may be the case that if it is too late for asubjective dream experience, then the idea of dreamwork comes in handy as a waking-life return to blindness.

Notes

1. "Traumarbeit: Gesamtheit der Operationen, die die Traummaterialen (körperliche Reize, Tagesreste, Traumgedanken) in ein Produkt umwendeln: den manifesten Traum. Die Entstellung ist das Ergebnis dieser Arbeit." (Laplache & Pantaks 1967).

References

Bataille, G. 1994. *The Absence of Myth. Writings on Surrealism.* transl. and ed. by M. Richardson, Verso, London.

Foucault, M. 1993. "Dream, Imagination, and Existence" in Foucault, M. and Binswanger, L. *Dream & Existence.* New Jersey: Humanities Press, (orig. 1954).

Globus, G. 1987. *Dream Life, Wake Life. The Human Condition through Dreams.* Albany: SUNY Press.

Laplache, J. and Pantaks, J.B. 1967. *Das Vokabular der Psychoanalyse*, Suhrkamp. Frankfurt am Main.

Libet, B. 1985. "Unconscious Cerebral Initiative and the Role of Conscious Will in Voluntary Action." *Behavioral and Brain Sciences* 8: 529–566.

Llinas, R. and Paré, D. 1991. "Of Dreaming and Wakefulness." *Neuroscience* 44(3): 521–535.

Index

In the series ADVANCES IN CONSCIOUSNESS RESEARCH (AiCR) the following titles have been published thus far or are scheduled for publication:

1. GLOBUS, Gordon G.: *The Postmodern Brain.* 1995.
2. ELLIS, Ralph D.: *Questioning Consciousness. The interplay of imagery, cognition, and emotion in the human brain.* 1995.
3. JIBU, Mari and Kunio YASUE: *Quantum Brain Dynamics and Consciousness. An introduction.* 1995.
4. HARDCASTLE, Valerie Gray: *Locating Consciousness.* 1995.
5. STUBENBERG, Leopold: *Consciousness and Qualia.* 1998.
6. GENNARO, Rocco J.: *Consciousness and Self-Consciousness. A defense of the higher-order thought theory of consciousness.* 1996.
7. MAC CORMAC, Earl and Maxim I. STAMENOV (eds): *Fractals of Brain, Fractals of Mind. In search of a symmetry bond.* 1996.
8. GROSSENBACHER, Peter G. (ed.): *Finding Consciousness in the Brain. A neurocognitive approach.* 2001.
9. Ó NUALLÁIN, Seán, Paul MC KEVITT and Eoghan MAC AOGÁIN (eds): *Two Sciences of Mind. Readings in cognitive science and consciousness.* 1997.
10. NEWTON, Natika: *Foundations of Understanding.* 1996.
11. PYLKKÖ, Pauli: *The Aconceptual Mind. Heideggerian themes in holistic naturalism.* 1998.
12. STAMENOV, Maxim I. (ed.): *Language Structure, Discourse and the Access to Consciousness.* 1997.
13. VELMANS, Max (ed.): *Investigating Phenomenal Consciousness. Methodologies and Maps.* 2000.
14. SHEETS-JOHNSTONE, Maxine: *The Primacy of Movement.* 1999.
15. CHALLIS, Bradford H. and Boris M. VELICHKOVSKY (eds.): *Stratification in Cognition and Consciousness.* 1999.
16. ELLIS, Ralph D. and Natika NEWTON (eds.): *The Caldron of Consciousness. Motivation, affect and self-organization – An anthology.* 2000.
17. HUTTO, Daniel D.: *The Presence of Mind.* 1999.
18. PALMER, Gary B. and Debra J. OCCHI (eds.): *Languages of Sentiment. Cultural constructions of emotional substrates.* 1999.
19. DAUTENHAHN, Kerstin (ed.): *Human Cognition and Social Agent Technology.* 2000.
20. KUNZENDORF, Robert G. and Benjamin WALLACE (eds.): *Individual Differences in Conscious Experience.* 2000.
21. HUTTO, Daniel D.: *Beyond Physicalism.* 2000.
22. ROSSETTI, Yves and Antti REVONSUO (eds.): *Beyond Dissociation. Interaction between dissociated implicit and explicit processing.* 2000.
23. ZAHAVI, Dan (ed.): *Exploring the Self. Philosophical and psychopathological perspectives on self-experience.* 2000.
24. ROVEE-COLLIER, Carolyn, Harlene HAYNE and Michael COLOMBO: *The Development of Implicit and Explicit Memory.* 2000.
25. BACHMANN, Talis: *Microgenetic Approach to the Conscious Mind.* 2000.
26. Ó NUALLÁIN, Seán (ed.): *Spatial Cognition. Selected papers from Mind III, Annual Conference of the Cognitive Science Society of Ireland, 1998.* 2000.
27. McMILLAN, John and Grant R. GILLETT: *Consciousness and Intentionality.* 2001.

28. ZACHAR, Peter: *Psychological Concepts and Biological Psychiatry. A philosophical analysis.* 2000.
29. VAN LOOCKE, Philip (ed.): *The Physical Nature of Consciousness.* 2001.
30. BROOK, Andrew and Richard C. DeVIDI (eds.): *Self-reference and Self-awareness.* 2001.
31. RAKOVER, Sam S. and Baruch CAHLON: *Face Recognition. Cognitive and computational processes.* 2001.
32. VITIELLO, Giuseppe: *My Double Unveiled. The dissipative quantum model of the brain.* 2001.
33. YASUE, Kunio, Mari JIBU and Tarcisio DELLA SENTA (eds.): *No Matter, Never Mind. Proceedings of Toward a Science of Consciousness: Fundamental Approaches, Tokyo, 1999.* 2001.
34. FETZER, James H.(ed.): *Consciousness Evolving.* n.y.p.
35. Mc KEVITT, Paul, Sean O'NUALLAIN and Conn Mulvihill (eds.): *Language, Vision, and Music. Selected papers from the 8th International Workshop on the Cognitive Science of Natural Language Processing, Galway, 1999.* n.y.p.
36. PERRY, Elaine, Heather ASHTON and Allan YOUNG (eds.): *Neurochemistry of Consciousness. Neurotransmitters in mind.* n.y.p.
37. PYLKKÄNEN, Paavo and Tere VADÉN (eds.): *Dimensions of Conscious Experience.* 2001.
38. SALZARULO, Piero and Gianluca FICCA (eds.): *Awakening and Sleep-Wake Cycle Across Development.* n.y.p.
39. BARTSCH, Renate: *Consciousness Emerging. The dynamics of perception, imagination, action, memory, thought, and language.* n.y.p.
40. MANDLER, George: *Consciousness Recovered. Psychological functions and origins of conscious thought.* n.y.p.
41. ALBERTAZZI, Liliana (ed.): *Unfolding Perceptual Continua.* n.y.p.